MODERN PERSIAN
COLLOQUIAL GRAMMAR

CONTAINING

A SHORT GRAMMAR, DIALOGUES AND EXTRACTS FROM NASIR-EDDIN SHAH'S DIARIES, TALES, ETC. AND A VOCABULARY

FRITZ ROSEN

GYAN

Published by

Gyan Publishing House
5, Ansari Road
Daryaganj, New Delhi-110002
Phone: 011-47034999, 9811692060
E-mail: books@gyanbooks.com

Distribution Network
gyanbooks.com
India, USA, Canada, UK, Australia, France

ISBN : 978-81-212-4565-4 (HB)
First Published, 1898

2nd Impression 2020

Printed at: Gyan Press, Delhi.

The book at your disposal is the edition of an old book originally published long back. The Text quality of this book may not be at par as compared to our other books but many readers approached us to reprint this important book so that it could satiate their hunger. We request all the readers of this book to help us to improve its quality by providing the necessary text of those pages which are not properly visible. Your valuable support in this case will be highly appreciated and acknowledged and our future readers will be benefitted immensely.

MODERN PERSIAN COLLOQUIAL GRAMMAR

CONTAINING

A SHORT GRAMMAR, DIALOGUES AND EXTRACTS FROM NASIR-EDDIN SHAH'S DIARIES, TALES, ETC. AND A VOCABULARY

BY

DR. FRITZ ROSEN.

LONDON:
LUZAC & Co.
PUBLISHERS TO THE INDIA OFFICE
46, Great Russell Street
1898.

To His Excellency

The Right Honble the Marquis of DUFFERIN and AVA,

G. C. B., K. P., G. C. S. I., G. C. M. G., G. C. I. E.

IN GRATITUDE FOR THE EXAMPLE SET BY HIM IN THE ACQUIREMENT OF THE PERSIAN LANGUAGE AND IN RECOLLECTION OF THE PLEASANT HOURS SPENT, LISTENING WITH HIM TO A PERSIAN STORY-TELLER IN INDIA

THESE PAGES ARE

DEDICATED BY

THE AUTHOR.

PREFACE.

The *"Modern Persian Colloquial Grammar"* is a translation and revision of my *"Neupersischer Sprachführer"* published at Leipzig by C. A. Koch in 1890. Its object is to assist the student in learning the language now spoken in Persia.

The Persian Grammars hitherto written in English have, like Forbes' Grammar and Clarke's Manual, dealt with the Persian of India, which differs in every respect from the language of Irân. A few English books, it is true, such as Finn's little vocabulary, Haggard and Lestrange's able edition of the Vazir of Lankuran and Wollaston's excellent dictionaries, have dealt with the Persian of Modern Persia, but I think that a work containing a grammar, dialogues and various specimens of colloquial prose together with some information regarding journeys and life in Persia will be found useful to all travellers and residents in that country as well as in Baluchistan and Afghanistan.

The principal additions to the German edition are

the introduction throughout the book of the Persian type along with the Latin transcription. This will enable the student to acquire the rudiments of reading as well as of speaking. Further-more an alphabetic vocabulary has been substituted for the tabulated collection of useful words contained in the German edition. Since publishing the "Neupersischer Sprachführer" a residence of six years in PERSIA has enabled me to make many corrections and amplifications.

The English translation of the diary of Nasir-Eddin SHAH'S journeys to Europe has been taken from Mr. REDHOUSE'S "The Diary of H. M. the Shah of Persia during his Tour through Europe in A. D. 1873. London, 1874".

I have much pleasure in thanking Prof. E. DENISON ROSS, of University College, London, for the kind assistance he has lent me by reading a great part of the proofsheets while I was in Persia.

Teheran, April 1897 *The Author.*

INTRODUCTORY REMARKS TAKEN FROM THE PREFACE TO THE GERMAN EDITION.

Persian, the most elegant and harmonious of all the languages of Muhammedan nations has, from the earliest days, enjoyed an importance far beyond the boundaries of the Shah's dominions and has still survived the many vicissitudes of Eastern history.

As early as the seventh century Persia lost her independence and fell under the successive sway of the Arab, the Turk and the Mongol. But it was under the foreign rule of the Turkish dynasties of the Ghaznevide and Seldjuk kings and their successors the Atabegs that Persian literature attained its highest development. It so far influenced the turkish conquerors as to render them instrumental in spreading Persian thought and speech over a great part of Asia. Even the Mongols fell beneath its charm. When they first invaded Irân under Jangiz Khan they had attempted to extirpate from its soil the inhabitants together with their civilization. But we see them not long afterwards when they invaded India under Babur — the great grandson of Tamerlane — in 1526, appearing as the bearers of Persian speech and thought and introducing into India the higher standard of Persian civilization; and the country, as it fell beneath their undisputed sway, attained an unprecedented degree of wealth and magnificence. The invaders introduced Persian art, Persian architecture and Persian industry, and *Persian* became the language of the court and government of the Moghuls. In fact, there can be no clearer illustration of Persian influence, than the transformation of a savage Tartar horde into the polished and magnificent courts of Dehli and Agra. To this day Persian is not only spoken at all the courts of India, but it is to a certain extent the official language of the Indian Foreign Office in its dealings with the native Princes, and it is taught in all the middle-class schools throughout Northern India. Out of the language of the Tartar conquerors has sprung up the language of the «*horde*» (*ordū* or *urdū*) or «*Royal camp*», the modern *Urdū* or *Hindūstānī*, which is itself three parts Persian.

Persian has exercised almost as much influence on the *Turkish* literature and language as on Hindustani, and the Persian classics are the foundation of higher education among the Turks both of Turkey and of Turkistan.

But though the Persian language has formed a bond of intellectual union between the nations of Islâm inhabiting the immense tract between the *Syr*, the *Brahmaputra*, the *Euphrates* and the *Danube*, yet it has had to yield considerably to foreign influences even on its original territory, the plateau of Irân: All Persian provinces are more or less populated by Turkish tribes. Several races of Mongols are settled in Afghanistan, who have however partially adopted the Persian language or in some instances the East Persian dialect Pukhtū, while in Baluchistan a distinct race, the Brahui talk a language of their own.

It is clear that this incroachment of foreign nations on Persian territory must have necessarily exercised an influence on the language. Already with the invasion of the Arabs and the conversion of Persia to Islâm a countless number of Arabic words and phrases had been adopted into the classical language. In the same manner, at a subsequent period, Turkish expressions found their way into the language and literature.

The addition of a considerable foreign vocabulary affected to some extent the original language. By far the greater number of foreign words were substantives and adjectives. The verb with its simple inflection remained for a long time untouched. But by degrees the Arabic or Turkish «*ism*» (noun or adjective), in conjunction with a Persian verb, supplanted the old *simple verb*. Thus there came into use a number of compound expressions formed by nouns and adjectives with auxiliary verbs, of which a list is given on page 47. This tendency produced a proportionate decrease in the number of simple verbs. E. g. آموختن *āmūkhtan*, *to learn* has been replaced by یاد گرفتن *yād giriftan* or درس خواندن *dars khāndan*, — بخشیدن *bakhshīdan*, *to bestow*, has been replaced by مرحمت کردن *marhamat kardan*.

A further change resulting from the foreign elements was the introduction of *adverbs*. No special form had existed for this part of speech in classical Persian, the meaning being expressed by an adjective used adverbially. In the modern language the arabic adverbs in اً, *an*, are the rule, whereas in the classical language they were the exception.

Another class of modifications might be styled *organic* and to these all languages are subject with the lapse of time. Two forces, a desire for lucidity and an inclination to laxity of expression, are especially powerful in producing this change. The old words lose their power and must either be strengthened or replaced by stronger expressions.

This phenomenon is most clearly marked in the case of the *prepositions*, for the prepositions of the classical language are now either doubled or strengthened or their place taken by simple concrete nouns. — It has been found necessary in a similar way to strengthen the *pronouns*, because like the prepositions, being small words, they were likely to be completely lost. Thus we now nearly always find *khudam*, *khudat khudash* used instead of the shorter form *khud* of the classical language. Double forms like: *chi kār* or *chi chīz* have replaced the simple form *chi*; *hīch kas na* is used for the original *kas na*; *chi vakht* for *key* etc.

Unfortunately the inclination towards laxity of expression has proved stronger in the development of modern Persian than the tendency towards lucidity. To this circumstance must be ascribed the great lack of rule and the partially apparent, partially real arbitrariness and inconsistency of the language, which renders the use of some parts of speech, especially the conjunctions and prepositions, a difficulty for the pupil and for the teacher. Also the inflection of the verb has lost some of its clearness and simplicity by the various forms being now frequently interchangeable, whereas in the classical language they were distinctly differentiated.

But vanity and love of effect, which, from the earliest days, have been weak points of the Persian character, have done even more harm to the language than inaccuracy of expression. It is owing to this love of display that the simplest subjects are mostly expressed in bombastic style, and quaint turns of speech are constantly drawn from the archaic or classical language and from Arabic. It is therefore, in dealing with the vocabulary and with the grammar, only possible to form a *general* distinction between the classical language and that of our own day. But such a distinction will not hold good in each particular case. *Modern Persian* must therefore to some extent be regarded as a mixture of *strictly modern Persian* and *classical Persian*. It is left to the taste of the individual to adopt whichever style he likes, the classical, the bombastic or the colloquial modern Persian. But it is always necessary to distinguish the language of Irân from the Persian which is still in use in *India*. The Persian of India may be looked upon as a petrification of the old classical language. It has also preserved the «*majhūl*» vowels *e* and *o* for *ī* and *ū* and many other differences in pronunciation. The Persian speaking Indians, whose studies are mostly confined to the classics and to poetic exercises, have followed none of the developments of the modern language.

In order to obtain a fixed standard in the midst of this confusion of styles, I have submitted nearly everything that has been written in purely modern Persian to a careful examination. The limited number of these publications has considerably lightened my task. Besides a few plays, of which the *Vazir of the Khān of Lankurān* is the best known, a small volume: *tādīb ul atfāl* (education of children) and the newspapers printed at Teheran, Isfahan and Constantinople, there are only the works of *Nāsireddīn Shāh* which are written in a modern and colloquial style. The excellent dialogues in Mirza Ibrahim's grammar of the Persian language (London 1841) belong half to the classical language, whose influence their author could not entirely shake off. In these it is only the uneducated people who use the style which Nāsireddīn Shāh has now raised to the dignity of a written language.

The descriptions which the late Shah has published of his travels in Persia and Europe are the best and truest specimens of the modern colloquial language spoken at the Persian court and capital. I have often during audiences with His Majesty been able to ascertain, in the course of long conversations, that the Shah spoke in exactly the same manner as he wrote, and frequently, in reading his most entertaining diaries, the very intonation of his voice has come back to me.

It is because the language of the Shah is the simple colloquial language committed to writing, that I have made it the foundation of the vocabulary, the grammar and the conversational parts of this book. All the examples given and all the dialogues are in strict accordance with the style used by the late Shah in his diaries.

As regards the *Turkish words* in the language, they follow the same rules in forming the plural etc. as purely Persian words. It has not therefore been necessary to devote a special chapter to them, as has been the case with the arabic words.

In drawing up the vocabulary and the conversations I have chiefly kept in view the requirements of the traveller. He may also derive useful information from particular chapters, as «a walk in the bazar» and «a journey through Persia» and others. I have taken especial pains to give such information as I have found useful in my first ride across the country, from the Persian Gulf to the Caspian Sea. A knowledge of the distances of the posthouses one from another, as given in the tables, may frequently save the «tāza vārid» (new arrival) from overcharge.

I would finally venture to express the hope that this *Grammar of Colloquial Persian* may awaken amongst some of my readers a certain interest in the modes of Persian thought and Persian expression, and that, after conquering the difficulties of the Persian characters, they may become acquainted with the very rich and fascinating classic literature, a knowledge of which is indispensable to the thorough mastery of the modern language.

F. R.

CONTENTS.

CONTENTS

CHAPTER I.

ALPHABET AND PRONUNCIATION.

The Persian alphabet consists of 32 letters which differ according to their position at the beginning, middle or end of a word or group of letters. The letters are written from right to left and, when made into words form a sort of shorthand.

As the table of the alphabet shows, some letters: ا د ذ ر ز ژ and و are never joined to the following letter. If they occur in the middle of a word, a gap is formed, similar to the interval between two separate words ex: برادر *bar ā da r* (*barādar*), brother.

In the so called شکسته *shikasta*, writing, all letters forming *one word* are connected. This greatly facilitates quick writing, but renders reading very difficult.

A number of letters, as may be seen in the table, represent *identical* sounds in Persian, f. i. ث, س and ص = s, or ح and ه = h, or ذ, ز, ض and ظ = z, ت and ط = t, ا and ع = spiritus lenis. — In *Arabic*, from which language the Persian alphabet is taken, these letters represent *different* sounds, but in Persian no distinction whatever is made between them. It is therefore useless for the student to trouble about the pronunciation of arabic sounds like ح, ظ or ض.

Persian names of letters.	not connected.	connected with the preceding only.	connected with the preceding a with the following.	connected with the following only.	EXAMPLES.			
					connected with the preceding only.	connected with the preceding a with the following.	connected with the following only.	
alif	ا	ـا	....	....	با bā	....	....	(see p.) spiritus lenis or long ā.
be	ب	ـب	ـبـ	بـ	شب shab	صبر sabr	بز buz	= English b.
pe	پ	ـپ	ـپـ	پـ	چپ chap	سپر sipar	پر par	= » p.
te	ت	ـت	ـتـ	تـ	دست dast	ستم sitam	تو tu	= » t.
se	ث	ـث	ـثـ	ثـ	ثالث sālis	مثل misl	ثم sum̃	= » s.
jīm	ج	ـج	ـجـ	جـ	کج kaj	هجر hijr	جا jā	= » j.
chīm	چ	ـچ	ـچـ	چـ	هیچ hīch	بچه bacha	چنك chang	= » ch in *ch*at.
he	ح	ـح	ـحـ	حـ	فتح fath	بحر bahr	حج haj	= » h.
khe	خ	ـخ	ـخـ	خـ	یخ yakh	لخت lukht	خر khar	= german ch in Sa*ch*e or Scotch in Lo*ch*.
dāl	د	ـد	....	....	بد bad	....	....	= English d.
zāl	ذ	ـذ	....	....	کاغذ kāghaz	....	....	= » z.
re	ر	ـر	....	....	خر khar	....	....	= Italian r (slightly rolled).
ze	ز	ـز	....	....	خز khaz	....	....	= English z.
je	ژ	ـژ	....	....	کژ kaj	....	....	= French j in *j*our or *s* in Engl measur-

				سـ	بس ..	قسم qism	سر sar	= English s in mason.
shīn	ش	ـش	ـشـ	شـ	كش kash	پشم pashm	شه shah	= » sh.
sād	ص	ـص	ـصـ	صـ	رقص raqs	قصد qasd	صاف sāf	= » s in mason.
zād	ض	ـض	ـضـ	ضـ	بعض baᶜz	خضر khizr	ضد zidd	= » z.
ta	ط	ـط	ـطـ	طـ	خط khatt	بطن batn	طير teir	= » t.
za	ظ	ـظ	ـظـ	ظـ	حافظ hāfiz	نظم nazm	ظلم zulm	= » z.
ᶜain	ع	ـع	ـعـ	عـ	مع maᶜ	بعد baᶜd	عقل ᶜaql	= initial alif (see p. 5) i. e. spiritas lenis.
ghain	غ	ـغ	ـغـ	غـ	تيغ tīgh	بغل baghal	غل ghul	a very guttural g not unlike the french r grasseillée.
fe	ف	ـف	ـفـ	فـ	كف kaf	سفر safar	فردا fardā	= English f.
qāf	ق	ـق	ـقـ	قـ	حق haq	نقره nuqra	قرآن qurān	a very guttural k.
kaf	ك	ـك	ـكـ	كـ	يك yak	بكن bikun	كن kun	= English k.
gaf	گ	ـگ	ـگـ	گـ	رنگ rang	جگر jigar	گدا gadā	= » g in garden.
lam	ل	ـل	ـلـ	لـ	گل gul	معلوم maᶜlūm	لب lab	= » l.
mīm	م	ـم	ـمـ	مـ	سم sum	نماز namāz	من man	= » m.
nūn	ن	ـن	ـنـ	نـ	تن tan	بنده banda	نام nām	= » n.
vāf	و	ـو	....	....	شو shou	....	....	= » v
he	ه	ـه	ـهـ	هـ	نه nuh	شبها shabhā	هنر hunar	= English h and = a at the end of words.
ye	ى	ـى	ـيـ	يـ	بى bī	بيد bīd	يورت yūrt	= English y in yard when a pure consonant; ى as a vowel see p. 5

The arabic alphabet contains no vowels proper. The three letters ا, و and ى are semivocalic consonants, viz: ا = spiritus lenis, i. e. the sound, not written in English, which introduces every initial vowel. — و = *v* and ى = *y* in *y*ard.

The vowel sounds short *a* 1) *u* and *i* are expressed by the signs ◌َ *fat'ha* or *zabar* for *a*, ◌ُ *zamma* or *pīsh* for *u* and ◌ِ *kasra* or *zīr* for *i*.

If these signs are added to the corresponding semivocalic consonants mentioned above, they form the long vowels *ā* 2), ī and ū, ex: جَالِينُوس Jālīnūs (Galen).

If they are added to the other consonants, they express short vowels, by which these consonants are followed ex: مُنتَظِر *muntazir*, expecting.

If a letter is to be followed by no vowel sound at all, the sign ◌ْ (*jazm* or *sukūn*) is placed over it ex: مُشْتْ *musht*, fist, مُنْتَظِر *muntazir*, expecting.

As a matter of fact these signs are *hardly ever used*, either in print or in writing. The consequence is, that the reader must either *know* or *guess* the vowels. This

---

1) The *fatha* ◌َ transcribed by a ◌َ is a short vowel very nearly resembling the English *a* in "apple" or "hat". The final *a* represented by ه has the same sound, and *not* that of the Italian *a* in "Roma", as is the case in *Hindūstānī* and *Indian Persian*.

2) Long ā is pronounced very much like in the English word "*bard*". Sometimes the sound is a little nearer the *o*, but never as much as in the English words "*soft*" or "*hawk*".

difficulty however is diminished by the general rule that: ا, و and ى between consonants represent long ā, long ū and long ī respectively, ex: مار mār, snake موش mūsh, mouse, ميز mīz, table.

In the transcription used in this book the long vowels, are marked with —, all vowels not bearing this sign being short.

ا in the beginning of a word, as also ع, is a mere spiritus lenis which can introduce any vowel or diphthong, ex: اَسپ asp, horse, اِنسان insān, man, اُردو urdū, camp, عَرب ʿArab, Arab, عِراق ʿIrāq [1]), عُرف ʿurf, civil code, عين ʿein, eye, اوقات ouqāt, times.

Long *initial* ā is expressed by آ (the sign ~ is called *madd*, prolongation) and by عا ex: آدم ādam, Adam, عادت ʿādat, custom.

ا which may be sometimes replaced by ء *hamza* in the middle of a word, is in some cases a spiritus lenis as it is when initial, ex: راس raʿs cape (pronounce ra-as), رئيس ra-ʿīs, director. Whenever the sign ʿ occurs in the *transcription*, a distinct hiatus must be heard, i. e. the word must be as it were, interrupted by a very short pause.

Initial و and ى are always pure consonants, ex: ورق *varag* leaf, ياور *yāvar* major.

Final short a is expressed by the letter ه ex: بنده *banda* slave, صفحه *safha* page. No *h*-sound is heard.

---

1) Vulgar ʿ*Arāq*.

If this final ه is to be followed by an ī or i, this is expressed by a ء *hamza*, over the ه, and the sound of a *y* is inserted, so as to avoid the hiatus, ex: صفحۀ *safha-yī* a page, بندۀ خدا *banda-yi khudā*, the slave of God.

The following words are spelt with a و as if they had a long ū, but pronounced with a short u.

دو	*du*	two
تو	*tu*	thou
خود	*khud*	self
خوردن	*khurdan*	to eat
آخور	*ākhur*	manger
خوراك	*khurāk*	food
خورش	*khurish*	stew
خورد	*khurd*	small
خورده	*khurda*	a little
خورشيد	*khurshīd*	the sun
خورسند	*khursand*	happy
خوش	*khush*	pleasant

The words چو and همچو are in modern Persian pronounced *chi* and *hamchi* as.

The syllables *ān* and *ām* are frequently pronounced *ūn* and *ūm*, especially in the South of Persia ex: نان *nān* or *nūn* bread, شام *shām* or *shūm* evening.

In the following words the و is not pronounced at all:

خواب	*khāb*	sleep
خوابيدن	*khābīdan*	to sleep

In some Arabic words final ā is represented by a ى Ex: مصطفى *Mustafā*, الى *ilā* until.

خواجه	*khāja*	eunuch
خوار	*khār*	abject
خوارزم	*khārizm*	the khanate of Khiva
خواستن	*khāstan*	to desire
خواهش	*khāhish*	desire
خوان, حوانچه	*khān*, *khāncha*	a tray
حواندن	*khāndan*	to read
خواهر	*khāhar*	sister

Diphthongs.

There are two diphthongs in Persian, *ei* and *ou*, ex: حَوض *houz* (not unlike English *hose*) a tank مَیل *meil* (not unlike English *mail*) inclination.

The Consonants proper and Orthographical Signs.

The consonants require no particular explanations beyond what is said in the table of the alphabet.

The only case where the pronunciation differs from the writing is the ه at the end of the words سه *si* three, به *bi* to چه *chi* what and كه *ki* who (و) where no aspiration is heard.

The ه standing for a short *a* at the end of words has been explained p. 5.

In order to show that a consonant is doubled, the sign ّ, *tashdīd* is placed over it, ex درّه *darra* valley, محمّد *Muhammad*.

Another orthographical sign much used in Persian is the *tanvīn* اً. It is originally the termination of arabic accusatives, used in Persian as adverbs ex: مثلاً *masalan* for instance, غالباً *ghāliban* mostly, اتّفاقاً *ittifāqan* accidentally. The ا preceding the *tanvīn* is a short *a*.

When the ل *l* of the arabic article ال *al* is assimilated with the following consonant, which is always the case before the dentals ت ث د ذ ر ز س ش ص ض ط ظ and ن, the sign ـ *vasla* is placed over the ل ex: اَلسلام *as salām* the greeting, هارون الرشيد *Hārūn ar Rashīd*, جبل الطارق *jabal at Tāriq* the mountain of Tāriq (Gibraltar) الشيطان *ash Sheitān* the devil.

All orthographical signs are frequently omitted in print and usually in writing.

The Accent.

The *accent* falls on the *last* syllable of all words except certain parts of the verb and some particles which are explained below.

The only Persian noun which has the accent on the first syllable is صنّار *sánnār* a penny, the contraction of صد دينار *sad dīnār* a hundred dinars.

The following parts of the verb have the accent on the first syllable:

1) All forms beginning by the prefixes مى *mī* and به *bi* ex: ميكيرد *mígīrad* he takes بپرسم *bípursam* shall I ask?

When either *mī* or *bi* are omitted, the accent remains on the first syllable, ex: كنم *kúnam* I may do كويد *gūyad* he will say.

The accent is particularly strong on the *bi* of the Imperative ex: بزن *bízan* strike! برويم *bívavīm* let us go!

2) The *negative* forms, beginning with نه *na*, ex: نکن *ná-kun* do not! نکردم *ná-kardam* I did not نمیکنم *ná-mīkunam* I do not.

In the *past tense* the syllable, which in the third person is either the last or the only one, keeps the accent throughout all the other persons of the tense ex: فرمود *farmúd* he ordered; the other persons are: *farmúdam*, *farmúdī*, *farmúdīm*, *farmúdīd*, *farmúdand.* داد *dād* he gave; the other persons are: *dádam*, *dádī*, *dádīm*, *dádīd*, *dádand* (compare conjugation table p. 49).

All other parts of the verb have the *accent* on the *last syllable.* These are:

1) The *infinitive*, full or shortened, ex: پرسیدن *pursīdán*, پرسید *pursíd* to ask.

2) The *participles*, *present* ex: کننده *kunandá* doing, خواننده *khānandá* singing,

and *past* ex: گرفته *giriftá* taken, برده *burdá* carried off.

3) The *gerund* ex: خوردنی *khurdaní* a thing to be eaten گفتنی *guftaní* a thing to be said.

A few *Arabic* and *Persian particles* have the accent on the *first* syllable:

آیا *áyā* interrogative particle	بلی *bálī* yes
امّا *ámmā* but	لیکن *líkan* but
ولی *válī* however	یعنی *yáʿnī* that is to say.

The ī at the end of a word, when it is the *indefinite article* is not accentuated. In this way words connected with the indefinite article are to be distinguished from abstract nouns or adjectives spelt and otherwise pronounced in the same way, ex: پادشاهی *pādisháhī* a king, *pādishāhí* royal power. — دولتی *douláti* a government, *doulatí* governmental. — شهری *sháhrī* a town, *shahrí* belonging to the town, municipal. — گدای *gadáī* a beggar, *gadāí* beggary.

There is a third ī in Persian, which may be called the *relative* ī. It connects the relative pronoun که *ki* with the preceding word. This relative ī has the accent, which makes it distinguishable from the ī of the indifinite article before mentioned, ex: شخصی که *shakhsí-ki the* person who, but *shákhsī ki a* person who اسپی که جو نخورده است *aspí ki jou nakhurda ast*, *the* horse which has eaten no barley, but *áspī ki jou na-khurda ast*, *a* horse which has eaten no barley.

A number of words are *enclytic*, i. e. they are so closely connected with the preceding word, that they have no accent of their own. These are:

1) The *suffixed pronouns* ام *am*, ات *at*, اش *ash*, مان *mān*, تان *tān*, شان *shān*, see p. 32, ex: مادرش *mādár-ash* his mother.

2) The *present* forms of the verb *to be* ام *am*, ای *ī*, است *ast*, ایم *īm*, اید *īd*, اند *and*, see p. 41, ex: چه ساعت است *chi sāᶜát-ast?* what is the time?

3) The short *i* called *izāfa* see p. 13.

CHAPTER II.

GRAMMAR.

The *grammar* of the Persian language is extremely simple, there being only *one* declension, *one* conjugation and *no* gender.

1. The Noun.

The *Plural* in *classical Persian* used to be ان *ān* for persons and ها *hā* for things, ex: پادشاهان *pādishāh ā n* kings, تختها *takht h ā* thrones.

Names of animals used to have their plurals formed both ways, ex: سگها *saghā* and سگان *sagān* dogs.

In *modern Persian* the plural in ان *ān* is almost obsolete and ها *hā* is generally used for persons as well as for things, ex: سرباز *sarbāz* soldier, plur: سربازها *sarbāzhā*, زن *zan* woman, plur: زنها *zanhā*, كتاب *kitāb*, book, plur: كتابها, گدا *gadā* beggar, plur: گداها.

The obsolete method of forming the plurals of Persian words in ه, viz: *agān* for persons and *ajāt* for things is still in use, especially in books and official writings, ex: بنده *banda* slave, plur: بندگان *bandagān* نوشته *navishta* writing, plural: نوشتجات *navishtajāt* روزنامه *rūznāma* newspaper, plural: روزنامجات *rūznāmajāt*. — كارخانه *kārkhāna* factory, plural: كارخانجات *kārkhānajāt*. — But at the same time the modern forms are used:

بندها *bandahā*, نوشتها *navishtahā*, روزنامها *rūznāmahā*, کارخانها *kārkhānahā*.

Some arabic collective nouns in ه form their plurals in ajāt. ex: عمله *'amala* workmen, plur: عملجات *'amalajāt*.

مرد *mard* man, has three plural forms: مردها *mardhā*, men مردم *mardum* and مردمان *mardumān*, people.

The *Accusative* is formed by adding را *rā* either to the singular or to the plural, ex: سگ *sag*, dog, acc: سگرا *sagrā*, noun plur.: سگها *saghā*, plural acc: سگهارا *saghārā*, سرباز *sarbāz* soldies, acc: سربازرا *sarbāzrā*, plur. nominat. سربازها *sarbāzhā*, plur accusative سربازهارا *sarbāzhārā*, زن *zan* woman, accus: زنرا *zanrā*, plur. nominat: زنها *zanhā*, plur. accusat: زنهارا *zanhārā*.

The accusative ending را *rā* is also added to the obsolete plurals mentioned above as well as to the arabic plurals.

The accusative ending را *rā* has the meaning of a *definite article* which otherwise does not exist in Persian. If *rā* is omitted, it leaves the word indefinite, ex: اسپرا دیدم *asprā dīdam* I saw *the* horse, but اسپ دیدم *asp dīdam* I saw *a* horse.

In order to express the *indefinite article* in the singular ی *ī* is added to the corresponding words. This *ī* is long and not accentuated, see pp. 9 and 10, ex: اسپی *aspī a* horse, خوب اسپی *khūb aspī* a good horse. If a noun is followed by an adjective, the *ī* of the indefinite article is added to the adjective ex: کوهِ بلندی *kūh-i bulandī* a high mountain, سگِ زردی *sag-i zardī* a yellow dog.

The izāfa.

1) The *genitive* is formed by adding a short *i* called *izāfa* to the governing noun, which generally precedes the noun governed.

The *i* of the *izāfa* is either not written at all or expressed by a ـِ (kasra).

Examples of the genitive.

اسپِ شاه *asp-i Shāh*, the horse of the King کوهِ نور *kūh-i nūr* the mountain of light زنِ وزیرِ پادشاهِ ایران *zan-i vazīr-i pādishāh-i Īrān*, the wife of the minister of the King of Persia.

When the governing word ends in a vowel, the *izāfa* is pronounced *yi*, so as to avoid the hiatus, and spelt with a ی, ex: پای فیل *pā-yi fīl* the foot of the elephant, روی زمین *rū-yi zamīn*, the surface of the earth.

If this vowel is the *a* expressed by ه, the *izāfa* takes the shape of a ء (hamza) over the ه, ex: خانهٔ درویش *khāna-yi darvīsh* the house of the dervish, بندهٔ خدا *banda-yi khudā* the slave of God.

2) *Adjectives* are connected in the same way with their nouns as the governed word with the governing in the case corresponding to the English genitive, ex: اسپِ شاه *asp-i shāh* the horse of the king, اسپِ سیاه *asp-i sīāh* the black horse — کوهِ نور *kūh-i nūr* the mountain of light کوهِ بلند *kūh-i buland* the high mountain. The above examples show that for the Persians there is no difference

between the possessive case and a noun connected with an adjective.

3) If several adjectives form attributes to the same noun, they are connected by the *izāfa* unless they are connected by the conjunction و *va*, and ex: اسپِ عربیِ سیاهِ خوبی *asp-i ʿarabī-yi sīāh-i khūbī* a good black arab horse. کوهِ بلندِ سنگیِ برفدار *kūh-i buland-i sangi-yi barfdar* a high, rocky, snow-covered mountain.

4) The *izāfa* is furthermore used to form *possessive pronouns*, by connecting the personal pronouns with the governing word, in the same way as adjectives are connected with their nouns, ex: (من *man*, I) اسپِ من *asp-i man*, my horse (ما *mā* we) خانهٔ ما *khāna-yi mā* our house.

Omission of the izāfa.

The *izāfa* is *omitted* in certain *arabic genitives* [1]) when the governing and the governed word form one compound noun or express one notion.

The most frequent governing words used in this way are: صاحب *sāhib* owner, possessor, امیر or میر *amīr* or *mīr* lord, ولی *valī* lieutenant, ابن *ibn* or بن *bin* son ex: صاحب منصب *sāhib mansab*, possessor of rank, officer.

صاحب قران *sāhib qarān* a Ruler over a space of 30 years.

صاحب کمال *sāhib kamāl* possessor of perfection.

---

1) In *Arabic* the genitive is formed by mere *juxta*-position ex: باب *bāb* gate, ال *al* the, وادی *vādī* valley باب الوادی *bāb al vādī*, the gate of the valley, ید *yad* hand ید محمد *yad Muhammad* the hand of Muhammad.

The great number of *arabic titles* now used in Persia are all formed in the same way, by mere juxtaposition, i. e. without the *izāfa*, ex:

صدر اعظم *sadr a^czam* most high chief, grand vizier.

ولی عهد *valī ᶜahd* lieutenant of the office, heir apparent.

ظلّ آلسلطان *zill as sultān* shadow of the King (title of the present Shah's eldest son).

نایب آلسلطنه *nāyib as saltana* lieutenant of royalty (the present Shah's third son).

بن سلطان *bin sultān* son of a king.

ولی نعمت *vali niᶜmat* lord of bounty, Sovereign.

اسد آلدوله *asad ad doula* lion of the state.

امین الملك *amīn al mulk* confidant of the Kingdom.

عزیز آلسلطان *ᶜazīz as sultān* favourite of the king.

صمصام آلسلطنه *samsām as saltana* scimitar of the kingdom.

عزّت الدوله *ᶜizzat ad doula* honour of the state } titles of princesses

عصمت الملوك *ᶜismat al mulūk* chastity of kings } titles of princesses

امیر تومان *amīr tūmān* lord over 10,000, general.

میر پنج *mīr panj* lord over 5(000).

میر غضب *mīr ghazab* lord of wrath, executioner.

میر شکار *mīr shikār* master of the hunt.

میر آخور *mīr ākhur* lord of the manger, master of the horse.

In the same way some *turkish-persian* genitives are used without the *izāfa*, ex:

نایب چاپار *nāyib chapar* postmaster.

شاگرد چاپار *shāgird chapar* postboy.

بیکلربیک *beiglarbeig* under governor (lit. chief of chiefs. but also with the turkish sign of the possessive case ex:

بیکلر بیکی *beiglar beig-ī* chief of chiefs.

دریا بیکی *daryā beig-ī* lord of the sea, admiral

In all the examples quoted above the two words connected without the *izāfa* express *one* notion and are to be considered as compound words. When this is *not* the case, the *izāfa must be used* ex: صاحب خانه *sāhib khāna* householder but *sāhib-i khāna the* owner of *the* house صاحب منصب *sāhib mansab* an officer, but صاحبِ منصبِ سرهنکی *sāhib-i mansab-i sarhangī* the holder of the rank of a colonel.

The *other cases* are formed by prepositions as in English or French:

به *bi*, to
برای *barāyi*, for
از *az* from
با *bā* with.
پیش *pīsh*, to, (used only for persons).

The following forms of frequently used verbs should be learnt by heart. They will be necessary in order to illustrate the formation of the cases.

آمد *āmad*, came
رفت *raft* went
گفت *guft* said
دید *dīd* saw
برد *burd* took away
آورد *āvurd* brought
گرفت *girift* took
داد *dād* gave

On the following page are given a few examples which will serve to illustrate some of the foregoing rules:

سرباز اسپ برای شاه آورد	sarbāz asp barāyi Shāh āvurd.	a soldier brought a horse for the King.
سگ نان گدارا برد	sag nān-i gadā-rā burd.	the dog carried off the beggar's bread.
کشتی انگلیس بایران آمد	kashtī-yi Inglīs bi Irān āmad.	an English ship came to Persia.
وزیر از طهران رفت به فرنگستان	vazīr az Tahrān raft bi Farangistān.	the minister went from Tehran to Europe.
مرد شمشیر شاهرا دید	mard shamshīr-i Shāhrā dīd.	the man saw the sword of the King.
شاه پول از وزیر گرفت و بگدا داد	Shāh pūl az vazīr girift va bi gadā dād.	the King took money from the minister and gave it to the beggar.
دوستِ من پیشِ من آمد	dūst-i man pīsh-i man āmad.	my friend came to me.
دوستِ تو بتو چه گفت	dūst-i tu bi tu chi guft?	what did your friend say to you?
کُتابرا بمن نداد	kitāb-rā bi man na dād.	he did not give me the book.
کتابی از من گرفت	kitābī az man girift.	he took a book from me.
شاه با وزیر بمسجد آمد	Shāh bā vazīr bi masjid āmad.	the King came with the minister to the mosque.
درویش از خانهٔ وزیر بحمام رفت	darvīsh az khāna-yi vazīr bi hammām raft.	the dervish went from the house of the minister to the bath.

2. Adjectives.

Adjectives generally follow nouns and in this case are joined to them by the *izāfa* (see p. 13) ex. اسپِ عربی *asp-i ʿarabī* the arabian horse, کوهِ بلند *kūh-i buland* the high hill, دستِ راست *dast-i rāst* the right hand, پای چپ *pā-yi chap* the left foot.

To form the accusative را *rā* is added to the *adjective* only, ex. اسپِ عربی‌را *asp-i ʿarabī-rā*, کوهِ بلند را *kūh-i buland-rā*, دستِ راست‌را *dast-i rāst-rā*, پای چپ را *pa-yi chap-rā.*

The termination of the plural is added to the *nouns* only, ex. اسپهای عربی *asphā-yi ʿarabī* arabian horses, کوه‌های بلند *kūhhā-yi buland* high hills, دستهای راست *dasthā-yi rāst* right hands, پاهای چپ *pāhā-yi chap* left feet.

Examples of the plural accusative:

اسپهای عربی‌را *asphā-yi ʿarabī-rā*
کوه‌های بلندرا *kūhhā-yi buland-rā*
دستهای راست‌را *dasthā-yi rāst-rā*
پاهای چپ‌را *pāhāyi chap-rā*

If a number of adjectives follow a noun, را *rā* is added to the last of these adjectives only, ex. قالیِ بزرگِ خوشرنگِ ترکمانی‌را *qālī-yi buzurg-i khushrang-i turkamānī-rā* the large finely coloured turkoman carpet.

A few adjectives sometimes precede the noun, which is generally followed by the indefinite article ی *i*, and in this case the *izāfa* is mostly omitted.

ex. عجب هوای *ʿajab havā-i*, (a) wonderful air خوب اسپی *khūb aspī*, a good horse.

In very few cases adjectives precede the noun *with* the *izāfa*. ex. پیر مرد *pīr-i mard* an old man, پیرِ زن *pīr-i zan* an old woman, پیرِ بازار *Pīr-i bāzār* the Saint's bazar, سبزِ میدان *sabz-i meidān* the green square.

Adjectives frequently precede nouns to form compounds, ex. بدبو *badbū* of bad smell, خوشرنگ *khushrang* of fine colour, سیاهبیشه *siāhbīsha* Black Forest, سفیدکوه *Safīdkūh* White Mountain.

The *degrees of comparison* are formed by adding to the adjective:

تر *tar* for the comparative and ترین *tarīn* for the superlative.

Examples.

خوب *khūb* good خوبتر *khūbtar* better خوبترین *khūbtarīn* best.

به *bih* good بهتر *bihtar* better بهترین *bihtarīn* best.

بد *bad* bad بدتر *badtar* worse بدترین *badtarīn* worst.

بزرگ *buzurg* large بزرگتر *buzurgtar* bigger بزرگترین *buzurgtarīn* biggest.

کوچك *kūchik* small کوچکتر *kūchiktar* smaller کوچکترین *kūchiktarīn* smallest.

Than is expressed by از *az* ex. بهتر از جان *bihtar az jān* better than life, بزرگتر از فیل *buzurgtar az fīl*, bigger than an elephant.

The *superlative construction* is the same as the genitive ex. بهترین مردم *bihtarīn-i mardum* the best of men, بزرکترین پادشاهها *buzurgtarīn-i pādishāhhā* the greatest of kings (the greatest king).

3. Numerals.

1. Cardinal Numerals.

١	یک	*yak*	1
٢	دو	*du*	2
٣	سه	*si*	3
٤	چهار	*chahār*	4
٥	پنج	*panj*	5
٦	شش	*shish*	6
٧	هفت	*haft*	7
٨	هشت	*hasht*	8
٩	نه	*nuh*	9
١٠	ده	*dah*	10
١١	یازده	*yāzdah*	11
١٢	دوازده	*davāzdah*	12
١٣	سیزده	*sīzdah*	13
١٤	چهارده	*chahārdah*	14
١٥	پانزده	*punzdah*	15
١٦	شانزده	*shunzdah*	16
١٧	هیفده	*hīvdah*	17
١٨	هیجده	*hījdah*	18
١٩	نوزده	*nuzdah*	19
٢٠	بیست	*bīst*	20
٢١	بیست و یک	*bīst u yak*	21
٢٢	بیست و دو	*bīst u du*	22
٢٣	بیست و سه	*bīst u si*	23

۲۴	بیست و چهار	*bīst u chahār*	24
۲۵	بیست و پنج	*bīst u panj*	25
۲۶	بیست و شش	*bīst u shish*	26
۲۷	بیست و هفت	*bīst u haft*	27
۲۸	بیست و هشت	*bīst u hasht*	28
۲۹	بیست و نه	*bīst u nuh*	29
۳۰	سی	*sī*	30
۳۱	سی و یك	*sī u yak*	31
۴۰	چهل	*chihil*	40
۵۰	پنجاه	*panjāh*	50
۶۰	شصت	*shast*	60
۷۰	هفتاد	*haftād*	70
۸۰	هشتاد	*hashtād*	80
۹۰	نود	*navad*	90
۱۰۰	صد	*sad*	100
۱۰۱	صد و یك	*sad u yak*	101
۲۰۰	دویست	*davīst*	200
۲۱۱	دویست و یازده	*davīst u yāzdah*	211
۳۰۰	سی‌صد	*sīsad*	300
۴۰۰	چهارصد	*chahārsad*	400
۵۰۰	پانصد	*punsad*	500
۶۰۰	ششصد	*shishsad*	600
۷۰۰	هفتصد	*haftsad*	700
۸۰۰	هشتصد	*hashtsad*	800
۹۰۰	نهصد	*nuhsad*	900
۱۰۰۰	هزار	*hazār*	1000
۲۰۰۰	دو هزار	*du hazār*	2000
۱۰۰۰۰	ده‌هزار	*dah hazār* [1]	10 000
۱۰۰۰۰۰	صد هزار	*sad hazār*	100 000

1) ۱۰۰۰۰۰ is also called لك *lak*. (The Indian lāk is 100 000.)

٥٠٠٠٠٠	کرور	*kurūr*	500 000
١٠٠٠٠٠٠	میلیون	*mīlīūn*	1 000 000

صدها *sadhā* hundreds, هزارها *hazārhā* thousands, یک یک *yak yak* or یک بیک *yak bi yak* one by one, یکایک *yakāyak* suddenly, دو دو *du du* or دو بدو *du bi du* by twos, etc.

جفت *juft* a pair, لنگه *linga* the other of a pair.

Rule After *cardinal numbers* the noun is employed in the *singular*, *not* in the plural, as in English ex. هفت لشکر *haft lashgar* seven armies (*not* haft lashgar*hā*, چهل ستون *chihil sutūn*, forty columns, پنجاه روز *panjāh rūz* fifty days.

Often, and more especially in writing, collective nouns follow the numerals, ex. دویست باب خانه *davīst bāb khāna*, 200 houses, پنج نفر فرّاش *panj nafar farrāsh* [1]) 5 footmen, یک دستگاه فنجان *yak dastgāh finjān* a set of cups, — ده رأس اسپ *dah raʿs asp* 10 horses.

چهارده رأس قاطر *chahārdah raʿs qātir*, 14 mules.
دو زنجیر فیل *du zanjīr fīl*, 2 elephants.
صد نفر شتر *sad nafar shutur*, 100 camels.
شش عراده توپ *shish ʿarrāda tūp*, 6 cannons.
یک دانه سرداری *yak dāna sardārī*, 1 coat.
دوازده عدد صندلی *davāzdah adad sandalī*, 12 chairs.
دو تا دستمال *du tā dastmāl*, 2 handkerchiefs.

In ordinary conversation نفر *nafar* is used for *persons* and generally تا *tā*, sometimes دانه *dāna* for things.

Learn the following idioms: دو سه تا *du si tā* two

---

1) It is difficult to translate the word *farrāsh*. A farrāsh may be called upon to act as housemaid or executioner.

or three; چهار پنج تا *chahār panj tā*, four or five; هفت هشت ده تا *haft*, *hasht*, *dah tā* some seven or ten (in this case نُه *nuh* 9 is always omitted.)

Ordinals.

یکم *yakum* first	هفتم *haftum* seventh
دویم *duyum* second	هشتم *hashtum* eighth
سیم *siyum* third	نهم *nuhum* nineth
چهارم *chahārum* fourth	دهم *dahum* tenth
پنجم *panjum* fifth	صدم *sadum* hundredth
ششم *shishum* sixth	هزارم *hazārum* thousandth.

Besides the Persian ordinals the *Arabic* ordinals are to a certain extent used:

اوّل *avval* first
ثانی *sānī* second
ثالث *sālis* third
رابع *rābiʿ* fourth
خامس *khāmis* fifth
سادس *sādis* sixth
سابع *sābiʿ* seventh, etc.

Of these *arabic ordinals* اوّل *avval* the first, is used in dates, ex. اوّلِ ماهِ رمضان *avval-i māh-i Ramazān* the first of the month of Ramazan.

The first day of the month is also called غرّه *ghurra* and the last day سلخ *salkh*.

The plural of اوّل *avval* is اوایل *avāyil*, which means the first days, the beginning.

The arabic ordinals are also used to distinguish sovereigns bearing the same name, ex. شاه عباس اول *Shāh Abbās-i avval*, Shah Abbas the First. شاه طهماسپ ثانی *Shāh Tahmāsp-i sānī*, Shah Tahmāsp II.

In *enumeration* the adverbial form of the arabic ordinals is mostly used: اولاً *avvalan* firstly, ثانیاً *sānian* secondly, ثالثاً *sālisan* thirdly, etc.

Adverbial numbers.

These are formed by adding دفعه *daf^ca*, بار *bār* or مرتبه *martaba* to the cardinals, ex. یك دفعه *yak daf^ca* once, دو بار *du bār* twice, سه مرتبه *si martaba* three times.

دو باره *du bāra* means: over again, once more.

2 × 2 = 4: دو تا دو چهار میشود *du tā du chahār mīshavad.*

Fractions.

½ نیم *nīm* or نصف *nisf*
⅓ ثلث *suls* or سه یك *si yak*
¼ ربع *rub^c* or چهار یك *chahār yak*
⅕ خمس *khums* or پنج یك *panj yak*, etc.
5% صد و پنج *sad u panj*
20% صد و بیست *sad u bīst*
20° (twenty degrees) بیست درجه *bīst daraja.*

4. Pronouns.

1) Personal pronouns.

من *man* I	ما *mā* we
تو *tu* thou	شما *shumā* you
او *ū* he, she, it	ایشان *īshān* they.

The second person singular تو *tu* thou, is used in speaking to inferiors only, especially to servants. Otherwise شما *shumā* you, is used like in English or *vous* in French.

In speaking of a person of superior rank, the plural ایشان *īshān* is used instead of the singular او *ū*.

The accusative of من *man* is مرا *marā*. Otherwise the declension of the personal pronoun is the same as that of the noun.

The personal pronoun *in the accusative* can also be expressed by adding the shorter form of the possessive pronoun to the word preceding the verb. Thus there is no distinction between the personal and the possessive pronoun in Persian.

2) Possessive pronoun, shorter form.

	Singular.	Plural.
1 person	ام *am* my, me.	مان *mān* our, us.
2 „	ات *at* thy, thee.	تان *tān* your, you.
3 „	اش *ash* his, hers, its, him.	شان *shān* their, them.

Examples of this pronoun used both as personal and as possessive:

دلم *dil-am*, *my* heart, ولم کن *vil-am kun*, let *me* go, صدات نشنیدم *sadā-at na-shanīdam* I have not heard *your* voice, صدات کردم *sadā-at kardam* I called *you*, میبینم اش *mībīnam ash* I see him, پیش اش بیار *pīsh-ash bīār* bring him forward.

These forms are also sometimes used for the *dative* (which in classical Persian was identical with the accusative), ex. نانم بده *nān-am bidih* give me bread, گفتِ شان *guft-i shān* he told them.

The *longer form* of *the possessive pronoun* is identical with the personal pronoun on page 24. ex. اسپِ من *asp-i man* my horse.

Illustration of the two forms of the possessive pronoun.

اسپم *aspam* or اسپِ من *asp-i man* my horse
اسپت *asp-at* „ اسپِ تو *asp-i tu* thy horse
اسپش *asp-ash* „ اسپِ او *asp-i ū* his horse
اسپمان *asp-i mān* „ اسپِ ما *asp-i mā* our horse
اسپتان *asp-i tān* „ اسپِ شما *asp-i shumā* your horse
اسپشان *asp-i shān* „ اسپِ ایشان *asp-i īshan* their horse.

The former of these two forms is the more frequent one in ordinary conversation.

In order to form the *accusative*, را *rā* is added to the pronoun: اسپمرا *aspamrā* or اسپِ مرا *asp-i marā.*

To form the *plural* ها *hā* is added to the noun ex. اسپهای من *asphā-yi man* or: اسپهام *asphā-am*.

The possessive case is often expressed by مال *māl* (property) ex. اسپ مالِ من *asp māl-i man* my horse كتاب مالِ حكيم *kitab māl-i hakīm* the doctor's book.

3. *The Reflexive Pronoun* in classical Persian is خود *khud.* Though this form is sometimes used in colloquial Persian, the following forms are much more usual:

خودم *khudam* myself
خودت *khudat* thyself

خودش *khudash* himself, herself, itself
خودمان *khudimān* ourselves
خودتان *khuditān* yourselves
خودشان *khudishān* themselves.

Rule: Personal and *possessive* pronouns must be replaced by the *reflexive* pronoun when they refer to the same subject, ex. من خودمرا نمیشناسم *man khudamrā na-mīshanāsam* I do not know myself, اسپ خودشرا دید *asp-i khudashrā dīd* he saw his horse.

In ordinary conversation this rule is not always strictly observed, ex. میخواهم دستمرا بشورم *mīkhāham dast-am-rā bishūram* I want to wash my hands, for دستِ خودمرا *dast-i khudam-rā.*

4. *Demonstrative Pronouns.*

این *īn* this آن *ān* (commonly pronounced *un*) that. When used as nouns they are declined in the ordinary way.

همین *hamīn* this same one
همان *hamān* (*hamun*) that same one
چنین *chunīn* همچنین *hamchunīn* such a one as this
چنان *chunān* همچنان *hamchunān* such a one as that
همچو *hamchu* generally pronounced *hamchi* so, such
چندین *chandīn* and چندان *chandān* so much.

5. *Relative Pronouns.*

که *ki* who, that, accusative: که .... اورا چه *chi* which.
ki .... *ūrā* or که .... اش *ki* .... *ash*. ex.

سربازکه اسپ اورا کشته بودند *sarbāz ki asp-i ūrā kushta būdand* the soldier whose horse they had killed, اسپیکه دمشرا بریدند *aspī-ki dum-ashrā burrīdand* the horse whose tail they cut off.

The *relative* pronouns کـه *ki* and چـه *chi* are often connected with the demonstrative pronouns:

اینکه *īnki*, آنکه *ānki* (*unki*), اینچه *īnchi* آنچه, *ānchi* (*unchi*). ex. اینـکه رفـت *īnki raft* this one who went, آنچه کفتی *ānchi guftī* that which you said.

If a noun is followed by a relative sentence which is to define it, a ی *ī* is added to that noun ex. شخصی کـه *shakhsí-ki* the person that, سگیرا کـه *sagīrā-ki* the dog which (accus.).

This relative ī must not be confounded with the ī of the indefinite article or the ī which serves to form adjectives and abstract nouns, see pp. 12 and 13.

Note the construction of the following examples: شخصی کـه بلو پـول داده بـودم *shakhsí-ki bi ū pūl dāda būdam* the person to whom I had given money, چـوبی که از او قاشق میسازنـد *chūbí-ki az ū qāshuq mīsāzand* the wood out of which they make spoons.

sháhrī-ki dar ū yak faqīrī na-bāshad a town in which there is not one poor person.

6. *Interrogative pronouns*. These are identical with the relative pronouns: که *ki* who? and چه *chi* what? The latter is generally followed by چیز *chīz* thing, کار *kār* business, حرف *harf* word.

که *ki* who?		
چه *chi*		
چه چیز *chi chīz* (thing)	}	what?
چه کار *chi kār* (business)		
چه حرف *chi harf* (word)		

Among the common people چه چی *chi chī* is often used for چه چیز *chi chīz*.

Note the construction of the following sentences: این اسپ کیست *īn asp-i kī-st?* (*ki ast*) whose horse is this? این چه حرف است *īn chi harf ast?* what word is this? (what do you mean by this?) آن مرد که بود *ān mard ki būd?* who was that man? از این چه بهتر است *az īn chi bihtar ast?* what is better than this?

کدام *kudām* which? ex: کدام شخص *kudām shakhs?* which person? کدام کتاب *kudām kitāb?* which book? چند *chand* how much? how many? چند نفر بودند *chand nafar būdand?* how many were they? این تفنگرا چند خریدی *īn tufang-rā chand kharīdī?* how much did you give for this gun?

چرا *chirā* (originally the accusative or dative of چه *chi*) why? ex. چرا نگفتی *chirā na guftī?* why did you not say (so)?

چرا *chirā* in vulgar Persian is very frequently used instead of the affirmative بلی *bálī* or آری *ārei* yes, ex. پول داری — چرا *pūl dārī?* — *chirā* have you any money? — yes. This is an abreviation of چرا نداشته باشم *chirā na dāshta bāsham?* why should I not have any?

کجا *kujā?* where?

کی *kei?* } when?
چه وقت *chi vakht?* }

کی *kei* is also used in the meaning of *how*, ex. کی میشود *kei mīshavad?* how can it be?

Table of Indefinite Pronouns and Adverbs.

همه *hama* all

همه همه *hama hama* all together

هر يك *har yak* every one

هر كدام *har kudām*
هر كه *har ki*
هر آنكه *har ān-ki*
هر كس *har kas*
هر كسيكه *har kasī-ki*
} whoever

چند نفر *chand nafar* some (persons)

چند تا *chand tā* some (things)

هر چيز *har chīz*
هرِ چيزى *har chīzī*
} everything

هرِ چه *har chi*
هر آنچه *har unchi*
هر چيز *har chīz*
هر چيزيكه *har chīzī-ki*
} whatever

همه‌جا *hama jā* everywhere

هرجا *har jā*
هر جايكه *har jāī-ki*
هرِكجا *har kujā*
} whereever

هر طرف *har taraf*
بهر سمت *bi har samt*
هر سو *har sū*
} whereever (in whatever direction)

هر طوريكه *har tourī-ki* in which ever way

هر وقت *har vakht* at any time

هميشه *hamīsha* always

هر روز *har rūz* every day

هر شب *har shab* every night

شب و روز *shab u rūz*
شبانه روز *shabāna rūz*
} day and night

همه روزه *hama rūza* all day long

هر دو *har du* both

بهر حال *bi har hāl* in any case, at all costs.

5. The Verb.

The *Persian verb* is particularly simple and easy to learn. There is only *one* conjugation. All tenses are formed from two fundamental parts, the *imperative* and the *infinitive.* The terminations added to these are the same in all verbs without any irregularities.

1. The auxiliary verb بودن *būdan* to be, is slightly irregular only in so far, as it has three radicals: هست *hast*, بود *būd* and باش *bāsh*.

Infinitive بودن *būdan* to be.

Indicative.

Present (weaker form).

ام *am* I am	ایم *īm* we are
ای *ī* thou art	اید *īd* you are
است *ast* he, she, it is	اند *and* they are.

Present (stronger form) [1])

هستم *hastam* I am	هستیم *hastīm* we are
هستی *hasti* thou art	هستید *hastīd* you are
هست *hast* he, she, it is	هستند *hastand* they are.

Present negative.

نیستم *nīstam* I am not	نیستیم *nīstīm* we are not
نیستی *nīstū* thou art not	نیستید *nīstīd* you are not
نیست *nīst* is not	نیستند *nīstand* they are not.

1) The stronger form is more emphatic than the weaker form ex. توی جنکل شکار است *tūyi jangal shikār ast*? Is there game in the forest? answer: هست there *is*. — وکرنه من همان خاکم که هستم *vagarna man hamān khāk am ki hastam* otherwise I am but the dust I (really) am. (Saadi).

Similarly words ending in a long vowel are contracted with forms of the present هستم *hastam* when followed by them, ex. ماست *māst* (for مااست) شماست *shumā-st* (for شما است *shumā ast*).

تو *tu* (thy, thine) and است *ast* form *tust* (with a short vowel)

كه *ki* (who, whose) and است *ast* form كيست *kīst*, the other forms with كه *ki* are: كيستم *kīstam*, كيستى *kīstī*, كيستيم *kīstīm*, كيستيد *kīstīd*, كيستند *kīstand*, ex. اين شخص كيست *īn shakhs kīst?* who is this person? ما سگِ كيستيم *mā sag-i kīstīm?* whose dogs are we? (idiom).

Very often this contraction is not expressed in writing, but exists none the less in pronunciation.

Preterite (French *je fus*)

بودم *būdam* I was	بوديم *būdīm* we were
بودى *būdī* thou wert	بوديد *būdīd* you were
بود *būd* he, she, it was	بودند *būdand* they were.

Imperfect (French *j'étais*).

ميبودم *mībūdam* I used to be
ميبودى *mībūdī* thou used to be
ميبود *mībūd* he, she, it used to be
ميبوديم *mībūdīm* we used to be
ميبوديد *mībūdīd* you used to be
ميبودند *mībūdand* they used to be.

Perfect.

بوده ام *būda am* I have been
بودهٔ *būda ī* thou hast been
بوده است *būda ast* he has been

بوده ایم *būda īm* we have been
بوده اید *būda īd* you have been
بوده اند *būda and* they have been

Pluperfect.

بوده بودم *būda būdam* I had been, etc.

Future.

(formed with the auxiliary verb خواستن *khāstan* and the shortened infinitive بود *būd*)

خواهم بود *khāham būd* I shall be
خواهی بود *khāhī būd* thou wilt be
خواهد بود *khāhad būd* he will be
خواهیم بود *khāhīm būd* we shall be
خواهید بود *khāhīd būd* you will be
خواهند بود *khāhand būd* they will be.

Infinitive.

بودن *būdan* } to be.
هستن *hastan* }

Past participle.

بوده *būda* been.

Imperative.

باش *bāsh!* be! The other persons of the imperative are identical with the corresponding persons of the subjunctive present.

Subjunctive.

Present.

باشم *bāsham* I may be	باشیم *bāshīm* we may be
باشی *bāshī* thou mayest be	باشید *bāshīd* you may be
باشد *bāshad* he may be	باشند *bāshand* they may be.

Imperfect.

میباشم *mībāsham* I might be
میباشی *mībāshī* thou mightest be
میباشد *mībāshad* he might be
میباشیم *mībāshīm* we might be
میباسید *mībāshīd* you might be
میباشند *mībāshand* they might be.

The *Pluperfect* of the *Subjunctive* is expressed by بودم *būdam*, میبودم *mībūdam*, or بوده باشم *būda bāsham*. See special usages of the tenses p. 43.

The *Optative* باد *bād* may he (she or it) be, is used in phrases expressing a wish e.g. عمرت دراز باد *ʿumrat dirāz bād!* may your life be long! مبارك باد *mubārak bād!* may it be blessed!

2. The *auxiliary verb* شدن *shudan*, to become, is a regular verb and as such forms its indicative and subjunctive present from the imperative شو *shou*, while all the other parts are derived from the shortened infinitive شد *shud*. The و of the imperative شو is pronounced *v* when a vowel is added, e. g. شویم *shavīm*, شوند *shavand*.

Indicative.

Present.

میشوم *mīshavam* I become
میشوی *mīshavī* thou becomest
میشود *mīshavad* he becomes
میشویم *mīshavīm* we become
میشوید *mīshavīd* you become
میشوند *mīshavand* they become.

Preterite (French *je devins*).

شدم	*shudam* I became	شدیم	*shudīm* we became
شدی	*shudī* thou becamest	شدید	*shudīd* you became
شد	*shud* he became	شدند	*shudand* they became.

Imperfect (French *je devenais*).

میشدم *mīshudam* I became
میشدی *mīshudī* thou becamest
میشد *mīshud* he became
میشدیم *mīshudīm* we became
میشدید *mīshudīd* you became
میشدند *mīshudand* they became.

Perfect.

شده ام *shuda am* I have become
شدهٔ *shuda ī* thou hast become
شده است *shuda ast* he has become
شده ایم *shuda īm* we have become
شده اید *shuda īd* you have become
شده اند *shuda and* they have become.

Pluperfect.

شده بودم *shuda būdam* I had become
شده بودی *shuda būdī* thou hadst become
شده بود *shuda būd* he had become
شده بودیم *shuda būdīm* we had become
شده بودید *shuda būdīd* you had become
شده بودند *shuda būdand* they had become.

Future.

خواهم شد *khāham shud* I shall become
خواهی شد *khāhī shud* you will become
خواهد شد *khāhad shud* he will become

خواهیم شد *khāhīm shud* we shall become
خواهید شد *khāhīd shud* you will become
خواهند شد *khāhand shud* they will become.

Infinitive.

شدن *shudan* to become.

Present participle.

شونده *shavanda* becoming (hardly ever used).

Past Participle.

شده *shuda* become.

Gerund.

شدنی *shudanī* what ought to become.

Subjunctive.

Present.

شوم *shavam* [1]) I may become
شوی *shavī* thou mayest become
شود *shavad* he may become
شویم *shavīm* we may become
شوید *shavīd* you may become
شوند *shavand* they may become.

The *Imperfect* of the *Subjunctive* is identical with the Imperfect or the Preterite of the Indicative.

The Pluperfect of the Subjunctive and of the Indicative are also identical, شده بودم *shuda būdam.*

The Regular Verb.

All infinitives end either in دن *dan* or in تن *tan.*

---

1) or بشوم *bishavam*, see p. 44.

In order to conjugate a verb, it is necessary to know its *infinitive* and its *imperative.*

The imperatives of all verbs in یدن *īdan* are obtained by cutting off this ending e.g. Infin: پرسیدن *pursīdan* to ask, imperative: پرس *purs!* ask!

From the *Imperative* are derived:

1) the Present of the Indicative, by prefixing the syllable می *mī* and adding the terminations م- *am*, ی *ī*, د- *ad*, etc. میپرسم *mī-purs-am*, میپرسی *mī-purs-ī*, etc.

2) the Present of the Subjunctive, by prefixing the syllable به *bi* and adding the same personal terminations: بپرسم *bi-purs-am*, بپرسی *bi-purs-ī*, etc.

All other forms are derived from the *shortened infinitive* i.e. the infinitive less the ending ن *an*, ex: پرسیدم *pursīd-am*, پرسیدی *pursīd-ī*, etc. — گفتن *guftan*, to speak, shortened infinitive, گفت *guft*, preterite, گفتم *guft-am*, etc.

Paradigm of the Regular Verb.

Active Voice.

Radicals { *Infinitive:* گرفتن *giriftan* to seize, to take.
Imperative: گیر *gīr!* take! [1]).

Indicative.

Present.

میگیرم *mīgīram* I take	میگیریم *mīgīrīm* we take
میگیری *mīgīrī* thou takest	میگیرید *mīgīrīd* you take
میگیرد *mīgīrad* he takes	میگیرند *mīgīrand* they take.

1) In colloquial Persian the form بگیر *bigīr* is always used, instead of گیر *gīr*.

Preterite (French *je pris*).

گرفتم *giriftam* I took	گرفتیم *giriftīm* we took
گرفتی *giriftī* thou tookest	گرفتید *giriftīd* you took
گرفت *girift* he took	گرفتند *giriftand* they took.

Imperfect (French *je prenais*).

میگرفتم *mīgiriftam* I took or used to take
میگرفتی *mīgiriftī* thou tookest
میگرفت *mīgirift* he took
میگرفتیم *mīgiriftīm* we took
میگرفتید *mīgiriftīd* you took
میگرفتند *mīgiriftand* they took.

Perfect.

گرفته ام *girifta-am* I have taken
گرفتهٔ *girifta-ī* thou hast taken
گرفته است *girifta ast* he has taken
گرفته ایم *girifta-īm* we have taken
گرفته اید *girifta-īd* you have taken
گرفته اند *girifta and* they have taken.

Pluperfect.

گرفته بودم *girifta būdam* I had taken
گرفته بودی *girifta būdī* thou hadst taken
گرفته بود *girifta būd* he had taken
گرفته بودیم *girifta būdīm* we had taken
گرفته بودید *girifta būdīd* you had taken
گرفته بودند *girifta būdand* they had taken.

Future.

خواهم گرفت *khāham girift* I shall take
خواهی گرفت *khāhī girift* thou will take

خواهد گرفت *khāhad girift* he will take
خواهیم گرفت *khāhīm girift* we shall take
خواهید گرفت *khāhīd girift* you will take
خواهند گرفت *khāhand girift* they will take.

Infinitive.

گرفتن *giriftan* to take.

Present Participle (rarely used).

گیرنده *gīranda* one who is taking.

Past Participle.

گرفته *girifta* taken.

Gerund.

گرفتنی *giriftanī* what must be taken.

Imperative.

بگیر *bigīr!* take! (obsolete: گیر *gīr*). The other persons of the Imperative are identical with the corresponding forms of the Subjunctive.

Subjunctive.

بگیرم *bigīram* I may take
بگیری *bigīrī* thou mayest take
بگیرد *bigīrad* he may take
بگیریم *bigīrīm* we may take
بگیرید *bigīrīd* you may take
بگیرند *bigīrand* they may take.

The *past tenses* of the *Subjunctive* are identical with the past tenses of the Indicative. The *Perfect of the Subjunctive* is گرفته باشم *girifta bāsham*. See: Special usages of tenses p. 43.

Passive Voice.

The passive voice is formed by adding the auxiliary verb شدن *shudan* to the past participle.

Indicative.

Present.

گرفته میشوم *girifta mīshavam* I am taken, etc.

Preterite (French *je fus pris*).

گرفته شدم *girifta shudam* I was taken, etc.

Imperfect (French *j'étais pris*).

گرفته میشدم *girifta mīshudam* I was taken, etc.

Perfect.

گرفته شده ام *girifta shuda am* I have been taken.

Pluperfect.

گرفته شده بودم *girifta shuda būdam* I had been taken.

Future.

گرفته خواهم شد *girifta khāham shud* I shall be taken.

Infinitive.

گرفته شدن *girifta shudan* to be taken.

Past Participle.

گرفته شده *girifta shuda* having been taken.

Imperative.

گرفته شو *girifta shou* be taken.

Subjunctive.

Present.

گرفته شوم *girifta shavam* I may be taken.

The *past tenses* of the *Subjunctive* are identical with those of the Indicative.

All Persian verbs are formed in the same way as گرفتن *giriftan*, by adding the verbal terminations to the two radical forms viz. the shortened infinitive and the imperative without به *bi*.

In the so called *irregular verbs* the irregularity consists only in the infinitive and imperative being derived from different roots, as دادن *dādan* to give, imperative: ده *dih*, or دیدن *dīdan* to see, imperative: بین *bīn*. Otherwise they offer no irregularity, the tenses being formed as in the case of regular verbs.

Thus in order to form all its parts, it is necessary to know the *infinitive* and the *imperative* of a verb, e. g. the verb *to see:* shortened infinitive: دید *dīd*, imperative: بین *bīn*, present: میبینم *mībīnam*, preterite: دیدم *dīdam*, subjunctive present: ببینم *bibīnam*, etc.

All verbs whose imperatives end in a long vowel (*ā* or *ū*) insert a ی *y* between these radical vowels and the termination, e. g.: گفتن *guftan* to say, imperative: گو *gū*, present: میگویم *mīgūyam*. نمودن *namūdan*, imperative: نما *namā*, present: مینمایم *mīnamāyam*.

In the same way verbs beginning with a vowel insert a ی *ī* between the prefix به *bi* and the initial vowel, thus giving the sound of *ī*, e. g.: آمدن *āmadan* to come, imperative: آ *ā* and بیا *bīā*. Mark the forms showing this inserted ى (*y* and *ī*) in the following couplet of *Saadī:*

گفته بودم چون بیایی غم دل با تو بگویم

چه بگویم که غم از دل برود چون تو بیایی

Gufta būdam chun bīāyī gham-i dil bā tu bigūyam,
Chi bigūyam, ki gham az dil biravad chūn tu bīāyī.

I had meant when thou shouldst come, to tell thee the sorrow of my heart. What shall I say, since sorrow flees from my heart when thou comest.

Obsolete Parts of the Verb.

Some parts of the verb are almost obsolete in modern Persian and are only occasionally used in speaking. These are:

1) The subjunctive بوم *buvam* I might be, for which باشم *bāsham* is used.

2) The negative imperative مه *ma*, ex.: مگو *magū* do not say مگیر *magīr* do not take. (In classical Persian the distinction between the two negatives مه *ma* and نه *na* is kept up exactly as in Hindustani: مت آؤ *mat āo*, do not come, and نہ آیا هی *na āyā hai* he did not come). In modern Persian the negative نه *na* is almost exclusively used: نگو *na-gū* do not speak, نگیر *na-gīr* do not take.

3) The *present participle* is almost obsolete. When it is used it mostly has the meaning of a noun or adjective, e. g.: بخشنده *bakhchanda* gracious.

4) The present participle in ان *ān* is only used in phrases like the following: صحبت کنان *suhbat kunān*

conversing, لند لند کنان *lund lund kunān* murmuring, کشان کشان *kashān kashān* dragging.

Special usages of Tenses.

The *Preterite* is used in narrating events which follow close on one another. Whenever the narration is interrupted by a description or a simultaneous action, the *Imperfect* is used, as in the following example: بشهر رسیدیم بازار رفتیم شخصی صدا کرد *bi shahr rasīdīm, bāzār raftīm, shakhsī sadā kard,* we reached the town, we went to the market, somebody shouted. In this case the three actions follow one another. But in the following sentence: بشهر رسیدیم بازار رفتیم شخصی صدا میکرد *bi shahr rasīdīm, bāzār raftīm, shakhsī sadā mīkard* we reached the town, we went to the market, someone was shouting, — the third action took place either simultaneously with or before the second one. The *preterite* corresponds with the French *passé défini* and the *imperfect* with the French *imparfait.*

Secondly the *Imperfect* is used to denote the duration or frequency of an action, ex. شخصی طوطیرا میپرورید *shakhsī tūtīrā mīparvarīd* a man was bringing up a parrot (duration) وقت صبح قران میخواند *vakat-i subh qurʿān mīkhānd* in the morning he used to read the Koran (frequency).

Thirdly the *Imperfect* is used to denote actions which are not real, but only supposed (Subjunctive), ex. شما میامدید *shumā mīāmadīd?* would you have come? اگر باران میامد خیلی بد میگذشت *agar bārān mīāmad, kheilī bad mīguzasht,* if it had rained it would have been very disagreable.

In the language of the common people the *imperfect* is sometimes used instead of the present tense, both in the indicative and in the subjunctive mood, ex.: چه میخواستید *chi mīkhāstīd?* or چه چی میخواستید *chi chī* [1]) *mīkhāstīd?* what do you want? — تا میشنیدند *tā mīshanīdand* for تا میشنوند *tā mīshanavand*, that they may hear.

Irregularities in the use of می *mī* and به *bi* are not unfrequent, but ought not to be imitated.

بودم *būdam* and باشم *bāsham* do not take the prefix می *mī*, e. g.: اگر بودم *agar būdam* if I was. اگر باشم *agar bāsham* if I were. اگر بوده باشم *agar būda bāsham* if I had been. Both forms شوم *shavam* and بشوم *bishavam* are in use.

داشتن *dāshtan* when it means *to have* never takes the prefix می *mī*, but only when it means *to keep*, *to hold*, ex.: پول دارم *pūl dāram* I have money; but پولرا نگاه میدارم *pūlrā nigāh mīdāram*, I keep the money.

As داشتن *dāshtan*, *to have* takes neither می *mī* nor به *bi*, there is no difference between the Indicative and Subjunctive present. In order to avoid this identity, the *perfect* of the subjunctive is used instead of the present, ex.: داشته باشم *dashta bāsham* I *may* have.

When خواستن *khāstan* means *to wish*, *to want*, the prefix می *mī* may *not* be omitted. The present خواهم *khāham* (without *mī*) has the meaning of *I shall* and is used to form the future, ex. خواهم گفت *khāham guft* I shall say, میخواهم بگویم *mīkhāham bigūyam* I want to say.

---

1) The common people often use *chī* for *chīz* چیز thing.

برخاستن *barkhāstan* to rise, برداشتن *bardāshtan* to lift and برگشتن *bargashtan* to return, take the prefix می *mī* after بر *bar*, ex. برمیخیزم *barmīkhīzam* I rise, برمیگردیم *barmīgardīm* we return. The prefix به *bi* in these verbs is omitted altogether, ex.: برخیز *barkhīz!* rise! اگر برگردم *agar bargardam*, if I return. In the same way the verbs composed with در *dar* have the *mī* and *bi* after the preposition. These verbs are: در کردن *dar kardan* to empty, در آمدن *dar āmadan* to get out, در آوردن *dar āvurdan* to bring out and در رفتن *dar raftan* to escape, ex.: چوب پنبه در بیار *chūb-i pamba dar biār* pull out the cork, توپ در میکنند *tūp dar mīkunand* they are emptying (firing) a cannon [1]).

The *shortened infinitive* (without *an*) is used:

1) with خواهم *khāham* (Future).

2) after the *impersonal verbs:*

میتوان *mītavān* it is possible
میشود *mīshavad* it is possible
میشد *mīshud* it was possible
باید *bāyad* it is necessary
بایست *bāyist* it was necessary

and their *negatives*, ex.: کمان رستم نمیتوان کشید *ka-mān-i Rustam na-mītavān kashīd*, it is impossible to draw Rustam's bow.

The *Subjunctive* is always used after میخواهم *mīkhā-ham* I want and میتوانم *mītavānam* I can, ex.: میخواهم

---

1) Verbs composed with وا *vā* follow the same analogy ex وا ایستادن *vā istādan* to stop, stand still, imperat. وا ایست *vā ist!* stop! — وا گذاشتن *vā guzāshtan* to leave to, وا کردن *vā kardan* to open.

میخواهم نان بخورم *mīkhāham nun bikhuram* I want to eat bread, نمیتوانم پا شوم *namītavānam pā shavam* I cannot rise.

The Subjunctive mood is generally employed when an *intention*, a *desire*, a *condition* or a *doubt* is to be expressed. It is immaterial in such cases, whether the conjunctions تا *tā*, تاکه *tā ki*, so that, اگر *agar*, if, کاش *kāsh*, would that! are added or not. These conjunctions are naturally often omitted in a language remarkable for its extreme terseness of expression.

Examples of the use of the Subjunctive.

ببینم *bibīnam* let me see
تا ببینم *tā bibīnam* that I may see
کاش ببینم *kāsh bibīnam!* would I might see!
بگو بیاید *bigū biāyad* tell him to come
باشد *bāshad* let it be.
برد بپوشد *burd bipūshad* he took it away to put it on
هر کتابیرا بگویند *har kitābīrā bigūyand* whatever book they might name
بده بخورم *bidih bikhuram* give (me something) that I may eat
دادم درست کنند پس بگیرم *dādam durust kunand, pas bigīram* I gave it them to repair that I might then take it back.

Causal Form.

The *causal verb* is formed by adding اندن *āndan* or انیدن *ānīdan* to the imperative root, ex. ترس *tars* fear ترساندن *tarsāndan* ترسانیدن *tarsānīdan* to frighten رو *rou* go, رواندن *ravāndan* or روانیدن *ravānīdan* to cause to go.

دو *dou,* run. دواندن *davāndan* or دوانیدن *davānīdan* to put to a gallop (a horse). The causal form نشاندن *nishāndan* to cause to sit down, to seat, from نشستن *ni-shastan* to sit, is irregular.

Compound Verbs.

In modern Persian the use of simple verbs is very limited. The original simple verbs have mostly been replaced by an auxiliary verb joined to a noun or adjective. These latter are not unfrequently arabic, especially the abstract nouns.

The verbs mostly used as auxiliaries are the following:

کردن *kardan* (imperat کن *kun*) to do
نمودن *namūdan* (نما *namā*) to show, to do
شدن *shudan* (شو *shou*) to become
بودن *būdan* (باش *bāsh*) to be
زدن *zadan* (زن *zan*) to strike
خوردن *khurdan* (خور *khur*) to eat, to be struck [1])
دادن *dādan* (ده *dih*) to give
گرفتن *giriftan* (گیر *gīr*) to take, to seize, to begin
آوردن *āvurdan* (آر *ār*) to bring
بردن *burdan* (بر *bar*) to take off, to carry
رسیدن *rasīdan* (رس *ras*) to arrive
رساندن *rasāndan* (رسان *rasān*) to make arrive, to cause

1) The passive voice of all verbs meaning: to hit, to knock, to strike, to throw, can be expressed by خوردن *khurdan*, ex.: زخم زدن *zakhm zadan* to strike a wound, passive زخم خوردن *zakhm khurdan* to be wounded. In a similar way the following expressions are used تکان خوردن *takān khurdan* to receive a push, زمین خوردن *zamīn khurdan* to fall on the ground, etc.

بستن *bastan* (بند *band*) to tie
افتادن *uftādan* (افت *uft*) to fall
انداختن *andākhtan* (انداز *andāz*) to throw
نهادن *nihādan* (نهِ *nih*) to place, to put
داشتن *dāshtan* (دار *dār*) to have, to hold
خواستن *khāstan* (خواه *khāh*) to wish, to want
کشیدن *kashīdan* (کش *kash*) to draw, to pull, to suffer
آمدن *āmadan* (آ *ā*) to come
رفتن *raftan* (رو *rou*) to go
ساختن *sākhtan* (ساز *sāz*) to make
دیدن *dīdan* (بین *bīn*) to see
فرمودن *farmūdan* (*farmā*) to order (used in speaking of anything done by superiors)
یافتن *yāftan* (یاب *yāb*) to find.

6. Prepositions.

The *Prepositions* form the only difficult chapter in Persian Grammar. The difficulty is caused by the fact that in cases where the classical language demands their use, modern Persian frequently discards them or else replaces them by various idiomatic expressions. The student would do well to commit the following examples to memory and to carefully observe the way in which the prepositions are used in the dialogues and Persian text given in this book.

The *original* and partly obsolete *prepositions* will be marked by brackets [ ]. They are *not* followed by the *izāfa*.

The words which, in the language as spoken at the present day, replace the original prepositions, are mostly concrete nouns like رو *rū* face, سر *sar* head, پهلو *pahlū* side, etc.

The secondary prepositions, which are really nouns, require the *izāfa* to connect them with the word they govern ex: روی میز *rū-yi mīz* on the table (surface of the table) پشتِ پرده *pusht-i parda* behind the curtain (back of the curtain).

Very frequently however the preposition is left out altogether:

1) [			
در	*dar*		in, into, (at, on)
تو	*tū*		
میان	*miān* (middle)		
در میان	*dar miān*		
داخل	*dākhil* (entering)		
اندرون	*andarūn* (inside)		
رو	*rū* (face)		
به	*bi*		

Of the above equivalents of the English prepositions *in*, *into*, etc. تو *tū* and the leaving out of the preposition are the most common.

در *dar* is mostly used with names of *towns* and *countries*, with *dates* or in connection with other prepositions conveying the same meaning.

Examples:

توی شیشه *tū-yi shīsha*, in (into) the bottle.
در طهران *dar Tahrān*, at Teheran.
در شهر *dar shahr*, in town.
در زمانِ خاقانِ مغفور *dar zamān-i Khāqān-i maghfūr*, in the days of the deceased monarch.

در روز عید *dar rūz-i īd*, on the day of the festival.

تفنگ دستِ او بود *tufang dast-i ū būd*, the gun was in his hand.

تبرزین در دست داشت *tabarzīn dar dast dāsht*, he had an axe in his hand.

در هوا *dar havā*, in the air.

روی هوا *rū-yi havā* in the air.

میانِ دریا *mīān-i daryā* in the sea.

در میانِ کاغذ *dar mīān-i kāghaz* in paper (wrapt).

روی رختِ خواب *rū-yi rakht-i khāb* in bed.

اندرونِ اوطاق *andarūn-i utāq* in (side) the room.

سوارِ کالسکه *savār-i kālaska* in a carriage.

بغلِ او *baghal-i ū* in his arms.

خانهٔ حکیم *khāna-yi hakīm* in the house of the doctor.

در نزدیکی سراپرده *dar nazdīkī-yi sarāparda* in the neighbourhood of the Royal tents.

رکاب شاه *rikāb-i shāh* } in the King's retinue.
در رکاب شاه *dar rikāb-i shāh* }

بقایق نشسته *bi qāiq nishasta* sitting in a boat.

بزمین فرود میرود *bi zamīn furūd mīravad* it penetrates into the earth.

اموالی که داخل ایران میشود *amvālī-ki dākhil-i Irān mīshavad* goods which are imported into Persia.

2) [بر	*bar*]		on, upon, over, across.
رو	*rū* (face)		
سر	*sar* (head)		
سوارِ	*savār*	(riding)	
سوار به	*savār bi*	(riding)	
بين	*bein* between		
در بين	*dar bein* between		on, upon, over, across.
بالا	*bālā* above		
دربالا	*dar bālā* above		

[بر *bar*] is hardly ever used alone in modern conversation.

Examples.

پلی بر روی رودخانه ساخته بودند *pulī bar rū-yi rūdkhāna sākhta būdand* They had built a bridge across the river.

پلی سرِ رودخانه ساخته بودند *pulī sar-i rūdkhāna sākhta būdand* They had built a bridge across the river.

پادشاه روی تاخت نشست *pādishāh rū-yi takht nishast* The King sat down on the throne.

روی صندلی *rū-yi sandalī* on a chair.

روی دریا *rū-yi daryā* on the sea.

سرِ میز *sar-i mīz* on the table.

زینی که سرِ اسپ بود *zīnī-ki sar-i asp būd* the saddle that was on the horse.

سرِ تاخته اسپ *sar-i tākhta asp* on a galloping horse.

خاکستر سرِ آتش بود *khākistar sar-i ātash būd* there were ashes on the fire.

صاحب منصب سوارِ اسپ بود *sāhib mansab savār-i asp būd* an officer was riding on a horse.

سوارِ شتر *savār-i shutur* on a camel.

سوارِ کشتی *savār-i kashtī* on board ship.

بینِ راه , دربینِ راه *bein-i rāh*, *dar bein-i rāh* on the way.

برف زمین مانده بود *barf zamīn mānda būd* snow had remained on the ground.

از رودخانه گذشتیم *az rūdkhāna guzashtīm* we went across the river.

از تمام ایران گذشتیم *az tamām-i Irān guzashtīm* we went across all Persia.

3) [به *bi*]
ظرف *taraf*
سمت *samt*
بسمت *bi samt*
سو *sū*
رو به *rū bi*
} to, towards.

به *bi* is often left out when it is the equivalent of English *to*, before names of places. ex منزل رفت he went *to* the house. In the language of the common people it is omitted also when it stands for the dative, ex: بده من *bidih man* give me, instead of: بده بمن *bidih bi man*.

The various ways in which به *bi* and its equivalents are employed, may be seen in the following examples:

کتابرا بمن بده *kitābrā bi man bidih*
کتابرا بده من *kitābrā bidih man*
} give me the book.

بکالسکه *bi kālaska* by carriage.

باردو رسیدیم *bi urdū rasīdīm* we came to the camp.

بشیراز *bi Shīrāz* to Shiraz.

بقدر یك انگشت *bi qadr-i yak angusht* one finger's breadth.

باب *bi āb* with water.

باحتیاط *bi ihtīāt* with care.

بپنج تومان میفروشم *bi panj tūmān mīfurūsham* I sell it for 5 tumans.

پنج تومان میفروشم *panj tūmān mīfurūsham* I sell it for 5 tumans.

بصرفِ جیبِ خودِ مان *bi sarf-i jīb-i khūd-i mun* from our own pocket.

طرفِ کوهستان *taraf-i kūhistān* towards the mountains.

بسمت اردو *bi samt-i urdū* towards the camp.

سوی منزل *sū-yi manzil* towards the station.

رو به بالا *rū bi bālā* upwards.

برو منزل *birou manzil*, go home.

طهران رفت *Tahrān raft*, he went to Tehran.

کنار دریای خزر رسیدیم *kanār-i Daryā-yi Khazir rasīdīm* we came to the shore of the Caspian Sea.

بازار میروی *bāzār mīravī?* are you going to the bazaar?

4) [با *bā*]
همراه *hamrāh* (same way) | with, by.

Examples.

اهل ایران بادست میخورند *ahl-i Irān bā dast mīkhurand* The people of Persia eat with their hands.

فرنکیها با کارد و چنکال میخورند *Farangīhā bā kārd u changāl mīkhurand* the Europeans eat with knife and fork.

حکیمرا همراه بیار *hakīmrā hamrāh biār* bring the doctor with you.

چند نفر همراهِ شاه فرنگستان رفتند *chand nafar hamrāh-i Shāh Farangistān raftand?* how many persons went with the Shah to Europe?

برادرم همراهم بود *barādar-am hamrāh-am būd*, my brother was with me.

همراهِ قافله رفتم *hamrāh-i qāfila raftam* I went *with* the caravan.

باقافله رفتم *bā qāfila raftam* I went *by* caravan.

با جان و دل *bā jān u dil* with heart and soul.

هرچه میشود بشود با خداست *har chi mīshavad bishavad, bā Khudā-st*, come what may, it is "with God".

با این همه علم باز خراست *bā īn hama ʿilm bāz khar ast* notwithstanding all this knowledge, he is an ass.

5) [بی *bī* | without.
بدون *bidūn* |

بی دوربین *bī dūrbīn* without a telescope.

بی زحمت *bī zahmat* without trouble.

بدونِ اطلاعِ من بیرون نرو *bidūn-i ittilāʿ-i man bīrūn na-rou* without my knowledge do not go out.

با *bā* and بی *bī* are much used to form compound *adjectives*, and بی *bī* also to form *nouns* and *adverbs* ex:

با صفا *bā safā* fine, lovely

بااطلاع *bā ittilāʿ* endowed with knowledge.

بامصرف *bā masraf* useful.

بی‌صفا *bī safā* ugly.

بی اطلاع *bī ittilāʿ* ignorant.

بی مصرف *bī masraf* useless.

بی‌ادبی *bīadabī* incivility.

بی‌ادبانه *bīadabāna* impolitely.

6) [جز *juz*]
الا *illā*
بجز *bi juz*
غیر از *gheir az*
باستثنا *bi istisnā*
} except, besides.

Examples.

غیر از من کسی نمیداند بجز دو نفر از دوستهای من *gheir az man kasī namīdānad bi juz du nafar az dūsthā-yi man* besides myself nobody knows it, except two of my friends.

نیست خدا الا خدا *nīst khudā illā khudā* there is no God but God.

همه کس از این کار راضی اند باستثنای بنده *hama kas az īn kār rāzī and, bi istisnā-yi banda* Everybody is pleased with this affair, except myself (*lit.* the slave).

7) [از *az*
از راه *az rāh* by way of
از رو *az rū* from, according to, (French *selon*)
} from, out of, by, of, (for)

از اصفهان آمدم *az Isfahān āmadam* I came from Isfahan.

این اسپ از دست میرود *īn asp az dast mīravad* this horse gets out of hand.

این کتاب از سعدی است *īn kitāb az Saᶜdī-st* this book is by Saadi.

از راهِ التفات *az rāh-i iltifāt* by way of kindness.

از روی کتابِ خوشخط مشق میکنم *az rū-yi kitāb-i khush-khatt mashq mīkunam* I am doing exercises from a well written book.

جمعیت زیاد از مرد و زن *jamᶜiat-i ziād az mard u zan* a large crowd of men and women.

از جان خودت نمیترسی *az jān-i khud-at na-mītarsī?* do you not fear for your life?

8) [تا *tā*]
[الی *ilā*] (arabic) } to, up to, until.
تا به *tā bi*

Examples.

از طهران تا اصفهان چند فرسخ راه است *az Tahrān tā Isfahān chand farsakh rāh ast?* How many farsakhs is it from Tehran to Isfahan?

ببین تفاوتِ راه از کجاست تا بکجا *bibīn tafāvut-i rāh az kujā-st tā bi kujā* see the difference (distance) of the way from where to where (Hafiz).

معطّلم تا پول برسد *muattal-am tā pūl birasad* I am waiting till the money comes in.

تا ببینیم *ta bibīnīm* until we may see.

از طهران الی قزوین بیست و پنج فرسخ راه است *az Tahrān ilā Qazvīn bīst u panj farsakh rāh ast* from Tehran to Kazvīn the distance is 25 farsakhs.

از صبح تا شام *az subh tā shām* from morning till night.

9) زیر *zīr*
بزیر *bi zīr*
در زیر *dar zīr*
پا *pā* (foot)
پاین *pāīn* (at the foot)
دامن *dāman* (skirt)
} under, below, down, at the bottom of.

Examples.

زیرِ درخت *zīr-i dirakht* under a tree.

زیرِ لب حرف نزن *zīr-i lab harf na-zan* do not speak under your lip (indistinctly).

در زیرِ ده *dar zīr-i dih* below the village.

دامنِ کوه *dāman-i kūh* on the skirts of the mountain.

پای منار *pā-yi manār* at the foot of the minaret (below the minaret).

پاینِ کوچه *pāīn-i kūcha* at the bottom of the street.

سرِ خودشرا بزیر انداخت *sar-i khudash-rā bi zīr andākht* he let his head sink.

10) از لا *az lā* through, across.

Examples.

چادرِ شمارا از لای درختها دیدم *chādur-i shumā-rā az lā-yi dirakhthā dīdam* I saw your tent across the trees.

گلوله از لای نیها بشکار خورد *gulūla az lā-yi neihā bi shikār khurd* The bullet hit the game through the reeds.

11) بیرون *bīrūn* / خارج *khārij* } outside.

Examples.

بیرون شهر *bīrūn-i shahr* / خارج شهر *khārij-i shahr* } outside the town.

12) نزد *nazd* (almost obsolete except in writing)
نزدیك *nazdīk*
نزدیکی *nazdīkī*
پهلو *pahlū* (side)
دم *dam* (breath)
لب *lab* (lip)
بیخ *bīkh* (root)
} by, close by, near, next to.

نزدیك شهر *nazdīk-i shahr*
نزدیك بشهر *nazdīk bi shahr*
نزدیکی شهر *nazdīkī-yi shahr*
} near the town.

پهلوی من بنشین *pahlū-yi man binshīn* sit by me.

دم دروازه *dam-i darvāza* near the gate.

لبِ دریا *lab-i daryā* near the sea (on the sea-shore).

طهران دامنِ کوهِ البرز واقع است *Tahrān dāman-i kūh-i Alburz vāqiʿ ast* Tahrān is situated at the foot of the Elburz mountains.

صندوق را بیخ دیوار بگذار *sandūq rā bīkh-i dīvār bugzār* place the box quite close to the wall.

13) پیش *pīsh*
قبل از *qabl az*
در پیش *dar pīsh*
پیشِ رو *pīsh-i rū* (before the face)
رو برو *rū bi rū* (face to face)
جلو *jilou* (bridle)
} before, in front of.

Examples.

بیار پیش *biār pīsh* bring (him) forward.

پیش از عید *pīsh az ʿīd*
قبل از عید *qabl az ʿīd*
} before the festival.

دررا پیش کن *darrā pīsh kun* shut the door.

پیشِ روی قاضی *pīsh-i rūyi qāzī* }
در پیشِ قاضی *dar pīsh-i qāzī* } before the judge.

رو بروی من گفت *rū bi rū-yi man guft* he said so before me.

پیشخدمت جلو رفت *pīshkhidmat jilou raft* the servant went in front.

فانوسرا جلو ببر *fānūsrā jilou bibar* carry the lantern to the front.

14) پس *pas* (back)
پس از *pas az* } after
بعد از *ba'd az* } after
عقب *'aqab* (heel)
پی *pei* (heel)
} back, backwards, after.

Examples.

پس از عیدِ نوروز *pas az 'īd-i nourūz* }
بعد از عیدِ نوروز *ba'd az 'īd-i nourūz* } after the New Year festival.

کتابرا پس بده *kitābrā pas bidih* give the book back.

بقاطرچی بگو جلو بـرود یا عقب بماند *bi qātirchī bigū jilou biravad yā 'aqab bimānad* tell the muleteer to go to the front or to keep at the back.

پشت *pusht* (the back) }
پشت سر *pusht-i sar* (the back of the head) } behind.

Examples.

پشت پرده *pusht-i parda* behind the curtain.

پشت سرم چه کار میکنی *pusht-i sar-am chi kār mīkunī?* what are you doing behind my back (my head).

پشت هم *pusht-i ham* one after (behind) the other.

رفت پی کره *raft pei-i kara* he went to fetch (lit. after) butter.

15) رو برو *rū bi rū* } opposite.
مقابل *muqabil*

رو بروی مساجد *rū bi rū-yi masjid* } opposite the mosque.
مقابلِ مساجد *muqābil-i masjid*

16) دور *dour* } around.
دورادور *dourādour* (all round)
اطراف *atrāf* } (surroundings)
حوالی *havālī*

فوج دورادورِ شهر حرکت میکند *fouj dourādour-i shahr harakat mīkunad* the regiment is marching all round the town.

اطرافِ شهر بیابان است *atrāf-i shahr bīābūn ast* all round the town there is desert.

از حوالیِ دریا بجنکل رسیدیم *az havālī-yi daryā bi jangal rasīdīm* from the neighbourhood of the lake we reached the forest.

کلهارا دورِ حوض بچیین *gulhārā daur-i houz bichīn* place the flowers round the tank.

17) برای *barāyi* } for, on account of, because of, out of.
از برای *az barāyi*
محض *mahz*
بجهت *bi jihat-i*
واسطه *vāsita* (middle)
بواسطه *bi vāsita*
خاطر *khātir* (mind)

Examples.

برای تو آمدم *barāyi tu āmadam* I came for you.

اسپ از برای وزیر آوردند *asp az barāyi vazīr āvardand* they brought a horse for the minister.

بجهت تاریکی *bi jihat-i tārīkī* on account of the darkness.

بواسطهٔ ارتفاع کوهها *bi vāsita-yi irtifāʿ-i kūhhā* on account of the height of the mountains.

چای واسطهٔ خانم کجاست *chāī vāsita-yi khānum kujā-st?* where is the tea for the lady?

محض احترام *mahz-i ihtirām* out of respect.

محض خاطر خانم *mahz-i khātir-i khānum* for the lady's sake.

7. Conjunctions.

The Conjunctions mostly used are the following:

اگر *agar* if

وگر *vagar* and if

وگرنه *vagarna* and if not, otherwise

مگر *magar* but, however

و *va*, *u* and

هم *ham*, نیز *nīz* } also

که *ki* that

چراکه *chirā-ki*, زیراکه *zīrā-ki* } because

بنا بر اینکه *binā bar īn-ki* in consequence of

اما *ammā*, ولی *valī*, ولیکن *va līkan*, لیکن *līkan* or *lākin* } but

از بس که *az bas ki* since (causal)

نه — نه *na — na* neither-nor

القصه *al qissa* } well, in short
خلاصه *khulāsa* }

بلکه *balki* perhaps

با وجود اینکه *ba vujūd-i īnki* } in spite of, although
اگرچه *agarchi* }

هر چند (که) *har chand* however much

پس *pas* consequently

بعد *baʿd* afterwards

یا *yā* or

یا — یا *yā — yā* either — or

خواه — خواه *khāh — khāh* either — or

چه — چه *chi — chi* what with — and

چون *chun* when

از آنکه *az ān ki* since

از وقتیکه *az vakhtī-ki* since

طوریکه *tourī-ki* thus

همین که *hamīn-ki* as soon as.

If و is used to connect two words which together form one notion, it is pronounced *u*, otherwise it is always pronounced *va*, ex: شب و روز *shab u rūz*, night and day, زن و مرد *zan u mard*, woman and man, گرد و خاك *gard u khāk* dust. — but: کتابها و صندوقها و صندلیها *kitābhā va sandūqhā va sandalīhā* books and boxes and chairs.

If a Dependent Clause begins with اگرچه *agarchi* although, the Principal Clause is, contrary to the rule in most European languages, generally introduced by امّا *ammā* or *līkan* but, باز *bāz* yet ex: اگرچه این را ندانست

اما خیلی با کمال است *agarchi īn-rā na-dānist, ammā kheilī bā kamāl ast* although he did not know this, (yet) he is very accomplished, اگرچه خلاف کرده است باز آدمِ خوبی است *agarchi khilāf harda ast, bāz ādam-i khūbī-st.* though he has failed, (yet) he is a good man.

8. Adverbs.

There are no Adverbs properly so called in Persian. Nouns with or without prepositions and especially adjectives are used adverbially.

Examples of nouns WITH prepositions used as adverbs.

از حدّ *az hadd* unlimitedly
با احتیاط *bā ihtīāt* carefully
بخوبی *bi khūbī* well
بی ملاحظه *bī mulāhaza* without paying attention to

Examples of nouns WITHOUT prepositions used as adverbs.

آسودگی *āsūdagī* safely
یاواشگی *yavāshagī* gently (vulgar)
راحت آمدیم *rāhat āmadīm* we came comfortably

Adjectives used adverbially require no explanation.

The *Arabic* adverbs in اً *an*, as e. g. یقیناً *yaqīnan* certainly or مثلاً *masalan* by way of example, etc., form a special class. They will be dealt with in the chapter on the *Arabic element in Persian* p. 72.

9. Construction.

The order of the parts of a simple sentence is, generally speaking, the same as in *Latin*, i. e. subject — object — verb. ex: اسپ جو میخورد *asp jou mīkhurad* (equus hordeum edit) the horse eats barley.

When there are two objects in a sentence, the accusative generally precedes the dative. ex: پدرم کتابرا بمن داد *padar-am kitābrā bi man dād*, my father gave me the book.

If however the accusative forms a part of the verb, it stands in close connection with the latter *after* the dative. ex: شخصی بما سلام گفت *shakhsī bi mā salām guft* somebody saluted us.

In cases where the *object* is a *pronoun* in English, it is *mostly omitted* in Persian. ex: دوست ندارد *dūst na dārad* he does not like *it*

نمیگذارد *na-mīguzārad* he does not let *me* (do it)
نداریم *na-dārīm* we have not got *it* or *any*
پاك كن *pāk kun* clean *it*
میخواهم بفروشم *mīkhāham bifurūsham* I want to sell *it*
دیگر نمیکنم *dīgar na-mīkunam* I shall not do *it* again
ندیدیم *na-dīdīm* we did not see *him*.

The *Verb* is almost always placed at the end of the sentence.

A few verbs sometimes precede their datives. There are: دادن *dadan* to give, گفتن *guftan* to say, رفتن *raftan* to go, رسیدن *rasīdan* to arrive, سپردن *supurdan* to entrust, ex:

رفتیم لار رسیدیم باردو چادر زدیم *raftīm Lār*, *rasīdīm*

bi urdū, chādur zadīm. We went to Lar, we reached the camp, we pitched the tents.

پولرا داد بفقیر *pūlrā dād bi faqīr* he gave the money to the poor man.

گفتم بنوکر *guftam bi noukar* I said to the servant.

برو بازار *birou bāzār* go to the market.

When the nominative of a sentence is the plural of an inanimate object, the verb is frequently used in the singular ex:

همهٔ مبل واسباب ما در سفر شکسته شد *hama yi mubl u asbāb-i mā dar safar shikasta shud*, all our furniture and things were broken on the journey. — جنگلهای مازندران در این فصل سالم نیست *jangalhā-yi Māzandarān dar īn fasl sālim nīst*, the forests of Mazandaran are not healthy in this season.

The *oblique narration* is hardly ever used in Persian. The words of another person are generally quoted in direct speech and introduced by که *ki* ex: میگوید که دیروز آمدم *mīgūyad ki dīrūz āmadam.* He says he came yesterday پرسید که آن شخص کیست *pursīd ki ān shakhs kīst?* he asked who that person was. — گفتند که میخواهیم صبر بکنیم *guftand ki mīkhāhīm sabr bi-kunīm*, they said they wanted to wait.

After گفتن *guftan* to say the conjunction *ki* is often omitted ex: گفت فردا میایم *guft fardā mīāyam* he said he would come tomorrow.

A construction resembling the oblique narration appears to be sometimes used when speaking of a given order; ex: بگو بیاید اینجا *bigū bīāyad īnjā* tell him to come here حکم دادم اردورا بر لب دریاچه بزنند *hukm dādam urdūrā bar lab-i daryācha bizanand.* I gave orders that they should pitch the camp on the bank of the lake.

In the above examples the forms بیاید *biāyad* and بزنند *bizanand* may be quite correctly regarded as imperatives. If this view be taken, the oblique narration may be said not to exist in Persian.

Dependent Sentences.

Dependent sentences are generally introduced by the conjunction که *ki*, which however may be omitted. ex: میخواستم بیاید *mīkhāstam bī-āyad*, I wish he had come.

Interrogative Sentences.

Interrogative sentences are sometimes marked by the interrogative particles مگر *magar* or آیا *āyā* ex: مگر تو سیّدی *magar tu Seiyid-ī?* are you a Seyid? (descendent of Muhammed). آیا دیروز آمدی *āyā dīrūz āmadī?* did you come yesterday?

مگر *magar* may also be placed at the end. ex: دیوانه شدهٔ مگر *dīvāna shuda-ī magar?* have you gone mad?

Another way of marking the interrogation is the adding of یا نه *yā na?* or یا خیر *yā kheir* or not. ex: پول داری یا نه *pūl dārī yā na?* have you got money or not? شما فارسی حرف میزنید یا خیر *shumā fārsī harf mīzanīd yā kheir?*

In most cases however *no* interrogative particle is used, the tone of the voice alone being sufficient.

All interrogative pronouns immediately precede the verb and are strongly accentuated. ex: حضور که بود

huzūr kí būd? who was in the (royal) presence? این خانهٔ کدام شاخص است *īn khāna-yi kudám shakhs ast?* whose house is this? این اسپِ کیست *īn asp-i kí-st?* whose horse is this? تا شهر چند فرسخ راه است *tā shahr chánd farsakh rāh ast?* how many farsakhs is it to the town? طولِ این راه چند فرسخ است *tūl-i īn rāh chand farsakh ast?* How many farsakhs long is this road? دیشب کجا بودی *dīshab kujā būdī?* where were you last night?

10. The Arabic Element in Persian.

Through the influence of Muhammedanism a great number of Arabic words have been introduced into Persian. As these words have preserved their own orthography and to some extent their Arabic inflexion, a certain acquaintance with Arabic grammar is clearly essential to the mastery of Persian. Students are therefore recommended to acquire some knowledge of Arabic and especially of the *Arabic verb* which is fully explained in any Arabic grammar. We shall here restrict ourselves to a few remarks on the *Arabic duals*, *plurals*, *adverbs* and *phrases* embodied in Persian.

Arabic Duals.

The *arabic dual* is used with words denoting things of which not more than two are supposed to exist. It is formed by adding *ein* to the singular ex:

Singular.	Dual.
جانب *jānib* side	جانبین *jānibein* both sides
طرف *taraf* side	طرفین *tarafein* both sides

كون *koun* existence	كونين *kounein* both existences
عالم *ʿālam* world	عالمين *ʿālamein* both worlds
يد *yad* hand	يدين *yadein* both hands
والد *vālid* parent	والدين *vālidein* both parents
حرم *haram* sanctuary	حرمين *haramein* both sanctuaries (Mekka & Medina)
نور *nūr* light	نورين *nūrein* both lights (sun and moon).

Arabic Plurals.

Arabic plurals are very much used both in writing and in speaking. They may be divided in two classes: *regular* and *irregular* or *broken plurals.*

1) The regular plurals are formed from the singular by adding *īn* for the masculine; and for the feminine gender by changing the termination ة, *at* into ات, *āt*; for the neuter by adding *āt.*

Examples of regular Arabic Plurals.

Masculine.

Singular.	Plural.
حاضر *hāzir* present.	حاضرين *hāzirīn* those present.
سایر *sāir* other	سایرین *sāirīn* the others
محبوس *mahbūs* prisoner	محبوسين *mahbūsīn* the prisoners
مسافر *musāfir* traveller	مسافرين *musāfirīn* the travellers
ناظر *nāzir* one who sees.	ناظرين *nāzirīn* those who see.

Feminine and Neuter.

Singular.	Plural.
حیوان *heivān* animal	حیوانات *heivānāt* animals
حضرت *hazrat* Highness	حضرات *hazarāt* gentlemen
ساعت *sā^cat* hour	ساعات *sā^cāt* hours.

Sometimes the ending *āt* is added to a plural, which gives it the meaning of "all sorts of" ex: جوهر *jouhar* precious stone, *simple plural* جواهر *javāhir* precious stones; *double plural* جواهرات *javāhirāt* all sorts of precious stones.

In imitation of these regular plurals of arabic feminines, Persian nouns in *ish* frequently form their plurals in *āt* ex:

Singular.	Plural.
فرمایش *farmāyish* an order	فرمایشات *farmāyishāt*
نگارش *nigārish* epistle	نگارشات *nigārishāt.*

The arabic plural of persian nouns in ه *a* as

Singular.	Plural.
نوشته *navishta* letter	نوشتجات *navishtajāt*
کارخانه *kārkhāna* factory	کارخانجات *kārkhānajāt*
میوه *mīva* fruit	میوجات *mīvajāt*

has been mentioned pp. 14 and 15.

Arabic plurals of some other persian words occasionally occur in the spoken language, though more often in writing, ex:

Singular.	Plural.
ده *dih* village	دهات *dihāt*
باغ *bāgh* garden	باغات *bāghāt*

کوهستان	*kūhistān* mountain-range	کوهستانات	*kūhistānāt*
شمران	*Shimrān* a district near Teheran	شمرانات	*Shimrānāt*
گیلان	*Gīlān* a province on the Caspian Sea.	گیلانات	*Gīlānāt*

2) The *broken* or *irregular* plurals are so numerous and anomalous, that it is impossible here to enter into a full explanation of them. They belong rather to the dictionary than to the grammar. In the vocabulary at the end of this work the broken plurals will be marked, and should be committed to memory as well as the corresponding singulars.

The number of broken plurals entirely depending on the whim of the writer or speaker, is unlimited.

Though an exhaustive list of broken plurals cannot be given here, yet some of those most frequently used are added as examples:

Singular.		Plural.	
شجر	*shajar* tree	اشجار	*ashjār*
برج	*burj* tower	بروج	*burūj*
قنات	*qanāt* subterranean watercourse	قنوات	*qanavāt*
ساحل	*sāhil* coast	سواحل	*savāhil* 1)
لوطی	*lūtī* a good for nothing	الواط	*alvāt*
فاکهه	*fākiha* fruit	فواکه	*favākih*
مسجد	*masjid* mosque	مساجد	*masājid*
لون	*loun* colour	الوان	*alvān*

1) From this plural *savāhil*, coasts, is derived the name of the language of the eastern coasts of Africa: Savāhili (Suaheli)

قسم	*qism* kind	اقسام	*aqsām*
اسم	*ism* name	اسامی	*asāmī*
ملك	*milk* landed property	املاك	*amlak*
مملكت	*mamlikat* province	ممالك	*mamālik*
معبر	*maʿbar* passage	معابر	*maʿābir*
ولد	*valad* child	اولاد	*oulād*
طفل	*tifl* infant	اطفال	*atfāl*
امر	*amr* affair, an order	امور	*umūr*
امير	*amīr* chief	امرا	*umarā*
فقير	*faqīr* indigent	فقرا	*fuqarā*
وزير	*vazīr* minister	وزرا	*vuzarā*
حكيم	*hakīm* doctor	حكما	*hukamā*
طبيب	*tabīb* physician	اطبّا	*atibbā*
قانون	*qānūn* law	قوانين	*qavānīn*
مكان	*makān* place	اماكن	*amākin*
بهيمه	*bahīma* beast	بهايم	*bahāyim*
وحش	*vahsh* wild beast	وحوش	*vuhūsh*
طير	*teir* bird	طيور	*tuyur*
قوم	*qoum* nation	اقوام	*aqvām*
طايفه	*tāyifa* tribe	طوايف	*tavāyif*
ملّت	*millat* community	ملل	*milal*
دكّان	*dukkān* shop	دكاكين	*dakākīn*
سبب	*sabab* thing, reason	اسباب	*asbāb*
يوم	*youm* day	ايّام	*ayyām*
بلد	*balad* town	بلاد	*balād*
خادم	*khādim* servant	خدّام	*khuddām*
شخص	*shakhs* person	اشخاص	*ashkhās*
قلب	*qalb* heart	قلوب	*qulūb*
بندر	*bandar* port	بنادر	*banādir*

Adverbs.

Arabic adverbs are formed by adding the accusative ending اً *an* to the noun or adjective ex:

	Adverbs.
تقریب *taqrīb* approach	تقریباً *taqrīban* approximately.
فرض *farz* supposition	فرضاً *farzan* supposing
ابد *abad* eternity	ابداً *abadan* never
مثل *masal* example	مثلاً *masalan* for instance
غالب *ghālib* most	غالباً *ghāliban* mostly
مستقیم *mustaqīm* straight	مستقیماً *mustaqīmam* straight
اقلّ *aqall* least	اقلّاً *aqallan* at least
مجدّد *mujaddad* renewed	مجدّداً *mujaddadan* renewedly

Gender.

The *Arabic Gender* is sometimes used with Arabic adjectives, especially in writing ex:

این زن در شهر مشهوره شد *īn zan dar shahr mashhūra shud*, this woman became celebrated in the town.
جهاتِ اربعه *jihāti arbaʿa* the 4 points of the compass.

It is, however, never necessary to use it in speaking.

Some Arabic Locutions commonly used in Persian.

بین الاثنین *bein ul isnein* between the two

کالنقش فی الحجر *ka an-naqshu fi'l' hajar* like the carving on the stone

وقس علی هذا *va qis ʿalā hāzā* and conclude from this

وغیره *va gheira* etc.

علی هذا القیاس *ʿalā hāzā 'l qīās* in the same way (lit. by this analogy)

و اللہ *v'Allāhi* or *v'Allāh* } by God

باللہ *b'Illāhi* or *l'Illāh* }

واللہ اعلم *v'Allāhu aʿlam* and God knows best

اللہ اکبر *Allāhu akbar* God is great

استغفر اللہ *istaghfir Ullāh* may God forgive, God forbid

بارك اللہ *bārik Allāh* may God bless you, bravo.

انشاء اللّٰہ *in shā Allāh* if God will

ما شاء اللّٰہ *mā shā Allāh* as God will

بسم اللہ *b'ism Illāh* in God's name

بسم اللّٰہ الرّحمن الرّحیم *b'ism Illāh ar Rahmān ar Rahīm* in the name of God the Mercyful, Bountiful.

الحمدُ للہ *al hamdu l'Illāh*! praise be to God!

لا حول ولا قوّة الاّ باللّٰہ *lā houla va lā qūvata illā b'Illāh* there is no help nor strength except in God.

يا امير المؤمنين *yā Amīr ul Muᶜminīn!* O Lord of the Believers! (Alī)

يا سيّد الشهدا *yā Seyid ash Shuhadā!* O Prince of Martyrs! (Husein)

يا سيّد المرسلين *yā Seyid ul Mursilīn!* O Prince of Prophets'. (Muhammad)

يا على *yā ʿAlī!* o Alī!

يا على مدد *yā ʿAlī madad!* o Alī help! (dervishes cry)

نعوذ بالله *naᶜūzu b' Illāh!* let us take refuge to God!

بينى و بين اللّه *beinī va bein Ullāh* between me and God (truly)

معهذا *maᶜ hāzā* all the same (lit. with this)

لهذا *li hāzā* therefore

هكذا *hakizā* thus

على الاتّصال *ᶜalā 'l ittisāl* continually

لاينقطع *lā yanqatiᶜ* without interruption

لم يزرع *lam yuzraᶜ* uncultivated (land)

بعينه *bi ᶜeinih* exactly alike (lit. as its eye).

CHAPTER III.

DIALOGUES.

دید و باز دید	*Dīd u bāzdīd.*	*Visiting.*
آقا تشریف دارد	Āghā tashrīf dārad?	Is your master at home?
بلی اقا خانه است	Bálī, aghā khāna ast.	Yes, my master is at home.
سوار شدند بیرون تشریف بردند	savār shudand, bīrūn tashrīf burdand.	He (they)[1]) has mounted, has gone out riding.
اندرون رفته است	andarūn rafta ast.	He is gone into the harem.
خلوت کرده اند	khalvat karda and.[1])	He has gone into his private apartment.
بسم الله بفرمائید	b'ism Illah, bifarmāyīd!	In the name of God, please walk in.
خوش آمدید صفا آوردید	khush āmadīd, safā avurdīd.	You are welcome, you have brought happiness.
بفرمائید بنشینید	bifarmāyīd binshīnīd.	Pray be seated.

1) Here the plural is used instead of the singular to denote respect.

سلامٌ عليكم	salāmun aleikum!	Peace be with you!
عليكم السّلام	aleikum assalām!	With you be peace!
احوال شريف چه طور است	ahvāl-i sharīf chi tour ast?	How are you? (lit. How is your august health?)
الحمد للّه	al hamdu l'Illāh.	Praise be to God! (i. e. Quite well, thank you.)
انشاء اللّه احوال شريف سركار خيلى خوب است	in shā Allāh ahvāl-i sharīf-i sarkār kheilī khūb ast.	I hope (If God will) your (worship's) august health is very good.
الحمد للّه از التفات سركار	al hamdu l'Illah, az iltifāt-i sarkār.	Thank God, by your kindness.
از مرحمت جناب عالى بسيار خوب است	az marhamat-i janāb-i ālī bisyār khub ast.	By your Excellency's kindness, very good.
خيلى زحمت كشيديد	kheilī zahmat kashīdīd.	You have had much trouble.
زحمتى نيست راحت است	zahmatī nīst, rāhat ast.	It was no trouble, it was a pleasure (rest).
فردا به بنده منزل تشريف خواهيد آورد	fardā bi banda-manzil tashrīf khāhīd āvurd?	Will you come (bring honour) to my (the slave's) house?

انشاء اللّه شرفیاب میشوم	in shā Allāh sharafyāb mī-shavam	I hope (if God will) to have the honour.
اکر مانعی پیدا نشود خدمت سرکار میرسم	agar mānīʿī peidā nashavad, khidmat-i sarkār mīrasam.	If I am not prevented, I will come to you (will wait upon you).
پریروز که سرکار بمنزل بنده تشریف آورده بودید من همان وقت منزل سرکار رفته بودم	parīrūz, ki sarkār bi manzil-i banda tashrīf āvurda budīd, man hamān vakht manzil-i sarkār rafta būdam.	The day before-yesterday, when your worship had come to the slave's dwelling, at that moment I had gone to your Excellency's house.
افسوس میخورم که ملاقات سرکار میسّر نشد از بد بختی من بود	afsūs mīkhuram ki mulāqāt-i sarkār muyassar na shud; az badbakhtī-yi man būd.	I am sorry that I did not meet (did not obtain a meeting with) your Excellency. It was my ill-luck.
بچه ها چای بیارید	bachahā! chāī bīārīd!	Servants! (children) bring tea.
قلیان میل میفرمائید یا سیکار بیارند	qaliān meil mīfarmāyīd, ya sigār bīārand?	Will you have a Kalian [1]), or shall they bring cigars?

1) The Persian water-pipe or hubble-bubble.

بقلیان هنوز عادت نگرفته ام	bi qaliān hanuz ādat na girifta am.	I have not yet got used to a Kalian.
یك قلیان کدوی با سلیقه چاق کن بیار صاحب ببیند	yak qaliān-i kaduī bā salīqa chaq kun‸ sāhib bibīnad.	Get ready a gourd Kalian with great care, so that the gentleman may try (see) it.
شربت بیار قهوهٔ شیرین بیار	Sharbat bīār, qahva-yi shīrīn bīār.	Bring something to drink (sherbet), bring sweet coffee.
قدری میل میفرمائید از این شیرینی	qadrī meil mīfarmāyīd az īn shīrīnī?	Will you take some of these sweets?
مرحمت شما زیاد همه چیز خوردم	marhamat-i shumā zīād! hama chīz khurdam.	Thank you! (your kindness is great!) I have eaten of everything.
حالا دیگر رفع زحمت میکنم مرخص میشوم	hala dīgar rafᶜ-i zahmat mīkunam, murakhkhas mīshavam.	Now I will remove the cause of trouble, I will take my leave.
باین زودی تشریف میبرید	bi īn zūdī tashrīf mībarīd?	You wish to go so soon?
ببخشید جائی وعده دارم	bibakhshīd, jāī vaᶜda dāram.	Excuse me, I have promised to go somewhere else.
خدا حافظ	Khudā hafiz!	Goodbye, (God keep you)

خدا حافظِ شما	Khudā hāfiz-i shumā!	Goodbye!
لطف شما زیاد	lutf-i shumā zīād!	Thank-you (your favor is great).
التفات شما زیاد	iltifāt-i shumā zīād!	Thank-you (your kindness is great).
مرحمت شما زیاد	marhamat-i shumā zīād!	Thank-you (your benevolence is great).
محبّت شما زیاد	mahabbat-i shumā zīād!	Thank-you (your friendship is great).
عزّت شما زیاد	izzat-i shumā zīād!	Thank-you (your glory is great).
سایهٔ شما کم نشود	sāya-yi shumā kam na shavad!	Thank-you (may your shadow never grow less.)
دست شما درد نکند	dast-i shumā dard na kunad!	Thank-you (may your hand not hurt you!)
از لطف شما	az lutf-i shumā!	Thank you (by your favor).
از التفات شما	az iltifāt-i shumā!	Thank you (by your kindness).
از شفقت شما	az shafaqat-i shumā!	Thank you (by your mercy).
از توجّه شما	az tavajjuh-i shumā!	Thank you (by your condescension).

احوال پرسی	*Ahval pursī.*	*Asking after health.*
احوال شریف شما امروز چه طور است	ahvāl-i sharīf-i shumā imrūz chi tour ast?	How is your august health to day?
قدری کسلم	qadrī kasil am.	I am rather unwell.
قدری ناخوشم	qadrī nākhush am.	I am rather ill.
خدا نکند	Khudā na kunad!	God forbid! (may God not do it!)
چه کسالت دارید	chi kasālat darīd?	What indisposition have you?
چند روز است سرم درد میکند و مزاجاً کسل هستم	chand rūz ast sar-am dard mīkunad va mizājan kasil hastam.	For several days I have had a headache and my health has not been good.
دیشب چه طور گذشت	dīshab chi tour guzasht?	What kind of a night did you have? (How did last night pass?)
بواسطهٔ کم خوابي دیشب خیلی کسل هستم و از امروز صبح درد سر شدّت کرده است	bi vāsita-yi kamkhābī-yi dī-shab kheilī kasil hastam, va az imrūz subh dard-i sar shiddat karda ast.	I am feeling very tired because I slept little last night, and since this morning my head-ache has become violent.

نبض شمارا ببینم تب نداشته باشید	nabz-i shumārā bibīnam, tap na dāshta bāshīd.	Let me feel (see) your pulse, I hope you have no fever.
در این فصل هوا بسیار بد و مورثِ امراضِ سخت است اینجاها دردِ چشم هم خیلی فراوان است	dar īn fasl havā bisyār bad va mūris-i amrāz-i sakht ast. īnjāhā dard-i chashm ham kheilī farāvān ast.	In this season the air is very bad, and is the cause of serious illnesses. In these parts also bad eyes are very common.
من هم چند روز است مبتلا به تب و نوبهٔ سخت بودم	man ham chand rūz ast mubtalā bi tap va nouba-yi sakht būdam.	I also have been troubled with fever and strong intermittent fever for some days.
معلوم است چایده باشید	ma'lūm ast chāīda bāshīd.	You must have caught a cold.
بلی آقا بشکار رفته از گرما عرقِ زیاد کرده بودم سرما خوردم زکام شدم وقتیکه بمنزل رسیدم سرم درد گرفت و نوبه آمد و لرز کردم وقتِ صبح بنوبهٔ شدیدی	Bálī āghā, bi shikār rafta az garmā araq-i zīād karda būdam va sarmā khurdam, zukkām shudam. vakhtī-ki bi manzil rasīdam, sar-am dard girift va nouba āmad va larz kardam. vakht-i subh bi nouba-yi shadīdī va tap,	Yes, sir, I had gone out shooting, and had perspired very much on account of the heat. I then took a chill and caught cold. When I got home, my head began to ache and I shivered. The next morning I had strong intermittent fe-

و تپ که مرضِ این ولایت است دوچار شدم بسیار بد و بکسالت گذشت	ki maraz-i īn vilāyat ast, duchār shudam; bisyār bad va bi kasālat guzasht.	ver, which is the illness of this country. I felt very ill and weak.
وقتِ صبح چه طور بودید	vakht-i subh chi tour būdīd?	How were you in the morning?
تپ تا صبح طول کشید صبح با سردردِ شدیدی از خواب برخاسته حکیمرا خواستم معالجه کرد	tap tā subh tūl kashīd; subh bā sardard-i shadīdī az khāb barkhāsta hakīm-rā khāstam, mu^cālija kard.	The fever lasted till the morning; I woke early with a very bad head-ache, and sent for the doctor, who cured me.
دوا بشما داد یا خیر	davā bi shumā dād yā kheir?	Did he give you any medicine?
حبِّ گنه گنه داد	habb-i gana-gana dād.	He gave me a quinine-pill.
شبِ دیگر هم باز نوبه کردم صبح بهتر شدم	shab-i dīgār ham bāz nouba kardam, subh bihtar shudam.	In the evening I had fever again; in the morning I felt better.
الحمد لله	al hamdu l'Illāh!	Praise be to God!
بسیار جای شکر است	bisyār jā-yi shukr ast.	It is a cause of thankfulness.
دیروز بجهتِ دردِ دل خیلی	dīrūz bijihat-i dard-i dil kheilī khasta būdam. chūn atibbā	Yesterday I felt very tired because I had indigestion

خسته بودم چون اطبّا منع از میوه و ترشی کرده اند هیچ چیز صرف نشد گردشِ باغ بیمزه بود و مثلِ شخصِ روزه‌دار بودم	man^c az mīva va turshī karda and, hīch chīz sarf na shud, gardish-i bāgh bī-maza būd va misl-i shakhs-i rūzadār būdam.	(lit. pain at the heart). As the doctors had forbidden me to eat fruit or anything acid, I could not eat anything. My walk in the garden gave me no pleasure, and I was like one who is fasting.
امروز احوالم الحمد لله خوب است حکیم از من خون گرفته است گفت باید بروید استحمامِ آبِ گرم معدنی بنمائید	Imrūz ahvāl-am al hamdu l' Illah khūb ast. hakīm az man khūn girifta ast; guft: bāyad biravīd istihmām-i āb-i garm-i ma^cdanī bina-māyīd.	Today, praise be to God! my health is good. The doctor bled me. He said "You must go and take baths of warm mineral water".
دندان‌سازِ خوبی در طهران هست	dandānsāz-i khūbī dār Tahrān hast?	Is there a good dentist in Teheran?
یک دندانسازِ فرنگی هست و دلاکهای ایرانی هم دندان کشی میکنند	yak dandānsāz-i farangī hast va dallākha-yi īrānī ham dan-dān-kashī mīkunand.	There is a European dentist there, and the Persian barbers also extract teeth.

آب و هوا	*āb u havā.*	*The Weather.* (lit. Water and Air).
امروز هوا بسیار صاف و بی ابر ومه است جای شکرِ بسیار است	imrūz havā bisyār sāf va bī abr u mih ast, jā-yi shukr-i bisyār ast.	To-day the air is very clear, and there are neither clouds nor mist. It is a cause of much thankfulness.
هوای مازندران پر مه و تاریک است رطوبتِ آن ولایت مشهور است	havā-yi Māzandarān pur mih va tārīk ast; rutūbat-i ān vilāyat mashhūr ast.	The air of Māzandarān is very cloudy and dark; that province is known for its moisture.
منتظر هستم که هوا باز شود	muntazir hastam ki havā bāz shavad.	I am waiting for the air to become clear.
شب باران و بادِ شدیدی آمد	shab bārān va bād-i shadīdī āmad.	In the evening it rained, and there was a strong wind.
دیشب باران و رعد و برقِ شدیدی بود و قدری تگرگ هم بارید حالا باران ایستاده است و هوا باز شد	dīshab bārān va raʿd va barq-i shadīdī būd va qadrī tagarg ham bārīd. hālā bārān īstāda ast va havā bāz shud.	Last night it rained, thundered, and lightened; it also hailed a little. Now the rain has stopped and the air has become clear.

چند روز پیش از تشریف آوردنِ شما اینجاها خیلی سرد بود کوههای بلندِ اطراف را برف زده بود وآب یخ بسته بود	chand rūz pīsh az tashrīf āvurdan-i shumā īnjāhā kheilī sard bud. kuhhā-yi buland-i atrāf-rā barf zada būd va āb yakh basta bud.	A few days before your arrival it was very cold in these parts. It had snowed on the high mountains near by, and the water was frozen.
یخ در ایران بسیار است یا کم	yakh dar Irān bisyār ast yā kam?	Is there much ice in Persia or little?
اغلبِ جاها پیدا میشود اهل ایران در یخچال انبار میکنند وقتِ تابستان توی آبِ خوردن می‌اندازند	aghlab-i jāhā peidā mīshavad. ahl-i Irān dar yakhchāl ambār mīkunand, vakht-i tabistān tū-yi āb-i khurdan mī-andāzand.	It is found in most places. The Persians keep it in an ice-cellar, and in the summer-time they put it in their drinking-water.
دیروز حوالیِ صبح بادِ سخت وزید و هوا پوشیده از ابر شد بیم باران بود امّا الحمد لله نبارید	dīrūz havālī-yi subh bād-i sakht vazīd va havā pūshīda az abr shud; bīm-i bārān būd, ammā al hamdu l'Illah na bārīd.	Yesterday at daybreak a strong wind was blowing, and the sky was cloudy. It looked like rain, but, thank God, it did not rain.
امروز هوا گرم و پوشیده از ابر و خفه است	imrūz havā garm va pūshīda az abr va khafa ast.	To day it is warm and the weather is cloudy and oppressive.

This morning the weather was very bad, it was cloudy, dreary, and oppressive. It rained unceasingly, sometimes much, sometimes little.	subh havā bisyār bad būd, pūshīda az abr va diltang va khafa. bārān muttasil mībārīd, gāhī shadīd, gāhī khafīf.	صبح هوا بسیار بد بود پوشیده از ابر و دلتنگ و خفه باران متصل میبارید گاهی شدید گاهی خفیف
I am waiting for the rain to stop.	muntazir-i īstādan-i bārān hastam.	منتظرِ ایستادنِ باران هستم
The rain comes down steadily. It depresses me. (lit. it makes my times bitter).	bārān nam nam mīāyad, ouqāt-am-rā talkh mīkunad.	باران نم نم میآید اوقاتم را تلخ میکند
On our journey across the mountains, the rain turned to snow. It snowed very much. On account of the height of the mountains, the sun did not shine at all on to the ground.	dar safar-i kuhistān bārān mubaddal bi barf shud. barf-i zīadī bārīd. bi vāsita-yi irtifāʿ-i kūhhā āftāb hīch bi zamīn na mītābīd.	در سفرِ کوهستان باران مبدّل به برف شد برفِ زیادی بارید بواسطهٔ ارتفاعِ کوه ها آفتاب هیچ بزمین نمیتابید
The water of the river is muddy on account of the excess of rain.	āb-i rūdkhāna az kasrat-i bārān gil-ālūda ast.	آبِ رودخانه از کثرتِ باران گل آلوده است

هوا از گرد و غبار تیره و تار است	havā az gard u ghubār tīra va tār ast.	The air is dark with the dust.
باد از جلو است	bād az jilou ast.	The wind is (blowing) from the front.
باد از عقب میوزد	bād az aqab mīvazad.	The wind is blowing from behind.
هوا مثلِ بهار است	havā misl-i bahār ast.	It is like Spring weather.
هوا مثلِ نسیمِ بهشت است	havā misl-i nasīm-i bihisht ast.	The air is like the zephyr from Paradise.
آب و هوای عراق مثلِ بهشت است هوا خشك است باران کم میبارد شبنم هیچ نیست	āb u havā-yi Irāq misl-i bihisht ast: havā khushk ast, bārān kam mībārad, shabnam hīch nīst.	The climate of Irāq is like Paradise: the air is dry, it rains little, and there is no dew.
آب و هوای تمامِ مملکتِ ایران همین است	āb u havā-yi tamām-i mamlikat Irān hamīn ast?	Is the climate of the whole country of Persia the same?
خیر آقا آب و هوای سواحلِ دریای خزر یعنی کیلان و مازندران و استراباد شبیه بآب و	kheir āghā, āb u havā-yi savāhil-i daryā-yi Khazir, yaʿnī Gīlān u Māzandarān u Astarābād shabīh bi āb u havā-	No, sir, the climate on the shores of the *Caspian Sea*, namely of *Gīlān*, and *Māzandarān* and *Astārābād* is

هـوای هند است هوا کرم و تر و خفه است	yi Hind ast, havā garm va tar va khafa ast.	like the climate of *India*. The air is hot, damp, and oppressive.
وقت و ساعت	***vakht va sāʿat.***	***The time and the hour.***
چه وقت است	chi vakht ast?	What time is it?
چهار ساعت بغروب مانده است	chahār sāʿat bi ghurūḱ munda ast.	It is four hours before sunset [1]).
سه ساعت از طلوعِ آفتاب کذشته است	si sāʿat az tulūʿ-i āftāb guzashta ast.	Three hours have passed since sunrise.
چند ساعت بظهر داریم	chand sāʿat bi zuhr dārīm?	How many hours have we till noon?
دو ساعت داریم بظهر	du sāʿat dārīm bi zuhr.	We have two hours till noon.
مطابقِ ساعتِ فرنکی ساعتِ ده است	mutābiq-i sāʿat i frangī sāʿat-i dah ast.	By European time it is ten o'clock.
قریب بظهر است توب هنوز	qarīb bi zuhr ast, tūp hanūz	It is near noon-day, the

1) The Persians reckon their time by sunrise, noon, and sunset.

نینداختهاند و ساعت نزده است	nayandākhta and va sāʿat na zada ast.	gun has not yet been fired and the clock has not struck.
امروز چه ساعت از خواب برخاستید	imrūz chi sāʿat az khāb bar-khāstīd ?	At what time did you wake to-day ?
دمِ صبح بیدار شدم باز خوابم برد وقتیکه دو باره بیدار شدم یك ساعت و نیم از آفتاب کذشته بود	dam-i subh bīdār shudam, bāz khāb-am burd. vakhtī-ki du bāra bīdār shudam yak sāʿat u nīm az āftāb guzashta būd.	At day-break I awoke, then I went off to sleep again. When I again awoke, it was an hour and a half after sunrise.
اولِ افتاب خوابیدن خوب نیست مسلمانان پیش از آفتاب برخاسته نماز میخوانند	avval-i āftāb khābīdan khūb nīst. Musalmānān pīsh az āf-tāb barkhāsta namāz mīkhā-nand.	It is not good to sleep after sunrise. The Mohammedans get up before sunrise and say their prayers.
بهتر است پیش از غذا یا بعد از غذا قدری راحت کنید	bihtar ast pīsh az ghazā ya baʿd az ghazā qadrī rāhat kunīd.	It is better if you rest a little before or after meals.
چه وقت میخواهید بیائید خزینهٔ شاهرا تماشا کنیم	chi vakht mīkhāhīd bīāyīd, khazīnā-yi Shāh-rā tamāshā kunīm ?	At what time do you wish to come to see the Treasury of the Shah ?
فردا و پسفردا فرصت ندارم	fardā va pasfardā fursat na-	To-morrow and the day after-

وچهار روز بیشتر بعید نداریم اکرمیل دارید تا یك هفتهٔ دیکر خدمتِ شما خواهم رسید	dāram va chahār rūz bīshtar bi ʿīd nadārīm. agar meil dārīd tā yak hafta-yi dīgar khidmat-i shumā khāham rasīd.	to-morrow I have no time, and we have not more than four days till the festival. If you like I will come (will wait upon you) next week.
بسیار خوب معلوم است پیش از عید نمیشود رفت من هم بیشتر وقتها کار دارم بعد از چند روزِ دیکر انشاء الله فرصتِ زیاد خواهم داشت	bisyār khūb, maʿlūm ast pīsh az ʿīd namīshavad raft. man ham bīshtar vakhthā kār dāram. baʿd az chand rūz-i dīgar in shā Allāh fursat-i zīād khāham dāsht.	Very well, of course we cannot go before the festival. I also am generally engaged. In a few days, please God, I shall have more time.
شما در روزِ عید چه کار دارید	shumā dar rūz-i ʿīd chi kār dārīd?	What do you do on the day of the festival?
خانهٔ دوستها عیدیه میفرستم و از هرکسی که میآید پذیرائی میکنم و تهنیت و تبریك عید	khāna-yi dūsthā ʿīdīa mīfiristam va az har kasī-ki mīāyad pazīrāī mīkunam va tahnīyat va tabrīk-i ʿīd mīgūyam,	I send presents to the houses of my friends, and I receive every one who comes. I congratulate them, (*lit*: I say con-

میگویم یعنی عید شما مبارك	yaᶜnī "ᶜīd-i shumā mubārak!"	gratulations and blessings for the feast) saying: "May your festival be blessed!"
امشب بمهمانیِ وزیر مختارِ انگلیس نمیروید باید لباسِ رسمی بپوشید دیر نشود	imshab bi mihmānī-yi vazīr mukhtār-i Inglīs na-mīravīd? bāyad libās-i rasmī bipūshīd, dīr nashavad.	Are you not going this evening to the English Minister's party? You must put on evening-dress before it gets late.
هنوز زود است اگر تا بعد از یك ربعِ دیگر تبدیلِ لباس بکنم سرِ وقت خواهم رسید	hanūz zūd ast. agar tā bᶜad az yak rubᶜ-i dīgar tabdīl-i libās bikunam, sar-i vakht khāham rasīd.	As yet it is too early. If I change my clothes in a quarter of an hour, I shall get there in time.
بناهای این شهر از کی بنا شده است	binahā-yi īn shahr az kei binā shuda ast?	When have the buildings of this town been erected?
مسجدِ جمعه در زمانِ سلطنت شاه صفیِ اول و حمام هفتاد سال قبل از این در زمانِ خاقانِ	masjid-i jumᶜa, dar zamān-i saltanat-i Shah Safī-yi avval va hammām haftād sāl qabl az īn, dar zamān-i Khāqān-i	The Friday Mosque [1]) was erected in the time of the reign of Shah Safī the First, and the bath was built seventy

1) The Principal Mosque, in which the Persians assemble on a Friday.

مغفور بنا شده است	maghfūr [1]) binā shuda ast.	years before this in the days of the Deceased Sovereign [1]).
سال گذشته پارسال	sāl-i guzashta, pārsāl.	Last year.
امسال	im-sāl.	This year.
سالِ آینده	sāl-i āyanda.	Next year.
سال بسال	sāl bi sāl.	Year after year.
در سنهٔ یك هزار و سیصد و سیزده هجری مطابقِ یك هزار و هشتصد و نود و پنج عیسوی	dar sana-yi yak hazār u sīsad u sīzdah hijrī, mutābiq-i yak hazār u hasht sad u navad u panj Isavī.	In the year 1313 of the Mahommedan era, which corresponds to the year 1895 of the Christian Era.
پسرِ شما چند سال دارد	pisar-i shumā chand sāl dārad?	How old is your son?
بچهٔ پنجساله است دخترِ چهارساله هم دارم	bacha-yi panjsāla ast, dukhtar-i chahārsāla ham dāram.	He is five years old; I also have a daughter, who is four years old.

1) This term is used in speaking of Fath Ali Shah, great-grandfather of the late Shah.

در خانهٔ من هیچ اطفالِ خوردساله نیست همه الحمد لله بزرك شده اند	dar khāna-yi man hīch atfāl-i khurdsāla nīst; hama al hamdu l'Illāh buzurg shuda and.	At home I have no very young children; thanks be to God, they have all grown up.
پس خودِ شما چند سال دارید	pas khud-i shumā chand sāl dārīd?	Well, how old are you yourself?
قریبِ پنجاه سال دارم	qarīb-i panjāh sāl dāram.	I am nearly fifty years of age.
باور نمیکنم از صورتتان همچو معلوم میشود که سنِّ تان از سی و پنج یا سی و شش سال بیشتر نیست	bāvar na-mīkunam! az sūrat-i tān hamchi maʿlūm mīshavad ki sinn-i tān az sī u panj yā sī u shish sāl bīshtar nīst.	I cannot believe it! From your looks it is plain that you are not more than 35 or 36 years old.
خیر آقا چرا دروغ بگویم لایقِ ریشِ من است	kheir gāhā! chirā durūgh bigūyam? lāīq-i rīsh-i man ast?	No sir! Why should I tell an untruth? Would it be worthy of me (of my beard)?
احوالِ والدِ شما خوب است	ahvāl-i vālid-i shumā khūb ast?	Is your father's health good?
الحمد لله اگرچه پیر است و ریشش سفید شده است لیکن	al hamdu l'Illāh, agarchi pīr ast va rīsh-ash safīd shuda	Thanks be to God! Though he is old and his beard has

مردِ قوی هیکل و با بنیهٔ است واحوالش از بچگی تا پیری همین بوده است	ast, līkan mard-i qavī heikal va bā bunya-ī-st va ahvāl-ash az bachagī tā pīrī hamīn būda ast.	become white, he is a powerful-looking and strong man, and his health has been the same from childhood to old age.
خدا عمرِ والدِ شمارا زیاد کند خدا پدرِ شمارا بیامرزد	Khudā ᶜumr-i vālid-i shumārā zīād kunad! khudā padar-i shumā-ra bīāmurzad!	May God augment the years of your father's life! May God forgive your father!
		Short sentences.
اسمِ تو چه چیز است	ism-i tu chi chīz ast?	What is thy name?
غلامِ شما خلیل	ghulām-i shumā Khalīl.	Your slave Khalīl.
اسمِ شریفِ شما	ism-i sharīf-i shumā?	What is your honoured name?
محمد حسین خان نوکرِ شما	Muhammad Husein Khān, noukar-i shumā.	Mohammed Hussein Khan, your servant.
یکی از دوستانِ من مشهدی رضا نام گویا با شما آشنا است	yakī az dūstān-i man Mashhadī Rizā nām gūyā bā shamā ashanā-st.	One of my friends named Mashhadi Riza is perhaps an acquaintance of yours.
بنده نمی‌شناسم	banda na-mīshanāsam.	I do not know him.

همسایهٔ من است بسیار تعریف از جنابِ عالی میکرد	hamsāya-yi man ast, bisyār ta^crīf az janāb-i ālī mīkard.	He is a neighbour of mine, he praised Your Excellency very much.
بنده قابل تعریف نیستم خیلی التفات دارند	banda qābil-i ta^crīf nīst, kheīli iltifāt dārand.	This slave is not worthy of praise, you have much kindness.
میخواهم شمارا با چند نفر دیگر از دوستانِ خودم معرّفی بکنم	mīkhāham shumārā bā chand nafar-dīgar az dūstān-i khudam mu^carrafī bikunam.	I want to introduce you to some other friends of my own.
کمالِ تشکررا خواهم داشت	kamāl-i tashakkurrā khāham dāsht.	I shall be most grateful.
میخواهم خدمتی بشما رجوع کنم	mīkhāham khidmatī bi shumā rujū^c kunam.	I would confide a certain service to you.
بفرمائید آقا با جان و دل برایِ انجامِ فرمایشاتِ سرکار حاضرم	bifarmāyīd āghā, bā jān u dil barāyi anjām-i farmāyishāt-i sarkār hāzir-am.	Be pleased to command, sir. I am ready, with life and heart, to carry out your worship's orders.
به به آفرین بر تو	bah bah! — āfarīn bar tu!	Bravo! — Bravo!
خوب نفهمیدم دو باره بفرمائید	khūb na-fahmīdam, du barā	I have not understood rightly,

در خدمت جنابعالی مقصّر نشوم	bifarmāyīd, dar khidmat-i janāb-i ālī muqassar na-shavam.	please say it once more, so that I should not fail in my service to Your Excellency.
عیب ندارد	ᶜeib na-dārad.	It does not matter (*lit:* there is no fault).
اگر جای دیگر دعوت نشده‌اید التفات بفرمائید به بنده منزل تشریف بیارید	agar jā-yi dīgar dᶜavat na shuda-īd, iltifāt bifarmāyīd bi banda-manzil tashrīf biārīd.	If you are not invited elsewhere, have the kindness to come to the dwelling of the slave.
اگرچه دیگر هیچ بمهمانی نمیروم لیکن با کمال میل دعوت سرکار را قبول میکنم	agarchi dīgar hīch bi mihmānī na-mīravam, līkan bā kamāl-i meil daᶜvat-i sarkār-rā qabūl mīkunam.	Though I otherwise do not go out to parties, yet with the greatest pleasure do I accept your worship's invitation.
چند روز است بملاقات برادر شما مشرف شدم جناب وزیر مارا با هم آشنا کرده بود	chand rūz ast bi mulāqāt-i barādar-i shumā musharraf na-shudam. janāb-i vazīr mā-rā bā ham āshanā karda būd.	For some days I have not had the honor of seeing your brother. His Excellency the Minister had made us acquainted with one another.

کجا بود	kujā būd?	Where was this?
در عمارتِ حضرتِ صدر اعظم که ما هر دو آنجا آمد و رفت داریم	dar ʿimārat-i hazrat-i Sadr-a'zam, ki mā har du āmad u raft dārīm.	In the Palace of His Excellency the Grand-Vizier, where we both have free access.
برادرم برای استقبالِ ایلچیِ انگلیس مهماندار شده است	barādar-am barāyi istiqbāl-i ilchī-yi inglīs mihmāndār shuda ast.	My brother has been appointed to receive the English Ambassador.
دیروز جنابِ وزیر مختار بملاقات وزرا وارکانِ دولت رفته بودند و امروز همه اعیان و نجبا ببازدیدِ ایلچیِ جدید آمدند	dīrūz janāb-i vazīr mukhtār bi mulāqāt-i vuzarā va arkān-i doulat rafta būdand, va imrūz hama aʿyān va nujabā bi bāzdīd-i ilchī-yi jadīd āmadand.	Yesterday His Excellency the Minister had gone to see the Viziers and Ministers of State, and to-day all the lords and nobles came to return the new Minister's call.
شما بحضور پادشاه رفته اید	shumā bi huzūr-i pādishah rafta-īd?	Have you had an audience with the King?
بلی شرفیاب شدم	balī, sharafyāb shudam.	Yes, I have had the honor.
وضعش چه طور بود	vazʿash chi tour būd?	What was it like?
ما همه صف کشیده در طالارِ تختِ	mā hama saff kashīda dar tā-	We were all standing drawn

مرمر ایستاده بودیم وقتیکه اعلیحضرت رسیدند ما همه تعظیم نمودیم شاه باهمه کس از آشنا و غریب با کمالِ مهربانی صحبت فرمودند بعد از آن مرخص شدیم	lār-i takht-i marmar īstāda budīm. vakhtī-ki aʿlāhazrat rasīdand mā hama taʿzīm namudīm. Shāh bā hama kas az āshanā va gharīb bā kamāl-i mihribānī suhbat farmūdand, baʿd az ān murakhkhas shudīm.	up in a line in the Hall of the Marble Throne. When His Majesty entered we all bowed. The Shah condescended to converse with everyone in the kindest possible way, as well with those whom he knew, as with the strangers. After that we were dismissed.
چه عرض کنم	chi ʿarz kunam?	What shall I say? (lit. what petition shall I make?)
دیگر چه عرض کنم	dīgar chi ʿarz kunam?	What else shall I say?
خلاف عرض نمیکنم	khilāf ʿarz na-mīkunam.	I am not telling an untruth.
عرضی دارم	ʿarzī dāram.	I have a petition.
زحمت میدهم که	zahmat mīdaham ki.	I beg you to ... (lit. I give you the trouble that ...)
دیگر زحمتی نیست	dīgar zahmatī nīst.	I will trouble you no more (lit. there is no more trouble).

بازار رفتن	*Bāzār raftan.*	*Going to the Bazaar.*
غریب راهِ بازار از کدام طرف است	*Gharīb.* Rāh-i bāzār az kudām taraf ast?	*Stranger.* Which is the way to the Bazaar?
بلد[1] از همین راه که میروید تا سبزِ میدان باید رفت آنجا اوّلِ بازار است	*Balad.* Az hamīn rah ki mīravīd, tā Sabz-i Meidān bāyad raft. ānjā avval-i bāzār ast.	*Native.* It is the same way that you are going. You must go to the «Green Square». That is the entrance to the Bazaar.
غریب دستِ چپ است یا دستِ راست	*Gharīb.* Dast-i chap ast yā dast-i rāst?	*Stranger.* Is it on the left hand side or on the right?
بلد پیشِ روی شماست راست راست که میروید میرسید ببازار کدام بازار میخواستید بروید	*Balad.* Pīsh-i rū-yi shumā-st, rāst rāst ki mīravīd, mīrasīd bi bāzār. kudām bāzār mī-khāstīd biravīd?	*Native.* It is in front of you; if you go quite straight, you will reach the Bazaar. Which Bazaar did you wish to go to?
غریب میخواهم بازارِ فرش فروشها بروم قالی و نمد بخرم و ساعت	*Gharīb.* Mīkhāham bāzār-i farsh furūshhā biravam, qālī u na-mad bikharam va sāʿat-i khu-	*Stranger.* I want to go to the carpet-sellers' Bazaar, and buy a carpet and a felt car-

1) derived from greek πολίτης, means a citizen, a native. Also one who knows his way about, a guide, and lastly, one who knows in the most general sense of the word. Ex: Har kas piano balad ast, bizanad. Whoever knows how to play the piano let him play.

خودمرا هم بدهم درست بکنند	dam-rā ham bidaham durust bikunand.	pet. I also want to give my watch to be repaired.
بلد خیلی خوب برای شما بلدی میکنم اوّل بازار بازار بزّازهاست بعد از آن بازار زرگرهاست دکّانهای ساعت‌سازها بآن متّصل است	*Balad.* Kheilī khūb! barāyi shumā baladī mīkunam. avval-i bāzār bāzār-i bazzāzhā-st, b^c^ad az ān bāzar-i zargarhā-st. dukkanhā-yi sa^c^atsāzhā bi un muttasil ast.	*Native.* Very well, I will be your guide. The nrst part of the Bazaar is the linendraper's bazaar; after this comes the goldsmith's bazaar. The watch-makers' shops are quite near this.
غریب خیلی خوب اوّل میرویم دکّانِ ساعت ساز آنجا کارِ خودم را انجام داده مشخّص میکنم که دکّانهای دیگر کجا است	*Gharīb.* Kheilī khūb! avval mīravīm dukkān-i sā^c^atsāz, ānjā kār-i khudam-rā anjām dādā mushakhkhas mīkunam ki dukkānha-yi dīgar-kujā-st.	*Stranger.* Very well! I shall first go to the watchmaker's shops. When I have given my work to be done there, I shall ascertain where the other shops are.
نوکر عرض میکنم دکان ساعت ساز رسیدیم	*Noukar.* ^c^Arz mīkunam dukkān-i sā^c^atsāz rasīdīm.	*Servant.* I beg to state that we have arrived at the watch-maker's shop.

ساعتساز چه چی میخواستید آقا	*Sāᶜatsāz.* Chi chī mīkhāstīd āghā?	*Watchmaker.* What did you wish for, sir?
آقا ساعتم هر روز بقدر ده یا دوازده دقیقه کند کار میکند و شیشه اش شکسته است میتوانید زود درستش کنید	*Aghā.* Sāᶜat-am har rūz bi qadr-i dah yā yāzdah daqīqa kund kār mīkunad, va shīsha-yash shikasta ast; mītavānīd zūd durust-ash kunīd?	*Master.* Every day my watch goesten or eleven minutes too slow, and its glass is broken. Can you quickly get it right?
ساعت ساز چرا تا فردا درست میکنم	*Sāᶜatsāz.* Chirā, tā fardā durust mīkunam.	*Watchmaker.* Why (not)? By to-morrow I will have it ready.
آقا نمیشود تا امشب پس بگیرم ساعتمرا بسیار لازم دارم	*Aghā.* Na-mīshavad tā imshab pas bigīram sāᶜat-am-rā bisyār lāzim dāram.	*Master.* Can I not have it back by this evening? I want my watch very badly.
ساعتساز خیلی خوب نوکرتان نیم ساعت بغروب مانده قدری قبل از بستن بازار بیاید بگیرد	*Sāᶜatsāz.* Kheilī khūb! noukar-i-tān nīm sāᶜat bi ghurūb munda qadrī qabl az bastan-i bāzār bīāyad, bigīrad.	*Watchmaker.* Very well! If your servant can come back half an hour before sunset, shortly before they shut the Bazaar, he can take it.
آقا (به نوکر) دهنه و رکاب اسپم را بگیر سوار شوم	*Aghā* (bi noukar). Dahana va ri-kāb-i aspam-rā bigīr, savār shavam.	*Master* (to the servant). Hold the horses' bridle and the stirrup, I want to mount.

نوکر چشم	*Noukar*. Chashm!	*Servant*. By my eyes!
آقا برو جلو و دکان قالیفروش سراغ کن	*Aghā*. Birou jilou va dukkān-i qālīfurūsh surāgh kun.	*Master*. Go on in front and find the carpet-seller's shop.
نوکر (سوارشده داد میزند که) خبردار خبردار بپا	*Noukar* (savār shuda dād mīzanad ki). Khabardār! khabardār! bipā!	*Servant*. (having mounted, calls out) Take care, take care! look out!
کسبهٔ دکاکین طرفین راه (متصل صدا میکنند که) آقا آقا چه چی میخواستید بیائید اینجا اسباب مارا سیل بکنید چیزی از من بگیرید	*Kasasba-yi dakākīn-i tarafein-i rāh* (muttasil sadā mīkunand ki). Aghā! āghā! chi chī mīkhāstīd? bīāyīd īnjā asbāb-i mārā seil (1) bikunīd, chīzī az man bigīrīd!	*Tradesmen in the shops on both sides of the road* (continually cry out) Sir! Sir! What were you wishing for? look at our things, buy something off us.
نوکر دکان فرش فروش همین است قالی میخواستید یا کلیم	*Noukar*. Dukkān-i farshfurūsh hamīn ast. qālī mīkhāstīd yā gilīm?	*Servant*. This is the carpet-seller's shop. Did you want a knotted carpet or a woven carpet?
آقا قالی و نمد لازم دارم کلیم هم بگو نشانم بدهند	*Aghā*. Qālī va namad lāzim dāram, gilīm ham bigū nishānam bidahand.	*Master*. I need a knotted carpet and a felt carpet; tell them also to show me some woven carpets.

1) *seil* vulg for *seir*.

نوکر بچه بیا دهنهٔ اسبهارا بکیر یك چیزی انعام بتو میدهم	*Noukar*. Bacha bīā, dahana-yi asphārā bigīr, yak chīzī inʿām bi tu mīdaham.	*Servant.* Boy, come here! Hold the horse's bridles. I will give you something as a reward.
تاجر عرض میکنم آقا که اکر قالیِ خوبی خواسته باشید چیزی نشانتان میدهم که مثلش را تا امروز هرکز ندیده باشید (بشاکرد) قالیِ بزرك ملِ کردستان‌را بیار واکن (بآقا) ملاحظه بفرمائید آقا چیزی غریبی خدمتِ سرکار حاضر کردم باغِ ارم از این قالی قشنکتر نیست ملِ کردستان است	*Tājir.* Arz mīkunam, āghā, ki agar qālī-yi khūbī khāsta bāshīd, chīzī nishun-i tun mīdaham, ki misl-ash-rā tā imrūz har giz na dīda bāshīd. (bi shāgird) qālī-yi buzurg māl-i Kurdistān-rā bīār, vā kun. (bi āghā) mulāhaza bifarmāyīd, āghā, chīzī gharībī khidmat-i sarkār hāzir kardam. Bāgh-i Iram az īn qālī qashangtar nīst, māl-i Kurdistān ast.	*Merchant.* I beg to state, sir, that if you wish for a good carpet, I will show you something, the like of which you have never seen until this day. (to his apprentice) Bring the large Kurdistan carpet, and spread it out. (to the gentleman) Please to look at it, sir. I have got ready a wonderful thing for your worship's service. The garden of Iram is not more beautiful than this carpet. It comes from Kurdistan.
آقا پشتش را ببینم جایِ	*Aghā*. Pusht-ash-rā bibīnam,	*Master*. Let me see its back.

وصله و رفو نشده باشد	jāı vasla va rufū na-shuda bāshad.	It has no join nor darn, I suppose.
تاجر خیر آقا هیچ جا یك سولاخ ندارد	*Tājir*. Kheir āghā, hıch jā yak sūlākh [1]) na-dārad.	*Merchant*. No, sir. It has not a hole anywhere.
آقا حالا گوشهٔ قالیرا زمین بگذار خوب پهن کن معلوم شود کجی دارد یاخیر میبینم کج است کیس دارد وصاف نمیشود	*Aghā*. Hālā gūsha-yi qālı-rā zamın bugzār, khūb pahn kun. ma'lūm shavad kajı dā-rad yā kheir. mıbınam kaj ast, kīs dārad va sāf na-mı-shavad.	*Master*. Now put down a corner of the carpet on to the ground, and spread it well, so that I can see whether it is uneven or not. I see that it is uneven; it makes a fold and does not lie smoothly.
تاجر عیب ندارد همهٔ قالیها چنین اند	*Tājir*. 'Eib na-dārad, hama-yi qālıhā chunin and.	*Merchant*. That does not matter all carpets are like that.
آقا رنکش هم جوهر است	*Aghā*. Rang-ash ham jouhar ast.	*Master*. It is also coloured with Aniline dyes.
تاجر نه خیر نشان بدهید رنکش ثابت است	*Tājir*. Na kheir, nishan bidahıd, rang-ash sābit ast.	*Merchant*. No, look at it, its colours are fast.
آقا قیمت این قالی چه چیز است	*Aghā*. Qımat-i ın qālı chi chız ast?	*Master*. What is the price of this carpet?

1) Vulg. for سوراخ *sūrākh*, hole.

تاجر بنده چه عرض کنم هرچه دلتان بخواهد بمن مرحمت بفرمائید پیشکش شما است ببرید	*Tājir*. Banda chi ʿarz kunam? har chi dil-i tun bikhāhad bi man marhamat bifarmāyīd. pīshkash-i shumā-st, bibarīd.	*Merchant*. What petition shall the slave make? Whatever your heart wishes, you can give me, by your kindness. I make you a present of it, take it.
آقا قیمت یک کلمه بگوئید فرصت گفتگوی زیاد ندارم کار دارم	*Aghā*. Qīmat yak kalama bigūyīd, fursat-i guftugū-yi zīād nadāram, kār dāram.	*Master*. Say the price in one word; I have not too much time for discussions. I have work to do.
تاجر قیمت این قالی پانزده تومان است امّا بسرکار دوازده تومان میدهم	*Tājir*. Qīmat-i īn qālī punzdah tuman ast, ámmā bi sarkār davāzdah tuman mīdaham.	*Merchant*. The price of this carpet is 15 tumans, but I will give it to your worship for 12 tumans.
آقا (بنوکر) ده تومان بده	*Aghā* (bi noukar). Dah tuman bidih.	*Master* (to his servant). Give (him) 10 tumans.
تاجر خیر آقا دوازده تومان عرض کرده بودم تمام بازار را بگردید باین خوبی قالیچه پیدا نمیشود	*Tājir*. Kheir āghā, davāzdah tuman arz karda būdam, tamām i bāzār bigardīd bi īn khūbī qālīcha peidā namīshavad.	*Merchant*. No sir, I had said 12 tumans. Go over the whole Bazar; you will not find such a good rug anywhere.

آقا بیشتر از ده تومان نمیارزد اگر میخواهید پولشرا بگیرید خوب است اختیار باشما است	*Aghā*. Bīshtar az dah tuman na-mīarzad. agar mīkhāhīd pūl-ash-rā bigīrīd, khūb ast. ikh-tiār bā shumā-st.	*Master*. It is not worth more than 10 tumans. If you like to take the money for it, all right. The decision rests with you.
تاجر چه عرض کنم از ده تومان خودم بیشتر خریدم اما نمیخواهم شما رنجیده بروید ده تومان و نیم بدهید آقا	*Tājir*. Chi arz kunam, az dah tuman khudam bīshtar kha-rīdam, ammā na-mīkhāham shumā ranjīda biravīd. dah tuman u nīm bidahīd, āghā!	*Merchant*. What shall I say? I bought it myself for more than 10 tumans, but I do not want you to go away displea-sed. Give (me) 10 tumans and a half!
آقا از حرفِ خودم بر نمیگردم (ببچه) اسبرا اینجا بیار سوار شوم	*Aghā*. Az harf-i khudam bar na-mīgardam (bi bacha) asp-rā injā biār, savār shavam!	*Master*. I never take my word back. (to the boy). Bring the horse here, so that I can mount.
تاجر بگیرید آقا ده تومان بدهید اگر چه ضرر من است تابحال دشت نکردم (نوکر پول را ادا میکند) خدا برکت بدهد	*Tājir*. Bigīrīd āghā, dah tuman bidahīd, agarchi zarar-i man ast; tā bi hāl dasht na-kar-dam. (noukar pūl-rā adā mī-kunad) khudā barakat bida-	*Merchant*. Take it sir, give me 10 tumans, although I lose by it. I have not yet struck a bargain to-day, (the servant pays the money) May God

لطفِ شما زیاد دیگر چه میخواستید قالیهای مالِ عربستان و مالِ کرمان و مالِ خراسان و مالِ ایلاتِ فارس خیلی دارم کلیمهای خوب هم هست که وقتِ سفر خیلی بکار میخورد یکی کلیمِ پشم اندر پشمِ مالِ شیروان دیگر پشم اندر پنبه مالِ شیراز و مثلِ گوشِ گربه گرم و نرم و سبك است	had! lutf-i shumā zīād! dīgar chi mīkhāstīd! qālīhā-yi māl-i Arabistān va māl-i Kirmān va māl-i Khurāsān va māl-i īlāt-i Fārs kheilī dāram. gilīmha-yi khūb ham hast, ki vakht-i safar kheilī bi kār mīkhūrad: yakī gilīm-i pashm andar pashm-i māl-i Shīrvān, dīgar pashm andar pamba māl-i Shīrāz va misl-i gūsh-i gurba garm va narm va sabuk ast.	bless you! Thank you! What else are you wishing for? I have many Arabian, Kirmān and Khorassan carpets; also carpets made by the Nomads of Fars. There are also good woven carpets, which are very useful for travelling purposes. One of them is a woven carpet from Shirvan, in which the warp and the woof are both of wool; the other one is a woven carpet from Shiraz, wool and cotton mixed, and it is like the ear of a cat: warm, soft and light.
آقا من که بسفر نمیروم کلیمِ سفری لازم ندارم	*Aghā.* Man, ki safar na-mīravam, gilīm-i safarī lāzim na-dāram.	*Master.* I who do not travel, do not need travelling carpets.
تاجر برای خانه نمد یزدی	*Tājir.* Barāyi khāna namad-i	*Merchant.* For the house, a

از همهٔ فرشها بهتر است ببینید چه قدر کلفت و نرم است	Yazdī az hamā-yi farshhā bihtar ast. bibīnīd chi qadr kuluft u narm ast.	Yezd felt carpet is better than any other carpet. Look how thick and how soft it is.
آقا امروز دیگر فرصت ندارم بعد از دو سه روزِ دیگر انشاء الله میآیم جنسِ شمارا میبینم خدا حافظ	*Aghā*. Imrūz dīgar fursat nadāram baᶜd az du sih rūz-i dīgar in shā Allāh mīāyam, jins-i shumā-rā mībīnam. Khudā hāfiz!	*Master*. I have no more time to-day. If God will, I shall come (back again) in two or three days to see your goods. Goodbye.
تاجر خدا نگهدار شما انشاء الله زودتر برمیگردید مرا سرافراز میفرمائید	*Tājir*. Khudā nigahdār-i shumā! in shā Allāh zūdtar bar mī-gardīd, marā sarafrāz mīfarmāyīd.	*Merchant*. May God be your keeper! I hope you will return very soon and condescend to honor me.
در سفره	*dar sufra.*	*Dinner-time.*
آقا اسمعیل	*Aghā*. Ismaᶜīl!	*Master*. Ismail!
اسمعیل بلی صاحب	*Ismaᶜīl*. Balī sāhib! [1])	*Ismail*. Yes, sir!
آقا عبد الله پیش خدمت هم بگو بیاید	*Aghā*. Abdullāh-i pīshkhidmat ham bigū biāyad.	*Master*. Tell Abdullah the butler to come also.

1) صاحب *sāhib*, Sir, is a title given to Europeans only.

اسمعیل عبدالله حاضر است	*Isma^cīl.* Abdullāh hāzir ast.	*Ismail.* Abdullah is ready.
آقا حالا برو غلام رضای فراش را با استاد مهدی آشپز حاضر کن و خودت هم بیا	*Aghā.* Hālā birou Ghulām Rizā-yi farrāsh-rā bā ustād Mehdī-yi āshpaz hāzir kun, va khudat ham bīā.	*Master.* Now go and tell Ghulam Riza, the second servant, and Master Mehdi, the cook to get ready, and then come back.
اسمعیل همه حاضراند صاحب	*Isma^cīl.* Hamah hāzir and, sāhib.	*Ismail.* All are ready, sir.
آقا خیلی خوب گوش کنید دیدم برای شما زحمت است یك شامِ مفصّلی بمن بدهید از این جهت امشب نان و پنیر و کره چیزی دیگر نمیخواهم بخورم میتوانید بوقت و بی دردِ سر حاضر کنید	*Aghā.* Kheilī khūb, gūsh kunīd! dīdam barāyi shumā zahmat ast yak shām-i mufassalī bi man bidahīd. Az īn jihat imshab nun u panīr u kara chizī dīgar na-mīkhāham bikhuram. Mītavānīd bi vakht va bī dard-i sar hāzir kunīd?	*Master.* Very well, listen! I have seen that for you it is a great trouble to give me an elaborate dinner. For this reason, this evening I do not wish to eat anything but bread and cheese and butter. Can you get this ready at the right time and without troubling (me)? [1])
همهٔ نوکرها استغفر الله صاحب ما برای هر خدمتی حاضریم	*Hama-yi noukarhā.* Istaghfir Ullāh, sahib! mā barāyi har	*All the servants.* God forbid, sir! We are ready for any

1) litt.: without giving me a headache.

هرچه بفرمائید واسطهٔ تان پیدا میکنیم خدمت سرکار را بزرکترین نعمتها میدانیم	khidmatī hāzir-īm har chi bifarmāyīd vasaṭyi-tun (vulg. for vāsita-yi tān) peidā mīkunīm. Khidmat-i sarkār-rā buzurgtarīn-i ni^cmathā mīdānīm.	service; whatever you order, we will get for you. We consider it the greatest blessing to be in your service.
آشپز عرض میشود صاحب برای امشب یك خوراك خیلی خوبی میخواستم واسطهٔ سرکار درست بکنم بعد از سوپ آزاد ماهی و بعد از آن فسنجان چلو و بعد از آن کباب شکار با کاهو و نخود فرنکی ویك شیرینی بسیار اعلی که تا بحال نخورده باشید میخواستم درست کنم حالا میفرمائید	*Ashpaz.* Arz mīshavad, sāhib, barāyi imshab yak khurāk-i kheilī khūbī mīkhāstam vasayi sarkār durust bikunam: ba^cd az sūp [1]) āzād-māhī va ba^cd az un fisinjān chilou va ba^cd az un kabāb-i shikār bā kāhū va nukhud-i farangī va yak shīrīnī-yi bisyār a^clā ki tā bi hāl na khurda bāshīd mīkhāstam durust kunam. — hālā mīfarmāyīd durust na-	*Cook.* I make the petition, sir, that for this evening I wished to prepare a very good dinner for your Excellency. After the soup, salmon, then "fisinjanchilou" (a Persian rice dish), then some roast venison with lettuce and peas, and lastly, an excellent sweet dish, the like of which you have not yet tasted. Now if you order me not to

1) taken from the English or French.

درست نکنم نمیکنم اطاعت میکنم	kunam, durust na-mīkunam, itāʿat mīkunam.	get this ready, I will not do it, I will obey you.
آقا اسباب آن همهٔ خوراك حاضر است	*Agha.* Asbāb-i un hama-yi khurāk hāzir ast?	*Master.* Are the things ready for all these dishes?
آشپز چرا همهٔ اش توی آشپز خانه حاضر است بفرمائید تماشا بکنید	*Ashpaz.* Chirā! hama-y-ash tū-yi āshpazkhāna hāzir ast, bifarmāyīd, tamāshā bikunīd.	*Cook.* Certainly! Everything is ready in the kitchen. *If you wish to see.*
آقا پس نخود فرنگی و ماهی را بیار ببینم	*Aghā.* Pas nukhud-i farangī va māhīrā bīār bibīnam.	*Master.* Well then bring me the peas and the fish so that I may see them.
آشپز شاگردم رفته بازار حالا میآرد	*Ashpūz.* Shāgird-am rafta bāzār, hālā miārad.	*Cook.* My boy has gone to the bazar, he will bring them at once.
آقا پس حاضر نیست خوراك دیگر را هرچه هست بیار اینجا	*Aghā.* Pas hāzir nīst. khurāk-i dīgar-rā har chi hast bīār īnjā.	*Master.* Then they are *not* ready. Bring whatever else there is here.
آشپز چشم (میرود بیرون)	*Ashpaz.* Chashm! (mīravad bīrūn).	*Cook.* By my eyes! (very good Sir) (he goes out).

آقا حالا باز بشما میکویم ساعت هفت بعد از ظهر میخواهم شام بخورم نان و پنیر و کره باید حاضر باشد	*Aghā*. Hālā bāz bi shumā mīgūyam sāʿat-i haft baʿd az zuhr mīkhāham shām bikhuram. nun u panīr u kara bāyad hāzir bashad.	*Master*. Now once more I tell you that I want to have supper at seven hours after noon. The bread and cheese and butter must be ready.
همهٔ نوکرها چشم حاضر میکنیم (تعظیم کرده بیرون میروند)	*Hama-yi noukarhā*. Chashm! Hāzirm mīkunīm. (taʿzīm karda bīrun mīravand).	*All the servants*. Very well! We will get it all ready. (Having bowed, they go out).
آقا (صدا میکند) آشپز را بفرستید اینجا	*Aghā*. Sadā mīkunad) Ashpazra bifiristīd īnjā!	*Master* (calls) Send the cook here!
نوکرها (از بیرون) چشم	*Noukarha* (az bīrūn). Chashm!	*Servants*. (outside). By our eyes!
آشپز فرمایشی داشتید آقا	*Ashpaz*. Farmāyishī dāshtīd aghā?	*Cook*. Have you any orders, sir?
آقا آن خوراکی که کفتی آشپز خانه حاضر است کجا است	*Aghā*. Un khurākī, ki guftī āshpazkhāna hāzir ast, kujāst?	*Master*. Where is that food, which you said was ready in the kitchen?
آشپز فرمودید نان و پنیر میخواهم	*Ashpaz*. Farmūdīd nun u panīr	*Cook*. You said you wished to

بخورم خوراك دیکر پیدا نکردم	mīkhāham bikhuram, khurāk-i dīgar peidā na-kardam.	eat bread and cheese, so I did not get any other food.
آقا پس انچه کفتی همهٔ اش دروغ بود	*Aghā.* Pas unchi guftī hama-y-ash durūgh būd.	*Master.* Well then, all you said was a lie!
آشپز چه عرض، کنم شما میفرمائید دروغ است دروغ باشد ولی بنده حالا ده سال است نوکری فرنکی میکنم تا بحال هیچ کس از من خیانتی ندیده است	*Ashpaz.* Chi ʿarz kunam? Shumā mīfarmāyīd durūgh ast; durūgh bāshad, valī banda hālā dah sāl ast noukarī-yi farangī mīkunam, tā bihāl hīch kas az man khīānatī na-dīda ast.	*Cook.* What petition shall I make? If you order it to be an untruth, it probably is an untruth, but (your slave) I have been in European service for ten years, and until now no one has seen any dishonesty in me.
آقا (میخواهد چند تا شلاق بآشپز بزند) کویا عرق خوردی و مستی	*Aghā.* (Mīkhāhad chand tā shallāgh bi āshpaz bizanad) gūyā ʿaraq khurdī va mast-ī.	*Master.* (threatening the cook with a whip) Perhaps you have had some arak and are tipsy.
آشپز ببخشید صاحب کُه خوردم دروغ کفتم دیکر نمیکنم	*Ashpaz.* Bibakhshīd sāhib! guh khurdam, durūgh guftam, dīgar na-mīkunam.	*Cook.* Forgive me, sir! I have eaten dirt, I have told a lie, I will not do it again.

آقا کم شو (بیرونش میکند)	*Aghā*. Gum shou! (bīrūn-ash mīkunad).	*Master*. Be off! (turns him out).
آقا اسمعیل ساعت هشت است و شام هنوز حاضر نیست	*Aghā*. Isma^cīl! Sā^cat-i hasht ast va shām hanūz hāzir nīst.	*Master*. Ismail! It is eight o'clock, and the supper is not yet ready.
اسمعیل حاضر است صاحب	*Isma^cīl*. Hāzir ast, sāhib.	*Ismail*. It is ready, sir.
آقا چه طور حاضراست هنوز سفره نینداخته اید	*Aghā*. Chi tour hāzir ast? hanūz sufra na-y-andākhta-īd.	*Master*. How can it be ready? you have not yet laid the cloth.
اسمعیل میبندازم صاحب (سفره میارد)	*Isma^cīl*. Mīandāzam, sāhib (sufra mīārad).	*Ismail*. I will lay it, sir (he brings the table-cloth).
آقا خیلی طول میکشد عبد الله کجا است	*Aghā*. Kheilī tūl mīkashad. Abdullāh kujā-st?	*Master*. It is taking a long time. Where is Abdullah?
اسمعیل رفت حمّام	*Isma^cīl* Raft hammūm.	*Ismail*. He has gone to the bath.
آقا پس غلام رضا بیاید	*Aghā*. Pas Ghulām Rizā bīāyad.	*Master*. Then let Ghulam Riza come.

اسمعیل غلام رضا نیستش ([1]	*Ismaʿīl.* Ghulām Rizā nīst-ash.	*Ismail.* Ghulam Riza is not here.
آقا کجااست	*Aghā.* Kujā-st?	*Master.* Where is he?
اسمعیل رفت پی کره	*Ismaʿīl.* Raft pei-i kara.	*Ismail.* He has gone for the butter.
آقا آشپز بیاید	*Aghā.* Ashpaz biāyad.	*Master.* The cook is to come here.
اسمعیل رفت نان بگیرد	*Ismaʿīl.* Raft nun bigīrad.	*Ismail.* He has gone to fetch the bread.
آقا پنیر آوردید	*Aghā.* Panīr āvurdīd?	*Master.* Have you brought the cheese?
اسمعیل چه پنیری میفرمائید بیارم پنیر فرنکی یا پنیر ایرانی	*Ismaʿīl.* Chi panīrī mīfarmāyīd biāram? panīr-i farangī yā panīr-i īrānī?	*Ismail.* What kind of cheese do you wish me to bring? European cheese, or Persian cheese?
آقا بکو آوردهٔ یا نه	*Aghā.* Bigū āvurda-ī yā na?	*Master.* Say, have you brought it or not?

1) *nīst-ash* vulgar for *nīst*.

اسمعیل چه عرض کنم ببینم شاگرد آشپز آورده است یا خیر	*Isma*ᶜ*īl.* Chi ᶜarz kunam? bibīnam shāgird-i āshpaz āvurda ast yā kheir.	*Ismail.* What petition shall I make? I will see whether the cook's boy has brought it or not.
آقا شاگرد آشپز بگو بیاید تو	*Aghā.* Shāgird-i āshpaz bigū bīāyad tū.	*Master.* Tell the cook's boy to come in.
اسمعیل چشم	*Isma*ᶜ*īl.* Chashm!	*Ismail.* By my eyes!
شاگرد آشپز سلام	*Shāgird-i āshpaz.* Salām!	*The cook's boy.* Salaam!
آقا استاد مهدی کو	*Aghā.* Ustād Mehdī kū?	*Master.* Where is Master Mehdi?
شاگرد از ظهری که کم التفاتی فرمودید احوالش بهم خورده [1] تب کرده رفته منزل افتاده خوابیده	*Shāgird* Az zuhr, ki kam iltifatī farmūdīd ahvāl-ash bi ham khurda [1]), tap karda, rafta manzil, uftāda, khābīda.	*The cook's boy.* From the time of noon, when you showed him a lack of kindness, his health became bad, he got fever, went home, lay down and slept.
آقا برو گم شو زهرمار	*Aghā.* Birou, gum shou, zahr-i mār!	*Master.* Be off, disappear, serpent's poison!

1) The omitting of the copula *ast* is very frequent among the common people

اسمعیل شیخ حسن آمد خدمت سرکار	*Ismaʿīl.* Sheikh Hasan āmad khidmat-i sarkār.	*Ismail.* Sheikh Hassan has come to see your Excellency.
آقا بسم اللّٰه تشریف بیارد	*Aghā.* B'ism Illāh! tashrīf biārad.	*Master.* In the Name of God! let him come in.
شیخ حسن سلام علیکم انشاء اللّٰه کسالتی ندارید	*Sheikh. Hasan* Salāmun ʿaleikum! in shā Allāh kasālatī na-dārīd.	*Sheikh Hassan.* Good evening! (Peace be with you!) I hope you are not indisposed.
آقا خیر احوالم از التفات شما خوب است اما اوقاتم مثل سك تلخ است	*Aghā.* Kheir, ahvāl-am az iltifāt-i shumā khūb ast, ammā ouqāt-am misl-i sag talkh ast.	*Master.* No, my health is good, thanks to your kindness, but my times are bitter like those of a dog.
شیخ حسن پس چه شده است	*Sheikh. Hasan.* Pas chi shuda ast?	*Sheikh Hassan.* Well, what has happened?
آقا چون نوکرها هیچوقت شام و نهار بوقت معیّن نمیدادند گفتم امشب یك خوراك خیلی مختصری بخورم نان و پنیر	*Aghā.* Chun noukarhā hīch-vakht shām u nahār bi-vakht-i muʿeiyan na-mīdādand, guftam imshab yak khurāk-i kheilī mukhtasarī bikhuram,	*Master.* As the servants never gave dinner and lunch at the appointed time, I said that this evening I would eat very simple food: bread, cheese,

وکره چیزی دیگر نخواسته بودم اینرا هم بمن ندادند با این جور مردم چه کار بکنم	nun u panīr u kara chīzī dīgar na-khāsta būdam. Inrā ham bi man na-dādand. bā īn jūr mardum chi kār bikunam?	and butter. Anything else I did not want. Even this they did not give me. What shall I do with such men?
شیخ حسن میدانید آقا چیزی خواسته بودید که انجامش محال است	*Sheikh Hasan.* Mīdānīd, āghā, chīzī khāsta būdīd, ki anjām-ash máhāl ast.	*Sheikh Hassan.* Do you know, sir, you have asked for something, the accomplishment of which is impossible.
آقا چه طور نان و پنیر در تمام طهران پیدا نمیشود	*Aghā.* Chi tour? nun u panīr dar tamām-i Tahrān peidā na-mīshavad?	*Master.* How is that? Is it impossible to find bread and cheese in all Tehran?
شیخ حسن نان و پنیر از فضل خدا فراوان است امّا نوکر درست کاری یافت نمیشود این همه نوکرها مواجبی که دارند کفایتشان نمیکند گرانی هم هست همه میخواهند در خرید و فروش مداخل زیادی	*Sheikh Hasan.* Nun u panīr az fazl-i Khudā faravān ast, ammā noukar-i durustkārī yāft namīshavad. In hama noukarhā mavājibī-ki dārand kafāyat-i-shun namīkunad; girānī ham hast. Hama mī-khāhand dar kharīd u furūsh	*Sheikh Hassan.* Bread and cheese praise be to God! are plentiful, but honest servants are not to be found. All these servants cannot manage to live on their wages, living is also expensive nowadays. They all wish to make an

بکنند از این سبب است که نان و پنیر حاضر نکردند	madākhil-i zīādī bikunand. Az īn sabab ast, ki nun u panīr hāzir na-kardand.	enormous profit by buying and selling. For these reason they did not get the bread and the cheese.
آقا پس خوراك دیکر را چرا هیچ وقت خوب و بوقت فراهم نمیآرند و برای هرکاری که بآنها رجوع میکنم یك عذری دارند	*Aghā.* Pas khurāk-i dīgar-rā chirā hīch vakht khūb va bi-vakht farāham na-mīārand va barāyi har kārī ki bi unhā rujū^c mīkunam yak ^cuzrī dārand?	*Master.* Well then, why do they not serve other dishes properly and punctually? And why do they have an excuse for anything I tell them to do?
شیخ حسن این طبیعتشان است آدم تنبل عوض یك کار هزار عذر میآرد اکر در ایران میخواهید بمانید باید خیلی صبر و حوصله داشته باشید	*Sheikh Hasan.* In tab^cīat-i-shun ast. Adam-i tambal ^cavaz-i yak kār hazār ^cuzr mīārad. Agar dar Irān mī-khāhīd bimānīd, bāyad kheilī sabr u housala dāshta bāshīd.	*Sheikh Hassan.* That is their nature. A lazy man will give a thousand excuses instead of doing one thing. If you wish to remain in Persia, you must have much patience.

در سواری	*dar savārī.*	*About riding.*
آقا دو ساعت بعد از ظهر اسپ کهر را برای من و قزل را برای خودت زین کن	*Aghā*[1]). Du sāʿat baʿd az zuhr asp-i kahar-rā barāyi man va qizil-rā barāyi khudat zīn kun.	*Master.* At two o'clock in the afternoon you must saddle the bay horse for me and the grey horse for yourself.
جلودار چشم برای سرکار دهنه بزنم یا آبخوری	*Jiloudār.* Chashm! barāyi sarkār dahana bizanam yā ābkhurī?	1st *Groom.* By my eyes! — Shall I put on a curb or a snaffle for your Excellency?
آقا آبخوری بزن	*Aghā.* Abkhurī bizan.	*Master.* Put on the snaffle.
جلودار آبخوری شکسته است	*Jiloudar.* Abkhurī shikasta ast.	1st *Groom.* The snaffle is broken.
آقا پس همان دهنه را بزن	*Aghā.* Pas hamun dahana rā bizan.	*Master.* Then just put on the curb.
جلودار دهنه زنجیرش کم شده است جلو هم پاره است	*Jiloudār.* Dahana zanjīr-ash gum shuda ast, jilou ham pāra ast.	1st *Groom.* The chin-chain of the curb is lost, the bridle is also torn.

1) اقا master and آغا ennuch are both pronounced alike.

آقا پس چه باید کرد عجالتاً یکی امانت بگیر تا فردا بده تعمیر کنند	*Aghā*. Pas chi bāyad kard? — ʿijālatan yakī amānat bigīr, tā fardā bidih taʿmīr kunand.	*Master*. Well then, what is to be done? for the present borrow one, and get ours mended by to-morrow.
جلودار خیلی خوب	*Jiloudār*. Kheilī khūb!	1st *Groom*. Very well!
آقا اسبِ سمند چه طور است	*Aghā*. Asp-i samand chi tour ast?	*Master*. How is the dun horse?
جلودار عیب ندارد قدری سینه گیر شده است	*Jiloudār*. ʿEib na dārad, qadrī sīna-gīr shuda ast.	1st *Groom*. There is nothing the matter with him, he has only caught cold.
آقا خانم میخواست سمندرا سوار شود زینِ زنانه به اسبِ کرند بزن	*Aghā*. Khānum mīkhāst samand-rā savār shavad, zīn-i zanāna bi asp-i kurand bizan.	*Master*. Your mistress wished to ride the dun horse. Put the lady's saddle on the chestnut horse.
جلودار کرند قدری میلنگد	*Jiloudār*. Kurand qadrī mīlan-gad.	1st *Groom*. The chestnut is rather lame.
آقا از کی میلنگد	*Aghā*. Az kei mīlangad?	*Master*. Since when is he lame?

جلودار از دیروز که نعلش کردند میلنگد میخ خورده است و دستش را زمین نمیگذارد	*Jiloudār.* Az dīrūz, ki naʿl-ash kardand, mīlangad, mīkh khurda ast va dast-ash-rā zamīn na-mīguzārad.	*1st Groom.* Since yesterday, when they shod him, he limps, a nail has gone into his hoof (lit. he has eaten a nail) and he does not put his leg on the ground.
آقا پس اسب قره کهر را بیرون بکش خیلی بد تیمار شده است	*Aghā.* Pas asp-i qara kahar-ra bīrūn bikash. — kheilī bad tīmār shuda ast.	*Master.* Then bring out the dark bay. — He has been very badly groomed.
مهتر بسر شما هر روز سه دفعه تیمار میکنم شال میمالم یال و دمش را هر روز میشورم	*Mihtar.* Sar-i shumā! har rūz si dafʿa tīmār mīkunam, shāl mīmālam. yāl u dum-ash-rā har rūz mīshūram.	*2d Groom.* By your head! Every day I groom him three times, I rub him down. I wash his mane and his tail every day.
آقا پس چرا اینقدر کثیف است خیلی هم لاغر است یقیناً جوش را تمام نمیدهی	*Aghā.* Pas chirā īnqadr kasīf ast? kheilī ham lāghir ast yaqīnan jou-ash-rā tamām na-mīdahī.	*Master.* Well then, why is he so dirty? He is also very lean. Surely you do not give him the whole of his barley.
مهتر والله بسر شما و جان خانم یک دانه جو خیانت	*Mihtar.* Vallāh! bi sar-i shumā va jān-i khānum yak dāna	*2d Groom.* By God! By your head and by the soul of my

نمیکنم نمك بحرامی نکردم اکر میخواهید این اسپ چاق شود باید بقصیل ببندید	jou khīānat na-mīkunam na-mak bi harāmī na-kardam. Agar mīkhāhīd īn asp chāq shavad, bāyad bi qasīl bi-bandīd.	mistress I do not steal a single grain of barley. I have not stolen your salt (i. e. I am not ungrateful). If you want to make this horse get fat, you must give it green fodder.
آقا حالا وقت قصیل نیست علف هنوز خیلی کران است یك هفتهٔ دیکر سبز میدهیم	*Aghā*. Hālā vakht-i qasīl nīst, ʿalaf hanūz kheilī girān ast. Yak hafta-yi dīgar sabz mī-dahīm.	*Master*. Now is not the season for green fodder. As yet grass is very dear. In a week we will give him green fod-der.
مهتر این اسبها هیچکدام نه جل دارد نه نمد همه اش تیکه پاره است میفرمائید بازار میروم تازه میخرم	*Mihtar*. In asphā hīch kudām na jul dārad, na namad, hama-y-ash tika pāra ast. Mīfarmāyīd, bāzār mīravam, tāza mīkharam.	*Groom*. Not one of these hor-ses have a cloth, nor a felt rug, all are torn. If you al-low it, I will go to the bazar and buy new ones.
آقا خیر بعد از چند روز دیکر جل پیراهن میبندیم هوا کرم	*Aghā*. Kheir, baʿd az chand rūz-i dīgar jul-pīrāhan mī-	*Master*. No, in a few days we will give the horses their

شده است	bandīm, havā garm shuda ast.	summer clothing (lit. shirt-covers) the weather has become warm.
مهتر یک پا بند و دو تا میخ طویله و یک افسار هم لازم است	*Mihtar*. Yak pāband u du tā mīkh-i tavīla va yak afsār ham lāzim ast.	*Groom*. A rope and two iron pegs and a halter are also necessary.
آقا هر روز میخواهی بازار بروی مداخل برای خودت پیدا بکنی آنچه هست خوب نگاهدار و تعمیر کن برای چند روز کاه و ینجه داریم	*Aghā*. Har rūz mīkhāhī bāzār biravī madākhil barāyi khudat peidā bikunī. Unchi hast khūb nigāh dār va taʿmīr kun. — Barāyi chand rūz kāh u yunja dārīm?	*Master*. Every day you want to go to the bazar to make a profit for yourself. Whatever we have you must look after well, and have it repaired. For how many days more have we got straw and hay?
جلودار برای امشب و فردا شب داریم میفرمائید فردا بروم میدان بخرم	*Jiloudār*. Barāyi imshab u fardā shab dārīm. Mīfarmāyīd fardā biravam meidān bikharam?	1st *Groom*. We have (enough) for this evening and to-morrow evening. Do you wish me to go to-morrow to the market to buy some?
آقا بسیار خوب بخر	*Aghā*. Bisyār khūb, bikhar.	*Master*. Very well, buy some.

جلودار پس پول التفات کنید کاه و جو بخرم و اسپهارا هم نعل بندی بکنم	*Jiloudar*. Pas pūl iltifāt kunīd kāh u jou bikharam, asphārā ham naᶜlbandī bikunam.	1st *Groom*. Then please give me some money to buy straw and barley. I must also get the horses shod.
آقا تخته پهین خیلی کم است گویا پهین‌را همه فروختی بحمامی خیلی هم کاه قاتی کردی بهتر توجه بکنید اگر فردا طویله مثلِ امروز شلوق است شمارا پنج هزار جریمه میکنم	*Aghā*. Takhta-pahīn kheilī kam ast, gūya pahīn-rā hama furūkhtī bi hammāmī. Kheilī ham kāh qātī kardī. Bihtar tavajjuh bikunīd! Agar fardā tavīla misl-i imrūz shulūq ast, shumārā panj hazār jarīma mīkunam.	*Master*. The dung-litters [1]) are very scanty; I suppose you have sold the dung to the bath-man [2]). You have also mixed it with much straw. You must take more care! If to-morrow the stable is in disorder as it is to-day, I will fine you five qarāns. (lit. five thousand dinars).
مهتر چشم اطاعت میکنم	*Mihtar*. Chashm! itāᶜat mīkunam.	2d *Groom*. By my eyes! I will obey.
آقا رکاب و دهنه خیلی زنگ	*Aghā*. Rikāb u dahana kheilī	*Master*. The stirrups and the bit

1) In Persia, dried dung is used for the horses' litter.

2) In Persia, the baths are heated with dung.

زده است و زینها پر از کرد و خاك شده است	zang zada ast va zīnhā pur gard u khāk shuda ast	are very rusty and the saddles are full of dust and earth.
جلودار سمباده نداریم و زره هم از اصل نداشتیم	*Jiloudār.* Sambāda na-dārīm va zara ham az asl na-dāshtīm.	1st *Groom.* We have no emery paper, and we have never had a polishing-chain.
آقا عذر بدتر از کناه نیار با خاك آجر خوب پاك میشود خوب مواظبت کن اسبابها ضایع نشود	*Aghā.* ᶜUzr badtar az gunāh na-y-ār! bā khāk-i ājur khūb pāk mīshavad. khūb mavāzi-bat kun, asbābhā zāiᶜ na-shavad.	*Master.* Do not give excuses worse than the faults. With brick-powder they will get quite clean. Take great care not to let my things get spoilt.

Extracts from Nāsir ed-Dīn Shāh's Diaries.

At an Exhibition in London.

صورت خری دیده شد پرسیدم قیمتش چند است رئیس اکسپوزیسیون که مرد فربه ریش سفیدی بود و قیمتهارا	Sūrat-i kharī dīda shud. Pur-sīdam: »qīmat-ash chand ast?" — Raīs-i akspūzīsyūn, ki mard-i farbih-i rīsh safīdī būd va qīmathārā mī-khund, guft: »sad līra-yi in-	The picture of a donkey was seen and I asked the price of it. The Director of the Ex-hibition, a fat, white-beard ed man, who gave information about the prices, told me it

میخواند کفت صد لیره انکلیسی که معادل دویست و پنجاه تومان ایران است کفتم قیمت خر زنده منتها پنج لیره است اینکه شکل خراست چرا باید باین کرانی باشد رئیس کفت چون خرجی ندارد جو و کاه نمیخورد کفتم اکرخرج ندارد بار هم نمیکشد و سواری نمیدهد بسیار خندیدیم

glīsī", ki muʿādil-i davīst u panjāh tumān-i Irān ast. Guftam: »Qīmat-i khar-i zinda muntahā panj līra ast; īn ki shikl-i khar ast, chirā bāyad bi īn girānī bāshad?" — Raīs guft: »Chun kharjī na dārad, jou va kāh na mīkhurad." — Guftam: »Agar kharj na dārad, bār ham na mīkashad va savārī na mīdahad. Bisyār khandīdīm.

was a hundred pounds sterling, equivalent to two hundred and fifty tumāns of Persia. I remarked: "The value of a live donkey is at the outside five pounds. How is it then, that this, which is but a picture of an ass, is to be paid so dearly for?" The Director said: "Because it is not a source of expense, as it eats neither straw nor barley (the eastern substitutes for hay and oats.)" I replied: »True; it is not a source of outlay; but neither will it carry a load, or give one a ride".

We laughed heartily.

سفر ایران	*Safar-i Irān.*	*Journey to Persia.*
فرنگی میخواهم سفر بروم	*Farangī.* Mīkhāham safar biravam.	*European.* I want to go on a journey.
ایرانی کجا انشاء الله خیال دارید بروید	*Irānī.* Kujā in shā Allāh khayāl dārīd biravīd?	*Persian.* Where, if God will, do you think of going?
فرنگی میخواهم بایران سفر بکنم	*Farangī.* Mīkhāham bi Irān safar bikunam.	*European.* I want to travel to Persia.
ایرانی برای کار مخصوصی میروید یا همین برای سیر و سیاحت	*Irānī.* Barāyi kār-i makhsūsī mīravīd, yā hamīn barāyi seir u sīāhat?	*Persian.* Are you going there with a special purpose, or only for the pleasure of sightseeing travelling?
فرنگی خیر آقا میخواهم زبان فارسی‌را یاد بگیرم	*Farangī.* Kheir āgha, mīkhāham zabān-i fārsī-rā yād bigīram.	*European.* No sir, I want to learn the Persian language.
ایرانی خیلی خوب برای تحصیل	*Irānī.* Kheilī khūb, barāyi tah-	*Persian.* Very well, for lear-

زبان هیچ چیز از سفر بهتر نیست بزودی میروید	sɪl-i zabān hɪch chɪz az safar bihtar nɪst. bi zūdɪ mɪravɪd?	ning a language, nothing is better than travelling. Do you start soon?
فرنگی انشاء الله بعد از یک ماهِ دیگر وخواهش دارم که بعضی اطلاعات از وضعِ مملکت و راه و رسمِ سفرِ ایران به بنده بدهید	*Farangī.* In shā Allāh baᶜd az yak māh-i dɪgar. va khāhish dāram ki baᶜzɪ ittilāᶜāt az vazᶜ-i mamlikat va rāh u rasm-i safar-i Irān bi banda bidahɪd.	*European.* If God will, in another month. I should like you to give me some information about the ways of the country, and its roads and the manner of travelling in Persia.
ایرانی بفرمائید آقا با دل وجان آنچه اطلاع دارم عرض میکنم چه چیز است میخواستید بفهمید	*Irānī.* Bifarmāyɪd āghā! bā dil u jān ānchi ittilāᶜ dāram ᶜarz mɪkunam. chi chɪz ast mɪkhāstɪd bifahmɪd?	*Persian.* Please to command, sir! With heart and soul I will give you any information I can. What were you wishing to know?
فرنگی میخواستم بدانم از کدام راه از انگلیس به ایران میتوان رفت	*Farangī.* Mɪkhāstam bidānam az kudām rāh az Inglɪs bi Irān mɪtavān raft.	*Europeau.* I want to know by which route one can go from England to Persia.
ایرانی اگر از راهِ دریا میل	*Irānī.* Agar az rāh-i daryā	*Persian.* If you like to go by

دارید بروید باید از لندن سوار کشتی بشوید آن کشتی از لندن میرود به جبل الطارق و از آنجا به جزیرهٔ ملت که میانِ دریای سفید واقع است از نهر سویس گذشته داخلِ دریای احمر میشوید بعد از آن میرسید به بندر عدن که از شهرهای عربستان است خلاصه از راهِ بحرالهند وارد بندرِ بمبئی میشوید که آنجا چند روز باید توقف نمود	meil dārīd biravīd, bāyad az *Landan* savār-i kashtī bishavīd. ān kashtī az Landan mīravad bi *Jabal ut Tāriq* va az ānjā bi jazīra-yi *Malt*, ki mīān-i *Daryā-yi Safīd* vāqi[c] ast. az *Nahr-i Savīs* guzashta dākhil-i *Daryā-yi Ahmar* mīshavīd. ba[c]d az ān mīravīd bi bandar-i [c]*Adan*, ki az shahr-hā-yi [c]Arabistān ast. khulāsa az rāh-i *Bahr ul Hind* vārid-i bandar-i *Bambaī* mīshavīd, ki ānjā chand rūz bāyad tavaqquf namūd.	sea, you must take a ship from *London*. That ship goes from London to *Gibraltar*, and from there to the island of *Malta*, which lies in the middle of the *Mediterranean* (the White Sea). Having passed through the *Suez Canal*, you enter the *Red Sea*. After that you go to the port of *Aden*, which is a town in Arabia. At last, crossing the *Indian Ocean*, you reach the port of *Bombay*, where you must stop for some days.
فرنگی از هندوستان میتوان از راهِ خشکی به ایران رسید یا خیر	*Farangī*. Az Hindūstān mītavān az rāh-i khushkī bi Irān rasīd, yā kheir?	*European*. Can I get from India to Persia by land, or not?
ایرانی چون میان هندوستان	*Irānī*. Chun mīān-i Hindūstān	*Persian*. As between India and

وایران ممالك افغانستان و بلوچستان واقع است که آدمهای آن طرف نمیکذارند خارجه از ملکشان عبور بکنند نمیشود از راهِ برّی بروید	va Irān mamālik-i *Afghānistān* va *Balūchistān* vāqi^c ast, ki ādamhā-yi ān taraf namīguzārand khārija az mulk-i-shān ^cubūr bikunad, namīshavad az rāh-i barrī biravīd.	Persia lie the countries of *Afghanistan* and *Beluchistan*, whose inhabitants do not allow strangers to pass through their country, it is impossible to go by land.
فرنگی پس از راهِ بحری باید رفت	*Farangī.* Pas az rāh-i bahrī bāyad raft?	*European.* Then I must go by sea?
ایرانی البتّه از بندرِ بمبئی تا بندرِ ابو شهر که لبِ خلیجِ فارس واقع است هر هفته یك دفعه یك کشتیِ بخارِ مالِ انکلیس میرود شما با کمال آسایش و راحت سفر خواهید کرد	*Irānī.* Albatta! az bandar-i *Bambaī* tā bandar-i *Abū-shahr*, ki lab-i khalīj-i Fārs vāqi^c ast, har hafta yak daf^ca yak kashtī-yi bukhār-i māl-i Inglīs mīravad. shumā bā kamāl-i āsāyish va rāhat safar khāhīd kard.	*Persian.* Of course! From the port of *Bombay* to the port of *Bushire*, which lies on the coast of the Persian Gulf, an English ship goes once a week. You will be able to travel in perfect ease and comfort.
فرنگی از سفرِ دریا هرکز خوشم	*Farangi.* Az safar-i daryā har	*European.* I never care for

نمیآید و از تکان و جنبشِ کشتی بیشتر وقتها حالتم بهم میخورد واوقاتم مثلِ سگ تلخ میشود	giz khush-am na-mīāyad va az takān u jumbish-i kashtī bīshtar-i vakhthā hālat-am bi ham mīkhurad va ouqāt-am misl-i sag talkh mīshavad.	a sea journey. The shaking and rocking of the ship generally upsets me and I become melancholy. (lit. my times are bitter like those of a dog).
ایرانی پس چرا سفر میروید	*Irānī.* Pas chirā safar mīravīd?	*Persian.* Then why do you go on a journey?
فرنگی نمیدانستم که این قدر سفرِ دریا باید کرد و گرنه شاید خیالِ این سفر هرگز نمیکردم	*Farangi.* Na-mīdānistam ki īn qadr safar-i daryā bāyad kard va garna shāyad khayāl-i īn safar hargiz na-mīkardam.	*European.* I did not know that one had such a long journey by sea. Had I known, I should never perhaps, have conceived the thought of (going on) this journey.
ایرانی خیر آقا سفر از هرچه باشد برای تربیتِ آدم بهتر است تا شخصی سفر نکند پخته	*Irānī.* Kheir āghā, safar az har chi bāshad barāyi tarbīat-i ādam bihtar ast. tā shakhsī safar na-kunad pukhta na-	*Persian.* No sir, a journey is better than anything else for the education of a man. Till a person has travelled, he

نمیشود و شیخ سعدی میگوید	mīshavad va Sheikh Saʿdī mīgūyad:	does not become experienced (lit. ripe), and Sheikh Sadi says:
تا بدکان خانه در گروی	“tā bi dukkān-i khāna dar girou-ī,	“As long as you remain a forfeit in the shop of the house.
هرگز ای خام آدمی نشوی	“hargiz, ei khām, adamī nashavī.	“Surely, you will not, oh unripe one! become a man.
برو اندر جهان تفرج کن	“birou andar jahān tafarruj kun,	“Go into the world and look about you.
پیش از ان روز کز جهان بروی	“pīsh az ān rūz k'az jahān biravī! —	“Before the time comes when you have to leave the world.
فرنگی درست است و شعرا هم گفته اند	*Farangi.* Durust ast, va shuʿarā ham gufta and:	*European.* That is true, and the poets have also said:
مشکلی نیست که آسان نشود	“mushkilī nīst, ki āsān nashavad,	“There is nothing difficult which may not become easy
مرد باید که هراسان نشود	“mard bāyad ki harāsān nashavad.	“A man must not be frightened.”
پس بفرمائید از بندر بمبئی تابندر ابو شهر چند روز راه است	pas bifarmāyīd az bandar-i *Bambaī* tā bandar-i *Abushahr* chand rūz rāh ast.	Now then, tell me, how many days' journey is there between *Bombay* and *Bushire*?

ایرانی اگر میخواهید مسقط را که شهر مشهورِ عربستان است به بینید دوازده روز طول میکشد	*Irānī*. Agar mɪkhᴀhɪd *Masqat*-rᴀ, ki shahr-i mashhᴜr-i ʿArabistᴀn ast, bibɪnɪd, davᴀzdah rᴜz tᴜl mɪkashad.	*Persian*. If you wish to see *Masqat*, which is a celebrated Arabian town, the journey takes 12 days. Otherwise it takes 10 days.
فرنکی میان بمبئی و بوشهر چند منزل است	*Farangī*. Mɪan-i Bambaɪ va Bushahr chand manzil ast?	*European*. How many stations are there between Bombay and Bushire?
ایرانی کشتی اول رو بشمال میرود تا بندرِ کراچی که یکی از بنادرِ معظم ممالکِ هند است وآنجا یك شب و یك روز توقف میشود اگر میل داشته باشید میتوانید در مهمانخانهٔ شهرِ کراچی منزل کنید	*Irānī*. Kashtɪ avval rᴜ bi shamᴀl mɪravad tᴀ bandar-i *Karāchī*, ki yakɪ az banᴀdir-i muʿazzam-i mamᴀlik-i Hind ast va ᴀnjᴀ yak shab u yak rᴜz tavaqquf mɪshavad. agar meil dᴀshta bᴀshɪd mɪtavᴀnɪd dar mihmᴀnkhᴀna-yi shahr-i *Karāchī* manzil kunɪd.	*Persian*. At first the ship goes in a northerly direction to the port of *Karāchi*, which is one of the most important Indian ports, there it stops for a night and a day. If you like you can stay at the hotel of the town of Karᴀchi.
فرنکی کراچی شهرِ بزرگی است یاخیر	*Farangī*. *Karāchī* shahr-i buzurgɪ-st yᴀ kheir?	*European*. Is Karᴀchi a large town or not?

ایرانی چرا شهر بزرگ و آباد است از صد و چهار هزار نفر بیشتر جمعیت دارد	*Irānī.* Chirā, shahr buzurg va ābād ast. az sad u chahār hazār nafar bīshtar jamʿīat dārad.	*Persian.* Yes, the town is large and populous. It has more than 104,000 inhabitants.
فرنگی اهالیِ شهر همهٔ شان مسلمان هستند	*Farangī.* Ahālī-yi shahr hama-yi-shān Musalmān hastand?	*European.* Are the inhabitants of the town all Mohammedans?
ایرانی خیر نصفشان مسلمان هستند و نصفِ دیگر هندی (یعنی بت‌پرست) و پارسی (یعنی گبر یا آتش پرست) و عیسوی	*Irānī.* Kheir, nisf-i-shān Musalmān hastand va nisf-i dīgar Hindī (yaʿnī butparast) va Pārsī (yaʿnī Gabr yā ātash parast) va ʿIsavī.	*Persian.* No, half of them are Mussulmans and the other half are Hindus (namely: idol-worshippers), Parsees (namely: fire-worshippers), and Christians.
فرنگی شنیده ام که تجارتگاه بزرگی است	*Farangī.* Shanīda am ki tijārat-gāh-i buzurgī-st.	*European.* I have heard that it is an important commercial town.
ایرانی درست است از هر طرف دنیا کشتیهای بخار و بادبانی	*Irānī.* Durust ast, az har taraf-i dunyā kashtīhā-yi bukhār va bādbānī mīāyand, māl va	*Persian.* That is true. From all parts of the world steamers and sailing-vessels come

میآیند مال وجنسِ هندوستان را بار کرده به ولایتهای دیکر میبرند مرکزِ تجارتِ عمدهٔ است	jins-i Hindūstān-rā bār karda bi vilāyathā-yi dīgar mība-rand. markaz-i tijārat-i ʿum-daī-st.	to fetch Indian goods and wares, and take them to other countries. It is an im-portant centre of commerce.
فرنکی پس از کراچی کجا باید رفت	*Farangī*. Pas az Karāchī kujā bāyad raft?	*European*. Well, where do we go to after Karāchi?
ایرانی اوّلاً بگوادر که بندرِ کوچکِ مکران است	*Irānī*. Avvalan bi *Gvādar*, ki bandar-i kūchik-i *Makrān* ast.	*Persian*. First to *Gvadar*, which is a small port in *Makran*.
فرنکی مکران چه مملکتی است	*Farangī*. *Makrān* chi mamli-katī-st?	*European*. What country is Makran?
ایرانی مکران اسمِ ساحلِ بلوچستان است از کوادر میروید بمسقط	*Irānī*. *Makrān* ism-i sāhil-i Ba-lūchistān ast. az Gvādar mī-ravīd bi *Masqat*.	*Persian*. Makran is the name of the coast of *Beluchistan* From Gvadar you go to *Mas-qat*.
فرنکی مسقط قابلِ دیدن است	*Farangī*. Masqat qābil-i dīdan ast?	*European*. Is Masqat worth seeing?
ایرانی بغیر از سنك و دریا	*Irānī*. Bi gheir az sang va daryā	*Persian*. There is nothing to

چیزی دیده نمیشود چهار پنج تا قصر و قلعه سر سنگ بنا کرده اند دو تا خانهٔ باصفا بیشتر ندارد یکی خانهٔ سفیرِ انکلیس و آن دیکر عمارتِ سیّد	chīzī dīda na-mīshavad. chahār panj tā qasr va qalʿa sar-i sang-binā karda and. du tā khāna-yi bā safā bīshtar nadārad, yakī khāna-yi safīr-i Inglīs va ān dīgar ʿimārat-i Seyyid.	be seen but rocks and sea. Four or five forts have been built on the rock. Masqat has only two fine houses; one is the house of the English resident, the other is the palace of the Seyyid.
فرنکی سید که را میکویند	*Farangī.* Seyyīd ki-rā mīgūyand?	*European.* Whom do they call Seyyid?
ایرانی سلطانِ مسقط را سید میکویند چرا که از خاندانِ پیغمبر است اسمِ سیّدِ مرحوم سید ترکی بود برادرِ سلطانِ مغفورِ زنگبار بود سیدِ حالیه پسرِ بزرگِ سید ترکی است اسمش سید فیصل است	*Irānī.* Sultān-i Masqat-rā Seyyid mīgūyand, chirā ki az khāndān-i Peighambar ast. ism-i Seyyid-i marhūm *Seyyid Turkī* būd. barādar-i sultān-i maghfūr-i *Zangbār* būd. Seyyid-i hālīa pisar-i buzurg-i Seyyid Turkī-st; ism-ash *Seyyid Feisal* ast.	*Persian.* They call the Sultan of Masqat Seyyid, because he is a descendant of the Prophet. The name of the deceased Seyyid was Seyyid Turkī. He was the brother of the deceased Sultan of *Zanzibar.* The present Seyyid is the eldest son of Seyyid Turkī; his name is *Seyyid Feisal.*

فرنکی تجارتِ مسقط زیاد است یا کم	*Farangī* tijārat-i Maskat ziād ast yā kam?	*European.* Is the commerce of Masqat great or small?
ایرانی چندان زیاد نیست بازارش هم کوچک است بنده فروشی بسیار است زنگی‌ها را از زنگبار میآرند به مسقط و از آنجا میفرستند بایران و ببغداد آبادیِ حوالیِ شهر کم است از اطرافِ شهر خرما میآورند میفروشند تاجرهای ینکی دنیا خرمای مسقط را با کشتی میبرند بولایتِ خودِ شان قریبِ شهر هیچ سبزی دیده نمیشود کاو و الاغِ آنجا عوضِ علف ماهیِ	*Irānī.* Chandān ziād nīst. bāzār-ash ham kūchik ast banda-furūshī bisyār ast. zangīhā-rā az *Zangbār* miārand bi *Masqat* va az ānjā mifiristand bi *Irān* va bi *Baghdād*. ābādī-yi havālī-yi shahr kam ast. az atrāf-i shahr khurmā miā-varand, mīfurūshand. tājirhā-yi Yangī Dunyā khurmā-yi Masqat-rā bā kashtī mībarand bi vilāyat-i khud-i shān. qa-rīb-i shahr hīch sabzī dīda na-mīshavad. gāv va ulāgh-i ānjā ʻavaz-i ʻalaf māhī-yi khushk mīkhurand. halvā-yi Masqat mashhūr ast; tā bi	*Persian.* It is not much, and the bazaar is small. There is much slave-trading. They bring the negroes from *Zanzibar* to *Masqat*, and from there they send them to *Persia* and to *Baghdad* There is little cultivation in the vicinity of the town. From the environs of the city, dates are brought, and are sold. American merchants take the Masqat dates in their ships to their own country. Near the town nothing green is to be seen. The cows and donkeys of those parts eat

خشك ميخورند حلواى مسقط مشهور است تا بهند و ايران حمل و نقل ميشود	Hind u Irān haml u naql mīshavad.	dried fish instead of fodder. The halvā (a sweet) of Masqat is famous and is exported to India and Persia.
فرنكى آب و هواى مسقط چه طور است	*Farangī.* Ab u havā-yi Masqat chi tour ast?	*European.* What is the climate of Masqat?
ايرانى مثلِ جهنّم است از هند هم گرم‌تر است با وجودِ اين امراضِ سخت در آنجا كم است	*Iranī.* Misl-i jahannam ast, az Hind ham garmtar ast. bā vujūd-i īn amrāz-i sakht dar ānjā kam ast.	*Persian.* It is like hell; it is hotter than India. Nevertheless, serious illnesses are rare there.
فرنكى در مسقط چند ساعت توقف ميشود	*Farangī.* Dar Masqat chand sā'at tavaqquf mīshavad?	*European.* How many hours do we stop at Masqat?
ايرانى دوازده ساعت صبح رسيده شام از آنجا ميرويد صبح ديگر انشاء الله ميرسيد	*Irānī.* Davāzdah sā'at. subh rasīda shām az ānjā mīravīd, subh-i dīgar in shā Allāh mī-rasīd bi Jāskh, ki langargāh-i	*Persian.* Twelve hours. You arrive in the morning and leave in the evening. If God will, you then reach *Jaskh*,

به جاشک که لنگرگاه کوچك مکران است	kūchik-i Makrūn ast.	which is a small landing-place in Makran.
فرنکی جاشك هم شهر عمدهٔ است	*Farangī.* Jāshk ham shahr-i ᶜumdaī-st?	*European.* Is Jashk also an important place?
ایرانی خیر قصبهٔ کوچکی است صفائی ندارد تلکرافخانهٔ انکلیس در جاشک است از جاشک تا بندر عباس یک شبانه روز راه است	*Irānī.* Kheir, qasaba-yi kūchikī-st, safāī na-dārad. talagrāf-khāna-yi inglīs dar Jāshk ast. az Jāskh tā *Bandar ᶜAbbās* yak shabāna rūz rāh ast.	*Persian.* No, it is a small village. It is not pretty. There is an English telegraph-office at Jaskh. From Jashk to *Bandar-Abbas* it is one night and one day's journey.
فرنکی شنیدم که بندر عباس را شاه عباس بنا کرده و در آن زمان شهرِ معتبری بوده است	*Farangī.* Shanīdam ki Bandar ᶜAbbās-rā Shāh ᶜAbbās binā karda va dar ān zamān shahr-i muᵓtabarī būda ást.	*European.* I have heard that Shah Abbas built Bandar Abbas, and that in his days, it was an important town.
ایرانی بلی احوالاتِ بندر عباس از تاریخ ایران معلوم است حالا هم مرکز تجارت است	*Irānī.* Balī ahvālāt-i Bandar ᶜAbbās az tārīkh-i Irān maᶜlūm ast. hālā ham markaz-i tijārat ast, ammā Linga az	*Persian.* Yes, the condition of Bandar Abbas is known from Persian history. It is still today a centre of commerce,

اما لنکه از بندرِ عباسی بزرگ تر و پر جمعیّت تر است	bandar-i ᶜAbbāsī buzurgtar va pur-jamᶜīattar ast.	but *Linga* is larger and more densely populated than Bandar Abbas.
فرنکی لنکه کجا واقع است	*Farangī.* Linga kujā vāqiᶜ ast?	*European.* Where does Linga lie?
ایرانی داخلِ خلیج فارس است ولنگرگاهش خوب است چرا که از بادِ شمال که بادِ سخت تمامِ خلیج فارس است محفوظ است بازارهای خوب دارد قالی و کلیم و نمد مالِ ایران از لنکه میبرند بمسقط و زنکبار کشتیِ خوب هم در لنکه میسازند	*Irānī.* Dākhil-i khalīj-i Fārs ast va langargāh-ash khūb ast, chirā ki az bād-i shamāl, ki bād-i sakht-i tamām-i *Khalīj-i Fārs* ast, mahfūz ast. Bāzārhā-yi khūb dārad qālī va gilīm va namad māl-i Irān az Linga mībarand bi Masqat va Zangbār. kashtī-yi khūb ham dar Linga mīsāzand.	*Persian.* It lies in the Persian Gulf, and its landing-place is good, because it is protected from the North Wind, which is very violent in the whole *Persian Gulf.* It has good bazaars. They export Persian woven and felt carpets from Linga to Masqat and to Zanzibar. They also build good ships at Linga.
فرنکی بعد از لنکه کدام منزل است	*Farangī.* Baᶜd az Linga kudām manzil ast?	*European.* Which is the station after Linga?

ایرانی جزیرهٔ بحرین است که مروارید در آنجا از تهِ دریا پیدا میکنند کویا شنیده اید که مرواریدِ خلیج فارس مشهور است اغلبش مالِ بحرین است زمینِ جزایرِ بحرین آباد و سبز و پر از درختِ خرما است اولاغهای بحرین بسیار قوی و بزرك و خوش ترکیب و تندرو و برای سواری از یابو بهتر اند از بحرین ببوشهر رو بشمال میروید	*Irānī.* Jazīra-yi *Bahrein* ast, ki murvārīd dar unjā az tah-i daryā peidā mīkunand. gūyā shanīda-īd ki murvārīd-i khalīj-i Fārs mashhūr ast. aghlab-ash māl-i Bahrein ast. Zamīn-i jazāyir-i Bahrein ābād va sabz va pur az dirakht-i khurmā-st. ulāghhā-yi Bahrein bisyār qavī va buzurg va khush tarkīb va tundrou va barāyi savārī az yābū bihtar and. az Bahrein bi *Būshahr* rū bi shamāl mīravīd.	*Persian.* It is the island of *Bahrein*, where they find pearls at the bottom of the sea. Perhaps you have heard that the pearls of the Persian Gulf are famous. Most of them come from Bahrein. The soil of the Island of Bahrein is well cultivated, and covered with verdure full of date-palms. The donkeys of Bahrein, are very strong, tall, well made, and swift. For riding they are better than ponies. From Bahrein to *Bushire* you teke a northerly direction.
فرنکی الحمد لله که در بوشهر	*Farangī.* Al hamdu l'Illāh ki	*European.* Thanks be to God

از عذابِ سفرِ دریا خلاص خواهم شد در بوشهر مهمانخانهٔ خوبی یافت میشود یاخیر	dar Būshahr az ᶜazāb-i safar-i daryā khalās khāham shud. Dar Būshahr mihmānkhāna-yi khūbī yāft mīshavad yā kheir?	that in Bushire I shall be delivered from the sufferings of this sea-journey. Is there a good Hotel at Bushire?
ایرانی خیر مهمانخانهٔ ندارد کاروان سرا دارد امّا برای شما بهتر است خانهٔ وکیل الدّولهٔ انکلیس منزل کنید	*Irānī.* Kheir, mihmānkhāna-yī na-dārad, kārvānsarā dārad, ammā barāyi shumā bihtar ast khāna-yi vakīl ad doula-yi Inglīs manzil kunīd.	*Persian.* No, there is no Hotel; there is a caravansery. But for you it is better to stop at the house of the English Resident.
فرنکی چه طور در خانهٔ وکیل الدّولهٔ انکلیس منزل کنم نمیشناسمش	*Farangī.* Chi tour dar khāna-yi vakīl ad doula-yi Inglīs manzil kunam? na-mīshanāsam-ash.	*European.* How can I stop at the house of the English Resident? I do not know him.
ایرانی او نمیکذارد جای دیکر منزل کنید هرکس از فرنکیها ببوشهر میآید مهمانِ وکیل الدوله میشود بسیار آدمِ	*Irānī.* U na-mīguzārad jā-yi dīgar manzil kunīd. har kas az Farangīhā bi Būshahr mīāyad, mihmān-i vakīl ad doula mīshavad. bisyār ādam-	*Persian.* He will not allow you to stay anywhere else. Whatever European comes to Bushire, becomes the guest of the Resident. He is a very

مهماندوستِ مهربانی است	i mihmāndūst i mihribānī-st.	hospitable and very kind man.
فرنکی دیکر از فرنکیها در بوشهر کسی هم هست	*Farangī.* Dīgar az Farangīhā dar Būshahr kasī ham hast?	*European.* Is there any other European at Bushire?
ایرانی بلی ده دوازده نفر تاجر دارد و چند نفر تلکرافچی هم در بوشهر ساکن اند خودِ شهر تجارتگاه بزرگی و پر جمعیت است خرید و فروش بسیار دارد هر مال التجاره که از طرف اصفهان و شیراز میبرند بلبِ دریا و هر چه از خارجه میآرند داخلِ ایران بنمایند از بوشهر میکذرد	*Irānī.* Balī dah davāzdah nafar tājir dārad va chand nafar talagrāfchī ham dar Būshahr sākin and. khud-i shahr tijāratgāh-i buzurg va pur jam'īat ast. kharīd u furūsh bisyār dārad. har māl at-tijāra ki az taraf-i Isfahān va Shīrāz mībarand bi lab-i daryā va har chi az khārija mīarand dakhil-i Irān binamāyand, az Būshahr mīguzarad.	*Persian.* Yes. There are ten or twelve merchants, and several telegraph-clerks living at Bushire. The city itself is an important commercial place and densely populated. There is much trade (buying and selling). All commercial goods, exported from Isfahan and Shiraz to the sea-coast, or imported from foreign parts into Persia, pass through Bushire.
فرنکی بغیر از بازار چیزی دارد	*Farangī.* Bi gheir az bāzār chīzī	*European.* Besides the bazaars,

که قابلِ دیدن باشد	dārad, ki qābil-i dīdan bā-shad?	is there anything worth seeing?
ایرانی چیزی ندارد بعد از توقّف چهار پنج روز باید راه بیفتید بروید شیراز	*Irānī*. Chīzī na-dārad. ba'd az tavaqquf-i chahār panj rūz bāyad rāh bīuftīd birāvīd *Shīrāz*.	*Persian*. There is nothing. After a stay of four or five days, you must set out for *Shiraz*.
فرنگی بفرمائید چه طور میتوان سفر کرد مگر کالسکه و ترمتاس پیدا میشود	*Farangī*. Bifarmāyīd chi tour mītavān safar kard? magar kālaska va turumtās peidā mīshavad?	*European*. Please tell me how I can make the journey? can I get a carriage or a tarantas?
ایرانی نه کالسکه دارد نه ترمتاس و نه راهِ آهن دو جور میتوان مسافرت کرد یکی با قافله میتوان رفت دیگری چاپاری	*Irānī*. Na kālaska dārad, na turumtās va na rāh-i āhan. du jūr mītavān masāfirat kard, yakī bā qāfila mītavān raft va dīgarī chāpārī.	*Persian*. There is no carriage, nor tarantas, nor railway. There are two modes of travelling; you can either go by caravan or with post-horses.
فرنگی بمن تعلیم بفرمائید بدانم چه طور باید رفت	*Farangī*. Bi man ta'līm bifarmāyīd bidānam chi tour bāyad raft.	*European*. Please to tell me all about it, so that I know which route to take.

ایرانی چشم بشما حالی میکنم میانِ بوشهر و شیراز چاپار نیست پس با قافله باید رفت یعنی دو سه راس قاطر برای بنه وبار و یك یابو برای سوارِی خودِتان کرایه کرده روزی یك منزل یعنی مسافت پنج شش فرسخ را طیّ میکنید	*Irānī.* Chashm! bi shumā hālī mīkunam: mīān-i Būshahr va Shīrāz chapar nīst, pas bā qāfila bāyad raft, yaʿnī du si rās qātir barāyi buna va bār va yak yābū barāyi savārī-yi khud-i tān kirāya karda, rūzī yak manzil, yaʿnī masāfat-i panj shish farsakh-rā tei mīkunīd.	*Persian.* With pleasure! (lit: by my eyes!) I will explain all to you. As between Bushire and Shiraz there are no posthorses, you must go by caravan; that is to say: you must hire two or three mules for the baggage and loads, and one pony for yourself to ride. Every day you can do one station, which is a distance of five on six leagues.
فرنگی همین را قافله میگویند بنده خیال کرده بودم که قافله جمعیّتِ بزرگی است از مرد و شتر و اسب و قاطر و غیره که باهم مسافرت میکنند	*Farangī.* Hamīn-rā qāfila mīgūyand? banda kheyāl karda būdam, ki qāfila jamʿīat-i buzurgī-st az mard u shutur u asp u qātir va gheira, ki bā ham musāfirat mīkunand.	*European.* I this what they call a caravan? I had thought that a caravan consisted of many men, camels, horses, and mules etc. that travel together.

ایرانی قافله عبارت است از این که با هر مالی که از محلّ حرکت سوار شدید تا محلِ مقصود تمامِ مسافتِ سفر را طیّ کنید و معنی چاپار این است که در هر منزل اسب عوض بکنید شما که بلدِ راه نیستید باید که یك نوکر که بلد باشد همراه بگیرید بنده بی نوکر رفته ام و شاگرد چاپار بقدرِ لزوم خدمت میکرد	*Irānī.* Qāfila ʿibārat ast az īn. ki bā har mālī ki az mahall-i harakat savār shudīd tā mahall-i maqsūd tamām-i masāfat-i safar rā tei kunīd; va maʿnī-yi chāpār īn ast, ki dar har manzil asp ʿavaz bikunīd. shumā ki balad-i rāh nīstīd, bāyad ki yak noukar ki balad bāshad hamrāh bigīrīd. banda bī noukar rafta am va shāgird chāpār bi qadr-i luzūm khidmat mīkard.	*Persian.* The meaning of caravan is this: that you should ride the whole way to your destination on the same animals which you started with. The meaning of travelling by post is this: that in each station you should change horses. You, who do not know the way, must take a servant with you who knows it. I (the slave) went without a servant, and the post-boy did the necessary service.
فرنگی عرض میکنم که حالیم بفرمائید سفر شما از بوشهر تا به شیراز چه طور کذشت	*Farangī.* ʿArz mīkunam ki hālī-am bifarmāyīd safar-i shumā az Būshahr tā bi Shīrāz chi tour guzasht.	*European.* I beg that you will tell me how you travelled from Bushire to Shiraz.

ایرانی چشم تفصیلِ سفرِ
خودمرا خدمتِ سرکار
مختصراً عرض میکنم با دو نفر
رفیق شده از بوشهر حرکت
نمودم که در عربی میگویند
الرّفیق ثم الطّریق یعنی اوّل
رفیق پیدا کن و بعد از ان
سفر برو خلاصه روزی اوّلِ
صبح سوارِ کرجی شده تا
شیف رفتیم که در طرفِ
دیگرِ مرداب بوشهر واقع است
آنجا چاروادار با مال منتظرِ
ما بود اسبابِ سفر را بار کرده
سوار شدیم براه افتادیم تا

Irānī. Chashm! tafsīl-i safar i khudam-rā khidmat-i sarkār mukhtasaran ʿarz mīkunam; bā du nafar rafīq shuda az Būshahr harakat namūdam, ki dar ʿarabī mīgūyand: "ar-rafīq thumm at-tarīq" yaʿnī avval rafīq peidā kun va baʿd az un safar birou. khulāsa rūzī avval-i subh savār-i karajī shuda tā *Shīf* raftīm, ki dar taraf-i dīgar-i murdāb-i Būshahr vāqiʿ ast. ānjā chārvādār bā māl muntazir-i mā būd. asbāb-i safar-rā bār karda savār shudīm, bi rāh uftādīm.

Persian. With pleasure! I will relate for your benefit all the particulars of my own journey. Together with two companions, I started from Bushire, for in Arabic they say "A companion, then the road", which means: find a companion before going on a journey.

Well, one day at day-break we took a boat and went to *Shīf*, which lies at the other end of the lagoon of Bushire. There the mule-driver was waiting for us with the mules. After having put up the loads, we mounted and started on our way. Till the foot of the mountain, there

بدامنهٔ کوه ریکستان است خیلی کرم بود جابجا آب پیدا میشد و لیکن اغلبش شور است درختِ خرما در آن صحرا که مشهور به کرمسیر است بیشمار است	tā bi dāmana-yi kuh rīgistān ast. kheilī garm būd. jā bi jā āb peidā mīshud va līkan aghlab-ash shūr ast. dirakht-i khurmā dar ān sahrā ki mashhūr bi *Garm·sīr* ast, bīshumār ast.	is a sandy soil. It was very hot. Here and there we found some water, but it was mostly brackish. The date-palms in that plain, which is known as *Garmsir*, are innumerable.
یک ساعت بغروب مانده رسیدیم به برازجون دهِ کوچکی است امّا کاروانسرای عظیمی دارد بنده در تلکرافخانه مهمان شدم و از تلکرافچی که ارمنی است مسافتِ راه را پرسیدم کفت که هفت فرسخ راه طیّ کرده اید	yak sāʿat bi ghurūb munda rasīdīm bi *Burāzjūn*. dih-i kūchikī st, ammā kārvānsarā-yi ʿazīmī dārad. banda dar talagrāf khāna mihmān shudam va az talagrāfchī, ki *Armanī*-st masāfat-i rāh-rā pursīdam. guft ki haft farsakh rāh tei karda-īd.	At one hour before sunset we arrived at *Burazjun*. It is a small village, but it has a large caravansery. I was a guest in the telegraph-office, and we asked the telegraph-clerk, who is an *Armenian*, about the distance of our way. He said: "You have travelled seven farsakhs".
صبح سوار شده رفتیم به کنار تخته شش فرسخ راه است	subh savār shuda raftīm. bi *Kunār Takhta*. shish farsakh	In the morning, having mounted, we went to *Kunar*

Takhta. It is a distance of six farsakhs. It is all stony, mountainous and bad. On the right was the mountain, and on the left the plain. At the foot of the hill, warm sulphur water springs forth; there are also several petroleum-springs there. In consequence of the quantity of horse-flies, it was very bad for man and beast.

Two hours before noon we reached the village of *Dalaki.* We had luncheon near the caravansery of *Dalaki.* From there the road went along the foot of the hills. There are dangerous defiles and dreadful precipices here.

rāh ast. tamām-ash sanglākh va kūh va bad ast, dast-i rāst kūh va dast-i chap dasht. az dāmana-yi kūh āb-i garm-i gūgird mīrīzad, bū-yi badī mīdahad. chand tā chashma-yi naft ham dar ānjā-st. bi jihat-i kasrat-i kharmagas bi mardum va bi mālhā kheilī bad guzasht. du sāʿat bi zuhr munda bi qarīa-yi *Dālakī* rasīdīm. nahār dam-i kārvānsarā-yi *Dālakī* sarf shud az ānjā rāh bi dāmana-yi kūh uftād: tangahā-yi makhūf va baghalahā-yi muhīb dārad. az rūdkhāna-yi *Khisht* guzashtīm, ki āb ash shūr ast.

تمامش سنگلاخ و کوه و بد
است دست راست کوه بود
دست چپ دشت از دامنهٔ
کوه آب گرم گوگرد میریزد
بوی بدی میدهد چند تا
چشمهٔ نفت هم در آنجاست
بجهت کثرت خرمگس بمردم
و بمالها خیلی بد گذشت دو
ساعت بظهر مانده بقریهٔ دالکی
رسیدیم نهار دم کاروانسرای
دالکی صرف شد از آنجا راه
بدامنهٔ کوه افتاد تنگههای
مخوف و بغلههای مهیب
دارد از رود خانهٔ خشت
گذشتیم که آبش شور است

پل سنگی بر روی رودخانه بسته اند بعد از آن رسیدیم بکوتل ملّو که بسیار پست و بلند است راه ساخته هم هست اما سنگ فرشش بطوری است که اسب نمیتواند راه برود بالا که رسیدیم میدانی پیدا بود صاف وهمند مانند سطح آب معلوم است آنجا قدیمًا دریاچهٔ بوده است بوته کنار و درخت خرما فراوان است	pul-i sangī bar rū-yi rūdkhāna basta and. baʿd az ān rasīdīm bi *kūtal-i Mallū*, ki bisyār past u buland ast, rāh-i sākhta ham hast, ammā sangfarsh-ash bi tourī-st, ki asp na-mītavānad rāh biravad. bālā ki rasīdīm meidānī peidā būd, sāf va humand mānand-i sath-i āb. maʿlūm ast unjā qadīman daryāchaī būda ast. buta-yi kunār va dirakht-i kharmā farāvān ast.	We passed the river *Khisht*, whose waters were brackish. A stone bridge has been built across the river. After that we reached the *Pass of Mallu*, which is exceedingly steep and elevated. There is also a built road there but its pavement is such that a horse cannot walk on it. When we got to the top, a plain was to be seen; it was flat and smooth, like an expanse of water. Evidently a small lake was there in olden times. Jujube-bushes and date-palms are there in plenty.
در تلگرافخانه که اتفاقًا خالی بود منزل کردیم	dar talagrāfkhāna, ki ittifāqan khālī būd, manzil kardīm. ghulām-i talagrāfkhāna	We stayed in the telegraph-office which happened to be empty. The servant at the

غلامِ تلگرافخانه هیزم و آب و برنج و پیاز و روغن و نان تازه حاضر کرد میانِ باغ آتش روشن کرده طعام پختیم خوردیم فرش وبالا پوش آنچه داشتیم روی بوریا انداخته راحت شدیم	hɪzum va ᴀb va birinj va pɪᴀz va roughan va nun-i tᴀza hᴀzir kard. mɪān-i bᴀgh ᴀtash roushan karda tuʿᴀm pukhtɪm, khurdɪm. farsh va bᴀlᴀpush unchi dᴀshtɪm rū-yi burɪᴀ andᴀkhta rᴀhat shudɪm.	telegraph-office brought wood, water, rice, onions, melted butter, and fresh bread. Having lit a fire in the middle of the garden, we cooked the food and ate it. Having spread all the rugs and over-coats, which we possessed on to the matting, we rested.
صبح زود برخاستیم سوار شدیم معلوم شد که امروز تا کازرون باید رفت هشت فرسخ سنگین	subh zūd barkhᴀstɪm, savᴀr shudɪm. maʿlum shud ki imrūz tᴀ *Kāzarūn* bᴀyad raft.	We rose very early, and mounted our horses. We knew we had to reach *Kazarun* that day.
راه است از رود خانه و از کوتل کمارج گذشتیم این	hasht farsakh-i sangɪn rᴀh ast. az rūdkhᴀna va az kūtal-i *Kamārij* guzashtɪm. ɪn gar-	It is 8 farsakhs and a hard road. We passed the river and the Pass of *Kamarij*.
گردنه هم خیلی پست و بلند و خطرناك است گاهی قاطرها پرت شده تا تهِ درّه میغلطند میمیرند پیاده	dana ham kheilɪ past u buland va khatarnᴀk ast. gᴀhɪ qᴀtirha part shuda tᴀ tah-i darra mɪghaltand, mɪmɪrand. pɪᴀda shuda bᴀlᴀ raftɪm. az	This pass is also very steep, high, and dangerous. Sometimes the mules fall and roll down to the bottom of the

شده بالا رفتم از آبادی ده
کمارج وگردنهٔ کوچکی کذشته
بجلگهٔ کازرون رسیدیم تمامش
باصفا و سبز و آباد است زمینش
خاكِ نرمِ خوبی است و یک
وجب زمین در تمام آن جلگه
خشك و لم یزرع نیست جابجا
آب از کوه های دست چپ
بقدرِ یک سنگ و دو سنگ
میریزد باغهارا مشروب میکند
اقسام و انواع میوهجات و
فواکهِ ممتاز عمل میآید

ābādī-yi dih-i *Kamārij* va gardana-yi kūchikī guzashta bi julga-yi *Kāzarūn* rasīdīm. tamām-ash bā safā va sabz va ābad ast. zamīn-ash khāk-i narm-i khūbī-st va yak vajab-i zamīn dar tamām-i ān julga khushk va lam yazraᶜ [1]) nīst. jā bi jā āb az kūhhā-yi dast-i chap bi qadr-i yak *sang* [2]) u du sang mīrīzad, bāghhā rā mashrūb mīkunad. aqsām u anvāᶜi [3]) mīvajāt va favākih-i [4]) mumtāz ᶜamal mīāyad.

pass and perish. We walked to the top. After we had passed by the fields of the village of *Kamarij*, and by a small pass, we reached the valley of *Kazarun*. It is all beauṭiful, green, and cultivated. Its soil is a soft, good earth, and not one span in the whole of that valley is dry or uncultivated. Here and there to the left, flows water from the mountains, enough for one or two stones [1]), and waters the gardens. (All) kinds and sorts of fruit are grown there.

1) arabic for "not cultivated".
2) The Persians measure water by the number of mill-stones it can drive.
3) arabic plurals of قسم qism and نوع nouᶜ, both meaning "kinds."
4) arabic plural of فاکهه fakiha, fruit.

کازرون	*Kazarūn.*	*Kazarun.*
سه ساعت بغروب مانده بشهر کازرون رسیدیم در تلگرافخانه پائین آمدیم بعد از صرفِ عصرانه گردش نمودیم میزبانِ ما بلدی میکرد بازار و کوچهارا تماشا کردیم بعد رفتیم به باغ مسمّی به باغ نظر باغیست مثل بهشت وتازه‌تر از گلستان ارم	si sāʿat bi ghurūb munda bi shahr-i *Kūzarūn* rasīdīm. dar talagrāfkhāna pāīn āmadīm. baʿd az sarf-i ʿasrāna gardish namūdīm. mīzbān-i mā baladī mīkard. bāzār va kūchahā-rā tamāshā kardīm, baʿd raftīm bi bāgh musammā bi *bāgh-i Nazar*. bāghī-st misl-i bihisht va tāzatar az gulistān-i *Iram*.	At three hours before sunset we reached the town of *Kazarun*. We stopped at the telegraph-office. After partaking of an afternoon meal, we had a walk. Our host was our guide. We saw the bazaars and the streets, then we went into a garden, called "The garden of Nazar." It is a garden like Paradise and fresher than the rose-garden of *Iram*.
نظم	*Nazm.*	*Verse.*
گلستانی چو گلزار جوانی	"gulistānī chi gulzār-i javānī,	"A flower-garden like the bed of roses of youth,

گلش سیراب زاب زندگانی	"gul-ash sīrāb 'z āb-i zindagānī,	"Its roses watered by the Water of Life,
نوای عندلیبش عشرت انگیز	"navā-yi ʿandalīb-ash ʿishrat angīz,	"The Song of its Nightingales causing delight,
نسیم عطرسایش راحت آمیز	"nasīm-i ʿitrsā-yash rāhatāmīz.	"Its perfumed Zephyr bringing peace".
میانِ چهار باغ حوضی است که آبش بسیار صاف و خوش گوار وخنك است جمیع درختهای چهار باغ مرکبات است یعنی نارنج و نارنگی ولیمو و پرتقال اوّل شکوفهٔ نارنج بود از بوی شکوفه‌ها و از آواز بلبلها مست شدم میگفتند هر درخت پرتقال زیاده از هزار دانه بار میدهد	mīān-i chahārbāgh houz-īst, ki āb-ash bisyār sāf va khush-gavār va khunak ast. jamīʿ-i dirakhthā-yi chahārbāgh murakkabāt ast, yaʿnī nāranj va nārangī va līmū va purtuqāl. avval-i shikūfa-yi nāranj būd. az bū-yi shikūfahā va az āvāzī-i bulbulhā mast shudam. mīguftand har dirakht-i purtuqāl zīāda az hazār dāna bār mīdahad.	In the middle of a cross-alley is a well, whose waters are very clear, agreeable to the taste, and cool. All the trees of this cross-alley bear golden fruits, such as bitter oranges, tangerines, lemons and sweet oranges. It was the beginning of the orange-blossom season. I was intoxicated by the smell of the blossoms and the singing of the Nightingales. We were told that each orange-tree

درخت خرما هم بسیار است از کازرون رو بشمال که رفتیم دیگر هیچ درختِ خرما دیده نشد	dirakht-i khurmā ham bisyār ast. az *Kāzarūn* rū bi shamāl ki raftīm dīgar hīch dirakht-i khurmā dīda na-shud.	bears more than a thousand fruits. There are also many date-palms. Going north from *Kazarun*, we saw no more date palms at all.
صبح زود ممکن نشد که بدون معطّلی راه بیفتیم قاطرچی میخواست بمال جو بدهد هر چه گشت جو گیر نیاورد فصلِ علف دادن بود امّا عجب اینکه در همهٔ کازرون یك من جو پیدا نشد	subh-i zūd mumkin na-shud ki bidūn-i muʿattalī rāh biuftīm. qātirchī mīkhāst bi māl jou bidahad. har chi gasht jou gīr nay-āvurd, fasl-i ʿalaf dādan būd, ammā ajab-īnki dar hama-yi *Kazarūn* yak man jou peidā na-shud.	Early next morning we found it impossible to continue our journey without delay. The mule-driver wished to give his animals some barley. However much he tried, he could nowhere get barley. It was the season for giving green-fodder. Yet it was wonderful, that in all *Kazarun*, not one single "*man*" of barley was to be found.

1) see page 123.

ار کازرون تا شیراز

دو ساعت و نیم بظهر مانده سوار شدیم باران متّصل میبارید راه از شدّت بارندگی پر گل و باطلاق شده بود و لباسهای ما در راه تا کلاه گلی میشد نزدیک کوه دستِ چپ که رسیدیم دریاچهٔ پیدا شد موسوم بدریای پریشان نیزار و لجن زار اطرافِ دریاچه بسیار است و پر از نوکدراز و اردک و مرغابی است پلِ چوبی روی یک گوشهٔ دریای پریشان بسته بودند که از او عبور

Az Kāzarūn tā Shīraz.

du sᴀʿat u nɪm bi zuhr munda savᴀr shudɪm. bᴀrᴀn muttasil mɪbᴀrɪd. rᴀh az shiddat-i bᴀrandagɪ pur gil va bᴀtlᴀq shuda bᴜd va libashᴀ-yi mᴀ dar rᴀh tᴀ kulᴀh gilɪ mɪshud. nazdɪk-i kᴜh-i dast-i chap ki rasɪdɪm, daryᴀchaɪ peidᴀ shud mousᴜm bi *Daryā-yi Parīshān.* neizᴀr va lajanzᴀr atrᴀf-i daryᴀcha bisyᴀr ast va pur az nᴜkdirᴀz [1]) va urdak va murghᴀbɪ-st. pul-i chubɪ rᴜ-yi yak gᴜsha-yi Daryᴀ-yi Parɪshᴀn basta bᴜdand, ki az ᴜ ʿubᴜr shud.

From Kazarun to Shiraz.

At two hours and a half before noon we mounted our horses. It rained incessantly. On account of the quantity of rain, the road was full of mud and mire, and on the road our clothes were covered with mud right up to our hats. As we approached the mountain, to the left, we saw a lake, called the *Parishan-Lake.* There are many reeds and much swamp round the lake. It is full of snipe, duck and water-fowl. A wooden bridge had been erected across

1) lit: long beak.

شد اکثر تختههای ان جسر شکسته و خراب شده بود امید است که تا امروز مرمّت کرده باشند	aksar-i takhtahā-yi an jisr shikasta va kharāb shuda būd, umīd ast, ki tā imrūz marammat karda bāshand.	a corner of the Parishan Lake. Over this we went. Many of the planks of that bridge were broken and rotten. Let us hope that they have now been repaired.
از آنجا راه بدرّهٔ کوه میافتد جمعیت از ایلات در راه و طرفینِ راه حرکت میکرد راه از عبور و مرورِ مردم و بنه بطوری باطلاق شده بود که پیاده نمیتوانستم راه برویم	az ānjā rāh bi darra-yi kūh mīuftad. jamʿīat az īlāt dar rāh va tarafein-i rāh harakat mīkard. rāh az ʿubūr u murūr-i mardum va buna bi tourī bātlāq shuda būd, ki pīāda namītavānistīm rāh biravīm.	From there the road goes into a mountain-valley. A quantity of Nomads moved along the way, and on both sides of the way. The road had got so muddy, on account of the traffic of man and beast, that we could not go on foot.
خلاصه به کوتل دختر رسیدیم کوهِ سنگیِ مرتفع و بسیار مهیب و سراشیب است اما سنگچینی کرده و سنگفرش و	khulāsa bi *Kūtal-i Dukhtar* rasīdīm. kūh-i sangī-yi murtafiʿ va bisyār muhīb va sarāshīb ast ammā sangchīnī karda va sangfarsh va	At last we reached the *Daughter's Pass*. The mountain is rocky, high, very imposing and precipitous, but they have removed all stones, and made a pavement and

درجها ساخته بودند بطوری که شتر با بار خوب و براحت میگذرد	darajahā sākhta būdand, bi tourī ki shutur bā bār khūb va bi rāhat mīguzarad.	steps, so that riders and camels with loads can pass quite well and easily.
سرِ گردنه که رسیدیم باران ایستاده و هوا صاف شد و دریای پریشان خوب پیدا بود قدری راحت کردیم باز براه افتادیم جنگلی مشهور بدشت برم بفاصله دو میدان اسب بود جنگل بلوط است وآنجا هم احتمال میرود قدیم دریاچهٔ بوده است	sar-i gardana ki rasīdīm bārān īstāda va havā sāf shud va *Daryā-yi Parīshān* khūb peidā būd. qadrī rāhat kardīm, bāz bi rāh uftādīm. jangalī mashhūr bi *Dasht-i Barm* bi fāsila-yi du meidān-i asp būd. jangal-i ballūt ast va ānjā ham ihtimāl mīravad qadīm daryāchaī būda ast.	When we reached the top of the Pass, the rain had stopped. The air had become clear and the *Parishan-Lake* was clearly to be seen. We rested a little, then continued our way. There was a forest called *Dasht-i Barm*, at the distance of the length of two gallops of a horse. It is a forest of oak-trees, and there was most probably a lake there formerly.
در کوههای اطرافِ دشتِ برم شیر دارد چند سال قبل یک شیر نرِ بسیار بزرگ بمردم	dar kūhhā-yi atrāf-i *Dasht-i Barm* shīr dārad. chand sāl qabl yak shīr-i nar-i bisyār buzurg bi mardum-i qāfila	In the mountains near *Dasht-i Barm* there are lions. Some years ago a male lion, very big, used to attack men

قافله حمله میآورد یك صاحب منصبِ انکلیس را هم نزدیك بود بدرد خیز زده چنکال بکفلِ اسب او زده بود صاحب منصب زمین خورده کریخت نمیدانست اسپش چه شد آخر الامر اسب را بمنزل آوردند زخم زیاد خورده بود همین شیرِ نر را که کفتم یك نفر از ایلات کشت ظلّ السلطان که حاکم اصفهان و فارس بود خلعت و هزار تومان به آن شخصِ دلاور انعام فرمودند

hamla mīāvurd. yak sāhib-mansab-i Inglīs-rā ham nazdīk būd bidarad. khīz zada changāl bi kafal-i asp-i ū zada būd. sāhib-mansab zamīn khurda gurīkht, na-mīdānist asp-ash chi shud. ākhir-ul-amr asprā bi manzil āvurdand zakhm-i zīād khurda būd. hamīn shīr-i nar-rā ki guftam yak nafar az īlāt kusht. *Zill as Sultān*[1], ki hākim-i *Isfahān* va *Fārs* būd, khalʿat va hazār tuman bi ān shakhs-i dilāvar inʿām farmūdand.

and caravans. He once nearly killed an English officer. Jumping, he thrust his claws into the horse's quarters. The officer fell to the ground, then fled, not knowing what had become of his horse. At last the horse was brought into the station very badly wounded. This same male lion that I have just mentioned, was killed by a Nomad. *Zill as Sultan*, who was Governor of *Isfahan* and *Fars*, gave this plucky man a cloak of honor and one thousand tumans reward.

1) "Shadow of the Sultan", the eldest son of the late Shah.

فرنگی حالاهم در آن سمتها شیر دیده میشود	*Farangī.* Hālā ham dar ān samt-hā shīr dīda mīshavad?	*European.* Does one still find lions in those parts?
ایرانی در سرِ جاده خیر اما در بیراهۀ کوهها تك تك پیدا میشود	*Irānī.* Dar sar-i jādda kheir, ammā dar bīrāha-yi kūhhā tak tak peidā mīshavad.	*Persian.* Not on the road itself, but in the mountain wildernesses one occasionnally finds them.
بعد از گذشتن از دشت برم راه باز سر بالا میرود کوه تمامش بی راه و سنگلاخ است اسمِ آنجا کوتلِ پیرِ زن است میگویند پیر زنی این معبر کوهها را احداث کرده و سنگچینی نموده است و قبرِ پیره زن در سرِ گردنه نمایان است	Ba^cd az guzashtan az *Dasht-i Darm* rah bāz sarbālā mīravad. kūh tamām-ash bī rāh va sanglākh ast. ism-i ān jā *Kūtal-i Pīr-i Zan* ast. mīgūyand pīr-i zanī īn ma^cbar-i kūhhā-rā ihdās karda va sangchīnī namūda ast va qabr-i pīra zan dar sar-i gardana namāyān ast.	After passing through (the forest) Dasht-i Barm, we again went up-hill. There are no roads on the mountain, which is covered with rolling stones. The name of this place is the *Old Woman's Pass.* They relate that an old woman discovered this passage over the Mountains and removed the stones from there; the tomb of the old woman is to be seen at the top of the Pass.

بواسطهٔ ارتفاعِ کوه و بدیِ راه نمیشد همان روز تابسر کوتل برسیم در کاروانسرای مشهور بمیان کوتل اطراق نمودیم که عمارتِ وسیعِ خوبیست و در توی طاقچهٔ آتش افروخته شام خوردیم چون هیچ حصیر و فرش نبود روی سنگ خوابیدیم اینقدر سرد شد که بعد از نصف شب از زور سرما بیدار شده پا شدیم	Bi vāsita-yi irtifā-ʿi kūh va badī-yi rāh na-mīshud ha-mān rūz tā bi sar-i kūtal bira-sīm. dar kārvānsarāī mash-hūr bi *Mīān Kūtal* utrāq namūdīm, ki ʿimārat-i vasī-i khūbī-st va dar tū-yi tāqcha-yī ātash afrūkhta shām khur-dīm. chun hīch hasīr va farsh na-būd rū-yi sang khā-bīdīm. īn-qadr sard shud, ki baʿd az nisf-i shab az zūr-i sarmā bīdār shuda, pā shudīm.	In consequence of the height of the mountain and the badness of the road, it was not possible to get that same day to the top of the Pass. We stopped at a caravansery known as "*Mian Kutal*. It is a fine spacions, building. Having made fire in a niche, we supped. As there were no mats nor carpets, we lay down on the stones. It got so cold, that after midnight we were awakened by the intensily of the cold, and so we rose.
آفتاب نزده راه افتادیم عبور از کوتل پیر زن بقدری مشکل است که هزارها قاطر سر راه	Aftāb na-zada rāh uftādīm. ʿubūr az *Kūtal-i Pīri Zan* bi qadrī mushkil ast, ki	Before sunrise we started on our way. The passing over the *Old Woman's Pass* is so

میمیرند تا چشم کار میکرد لاشه و استخوانِ قاطر ریخته شده بود باین جهت لاشخور در آنجا فراوان است	hazārhā qātir sar-i rūh mī-mīrand. tā chashm kār mī-kard lāsha va ustukhān-i qātir rīkhta shuda būd. bi īn jihat lāshkhūr dar ānjā farāvān ast.	difficult, that thousands of mules die on the road. As far as one's eyes could see, the place was strewn with carcasses and bones of mules. For this reason, vultures are plentiful in those parts.
طرفِ شمالِ این کوتل دشتی است موسوم بدشتِ ارجن دورادورش کوههای بلندِ برفدار است دستِ راست دریاچه و لجن زار و نیزار است و دستِ چپ چشمهٔ عظیمی است که آبش بقدرِ چهار سنگ از شکافِ کوهِ سنگی میریزد جمعیّت بزرگی از	Taraf-i shamāl-i īn kūtal dashtī-st mousūm bi *Dasht-i Arjan*. dourādour-ash kūhhā-yi buland-i barfdār ast. dast-i rāst daryācha va lajan-zār va neizār ast, va dast-i chap chashma-yi ʿazīmī-st ki āb-ash bi qadr-i chahār sang az shigāf-i kūh-i sangī mī-rīzad. jamʿīat-i buzurgī az	On the Northern side of this Pass there is a plain named *Dasht-i Arjan*. All round it are high mountains, covered with snow. To the right is a lake with reeds and swamps, and to the left is an excellent spring whose water is strong enough to drive four mill-stones, and which flows from a cleft in the mountain-rock. A great many Nomads were passing through

ایلات از آن آب عبور مینمود خیلی تماشا داشت بچها و برّه ها توی خرجین بسته روی گاو و اولاغ گذاشته بودند و مرغهارا سرِ بار بسته بودند زنها سوار اسپ بهمه کار مشغول بودند یکی کره درست میکرد دیگری پشم میرشت وغیره	Ilāt az ān āb ᶜubūr mīnamūd, kheilī tamāshā dāsht: bachahā va barrahā tū-yi khurjīn basta rū-yi gāv va ulāgh guzāshta būdand, va murghā-rā sar-i bār basta būdand. zanhā savār-i asp bi hama kār mashghūl būdand: yakī kara durust mīkard, dīgarī pashm mīrisht va gheira.	this water. It was a curious sight: children and lambs were tied up in the saddle-bags, which were placed on the backs of cows and donkeys. Fowls were tied on top of the loads. The women, on horseback, were occupying themselves in various ways: one was making butter, another was spinning wool, etc.
تلگرافخانهٔ دشتِ ارجن قریبِ همان چشمه واقع است قدری استراحت نموده بالای کوهِ کوچکی رفتیم راه خوب و بی سنك و بی گل بود	Talagrāfkhāna-yi *Dasht-i Arjan* qarīb-i hamun chashma vāqiᶜ ast. qadrī istirāhat namūda bālā-yi kūh-i kūchikī raftīm. rāh khūb va bī sang va bī gil būd.	The telegraph-office of *Dasht-i Arjan* lies near this spring. Having rested a little, we ascended a small hill. The road was good, and free from stones and mud.
نیم ساعت بغروب مانده به کاروانسرای خانه زنیون	Nīm sāᶜat bi ghurūb munda bi kārvānsarā-yi *Khāna Zan-*	Half an hour before sunset we reached the caravansery of

رسیدیم هوا بقدری سرد بود که آب یخ میکرد شب خیلی بد بما گذشت صبح تا دو ساعت از آفتاب گذشته ژاله روی زمین میماند	*yūn* rasīdīm. havā bi qadrī sard būd, ki āb yakh mīkard. shab kheilī bad bi mā guzasht. subh tā du saʿat az āftāb guzashta jāla rū-yi zamīn mīmānd.	*Khana Zanyun*. The air was so cold, that the water was frozen. We spent a very bad night. In the morning, until two hours after sunrise, the ground remained frozen.
از خانه زنیون تا شیراز هشت فرسخ سنگین راه است با وجودِ سرمای شبِ گذشته قریبِ ظهر هوا بسیار گرم شد قاطرها خیلی خسته شده بودند که نتوانستیم هیچ سوار بشویم تمام راه را پیاده طی کردیم	Az *Khāna Zanyūn* tā *Shīrāz* hasht farsakh-i sangīn rāh ast. bā vujūd-i sarmā-yi shab-i guzashta qarīb-i zuhr havā bisyār garm shud. qātirhā kheilī khasta shuda būdand, ki na-tavānistīm hīch savār bishavīm. tamām-i rāh-rā pīāda tei kardīm.	Between *Khāna Zanyun* to *Shiraz* there are eight farsakhs of hard road. Notwithstanding the cold of the previous night, near midday it became very warm. The mules were so tired that we could not ride them. We did the whole distance on foot.
دو ساعت از ظهر گذشته وارد دار العلم شیراز شدیم	Dū saʿat az zuhr guzashta vārid-i *Dār ul ʿilm-i Shīrāz* shudīm.	Two hours after mid-day, we arrived at the *"House of Science* [1]) *Shiraz"*.

1) The principal Persian towns have titles. Tehran is called "House of the Chalifate" (Dār al Khilāfa) Isfahan is called House of the Sultanate (Dār as Saltana).

فرنگی در شیراز شاید خانهٔ دوست خود تان پیاده شدید	*Farangī*. Dar shāyad Shīrāz khāna-yi dūst-i khud-i tān pīāda shudīd?	*European*. Did you stop at the house of your friend at Shiraz?
ایرانی بلی، دوستم قریب دروازهٔ شهر باغ و انگورستان و خانه دارد آنجا منزل کردیم	*Irānī*. Balī dūst-am qarīb-i darvāza-yi shahr bāgh va angūristān va khāna dārad. unjā manzil kardīm.	*Persian*. Yes, my friend has, near the gate of the town, a garden, a vineyard and a house. There we stayed.
فرنگی شما یقین از زحمتِ سفر بسیار خسته شده بودید	*Farangī*. Shumā yaqīn az zahmat-i safar bisyār khasta shuda būdīd?	*European*. I suppose you were much fatigued with the hardships of the journey.
ایرانی خیر آقا من که بار نکشیده بودم خسته هم نشدم ولی مالها نیم مرده بودند	*Irānī*. Kheir āghā, man ki bār na-kashīda būdam khasta ham na-shudam valī mālhā nīm murda būdand.	*Persian*. No sir, I who had not borne a load, was not tired, but the mules were half dead.
شیراز	*Shīrāz.*	*Shiraz.*
فرنگی شیراز میدانم که شهرِ بزرگ و مشهور و معروفِ دنیا	*Farangī*. *Shīrāz* mīdānam ki shahr-i buzurg va mashhūr va maʿrūf-i dunyā-st, ammā	*European*. I know that *Shiraz* is a large town, famous and celebrated all over the world.

است امّا شما بفرمائید که چه چیز در شیراز باید تماشا بکنم	shumā bifarmāyīd ki chi chīz dar *Shīrāz* bāyad tamāshā bikunam.	But please tell me what I ought to see at Shiraz.
ایرانی یکی حافظیّه و سعدیّه یعنی قبرِ خواجه حافظ و شیخ سعدی هرکسیکه شیراز میآید زیارتِ مزارِ این دو شاعرِ نامدار را مینماید هر دو در خارج شهر واقع اند و باغاتِ خوب هم در اطرافِ شهر دارد باید گردش کنید	*Irānī.* Yakī *Hāfizīya* va *Saʿdīya*, yaʿnī qabr-i *Khāja Hāfiz* va *Sheikh Saʿdī.* har kasī ki *Shīrāz* mīāyad, zīārat-i mazār-i īn du shāʿir-i nāmdārrā mīnamāyad. har du dar khārij-i shahr vāqiʿ and va bāghāt-i khūb ham dar atrāf-i shahr dārad, bāyad gardish kunīd.	*Persian.* Firstly the "*Hafizya* and *Sadiya*, namely, the tombs of *Khaja Hafiz* and of *Sheikh Sadi.* Everyone who comes to *Shiraz* makes a pilgrimage to the tombs of these two celebrated poets. Both lie outside the town; there are also pretty gardens round about the town, in which you should take a walk.
فرنگی خودِ شهر بناهای خوبِ قدیم دارد	*Farangī.* Khud-i shahr banāhā-yi khūb-i qadīm dārad?	*European.* Are there any fine old buildings in the town itself?
ایرانی عماراتِ شهر اکثرِ شان	*Irānī.* ʿImārāt-i shahr aksar-i shān az zamān-i *Karīm Khān-i*	*Persian.* Most of the buildings have remained from the time

از زمانِ کریم خانِ وکیل باقی مانده است که در سنهٔ ۱۱۹۳ هجری مطابق ۱۷۷۹ عیسوی فوت شده است همین است که بیوتات و باغات و مساجد و حمّامات و قلعه و حصار و خندق و دروازه ها و برکه‌ها و بازارها بنا کرده است شما که فرنگی هستید اجازهٔ دیدنِ مسجدها و حمامها بشما نخواهند داد اما باغها و بازارها و خصوصًا بازار وکیل را خوب تماشا باید بکنید

Vakīl bāqī munda ast, ki dar sana-yi hazār u yak sad u navad u si hijrī mutābiq-i hazār u haft sad u haftād u nuh ʿīsavī fout shuda ast. hamīn ast, ki buyūtāt [1]) va bāghāt [1]) va masājid [1]) va hammāmāt [1]) va qalʿa va hisār va khandaq va darvāzahā va birkahā va bāzārhā binā karda ast. shumā, ki *Farangī* hastīd, ijāza-yi dīdan-i masjidhā va hammāmhā bi shumā na-khāhand dād, ammā bāghhā va bāzārhā va khusūsan *bāzār-i Vakīl*-rā khūb tamāshā bāyad bikunīd.

of *Karīm Khan-i Vakil*, who died in the year 1193 of the Mohammedan era, which corresponds to the year 1779 of the Christian Era. It is he who built the houses, gardens, mosques, baths, forts, citadels, moats, gates, tanks, and bazaars. You, who are an European, will not be allowed to see the mosques and the baths; but the gardens and the bazaars, especially the *Vakil's Bazaar*, you must make a point of seeing properly.

1) Arabic plurals of بیت beit (house), باغ bāgh (garden), ساجد masjid (mosque), حمام hammām (bath).

فرنگی بسیار خوب من هرجای که ممکن باشد انشاء اللّه خواهم رفت	*Farangī.* Bisyār khūb, man har jāī ki mumkin bāshad in shā Allāh khāham raft.	*European.* Very well, I will go wherever it is possible to go, if God will.
ایرانی انشاء اللّه بعد از سیر شیراز باصفهان میروید	*Irānī.* In shā Allāh! baᶜd az seir-i *Shīrāz* bi *Isfāhan* mī-ravīd.	*Persian.* May it be God's will! After having seen *Shiraz*, you will go to *Isfahan.*
فرنگی آن راه را هم با قافله طیّ باید کرد	*Farangī.* An rāh-rā ham bā qāfila tei bāyad kard?	*European.* Must I make this journey also by a caravan?
شرح سفرِ چاپاری از شیراز و اصفهان و طهران و قزوین و رشت تا لب دریای خزر	*Sharh-i safar-i chāpārī az Shīrāz va Isfahān va Tahrān va Qazvīn va Rasht tā lab-i Daryā-yi Khazir.*	*Description of a post-journey from Shiraz to Isfahan, Tahrān, Qazvin and Resht, to the coast of the Caspian Sea.*
ایرانی از شیراز رو بشمال چاپار خانه دارد اگر میخواهید تند راه بروید چاپاری بروید	*Irānī.* Az *Shīrāz* rū bi shamāl chāpārkhāna dārad. agar mī-khāhīd tund rāh biravīd, chaparī biravīd.	*Persian.* From Shiraz, going north, you will find post-houses. If you wish to travel quickly, go with post-horses.

فرنگی سفرِ چاپاری چه طور میشود مرحمت فرموده بیان کنید	*Farangī*. Safar-i chaparī chi tour mīshavad? marhamat farmūda beyān kunīd.	*European*. How does one travel with post-horses? Please have the kindness to explain.
ایرانی چشم از چاپارخانهٔ شیراز یك تذکره برای دو رأس اسپ بگیرید	*Irānī*. Chashm! az chaparkhāna-yi *Shīrāz* yak tazkira barāyi du raʿs [1]) asp bigīrīd.	*Persian*. With pleasure! you must take, from the post-house at Shiraz, a pass for two horses.
فرنگی اگر تنها بروم یك اسب کفایت نمیکند	*Farangī*. Agar tanhā biravam yak asp kafāyat na-mīkunad?	*European*. If I travel alone, is not one horse sufficient?
ایرانی خیر شما سوارِ یك اسب میشوید و شاگردِ چاپار سوارِ اسپِ دیگر و او هم خرجینِ تانرا باخودش حمل مینماید بعد از ورود مقصد شاگرد چاپار مالهارا پس میبرد منزلِ	*Irānī*. Kheir, shumā savār-i yak asp mīshavīd va shāgird chapar savār-i asp-i dīgar, va ū ham khurjīn-i tun-rā bā khudash haml mīnamāyad baʿd az vurūd-i maqsad shāgird chapar mālhā-rā pas mībarad manzil-i khudash	*Persian*. No, you must ride one horse and the post-boy the other. He will also carry your saddle-bags. After arriving at your destination, the post-boy takes the horses back to their station.

1) see p,

جوش شما در هر منزل اسپ عوض میکنید	shumā dar har manzil asp ᶜavaz mīkunīd.	You, change horses, in each station.
فرنگی از منزل تا منزلِ دیگر چه قدر مسافت است	*Farangī.* Az manzil tā manzil-i dīgar chi qadr masāfat ast?	*European.* What is the distance between the stations?
ایرانی سه فرسخ الی هفت فرسخ و هشت فرسخ راه است	*Irānī.* Si farsakh ilā haft farsakh va hasht farsakh rah ast.	*Persian.* From three to seven or eight farsakhs.
فرنگی و کرایه اسپهای چاپار چند میشود	*Farangī.* Va kirāya-yi asphā-yi chāpārī chand mīshavad?	*European.* And as to the hire of post-horses, what does it come to?
ایرانی برای هر اسپی فرسخی یک قران	ᶜ*Irānī.* Barāyi har aspī farsakhī yak qarān.	*Persian.* For each horse one qaran a farsakh.
فرنگی روزی چند فرسخ میتوان طیّ نمود	*Farangī.* Rūzī chand farsakh mītavān tei namūd?	*European.* How many farsakhs can I do in one day?
ایرانی اگر آموخته باشید در یک روز بیست و پنج الی سی فرسخ راه میتوانید بروید	*Irānī.* Agar āmūkhta bāshīd dar yak rūz bīst u panj ilā sī farsakh rāh mītavānīd biravīd.	*Persian.* If you are used to it, you can do 20 or 30 farsakhs in one day.

فرنگی عجب این از تندی کالسکه بخار چندان کمتر نیست پس تمام روز را یورتمه یاچهار نعل باید رفت	*Farangī.* Ajab! In az tundi-yi kalaska-yi bukhar chandān kamtar nist. pas tamam-i ruz-ra yurtma ya chahārnaʿl bayad raft?	*European.* How wonderful! That is not much slower than a train. Then must I trot or gallop the whole day?
ایرانی خیر آقا یك میدانِ اسپ یورتمه یا چهار نعل که رفتید یك میدان قدم بروید تا مال نفس بگیرد	*Irānī.* Kheir agha, yak meidan-i asp yurtma ya chahārnaʿl ki raftid, yak meidān qadam bi-ravid ta mal nafas bigirad.	*Persian.* No sir, if you trot or gallop the length of a horse's canter, you must walk a bit afterwards, so that your horse may recover his breath.
فرنگی اسپهای چاپاری چه طوراند خوب یا بد	*Farangī.* Aspha-yi chapari chi tour and, khub ya bad?	*European.* Are the posthorses good or bad?
ایرانی خوب و بد دارد اکثرِ شان این قدر ضعیف و بد و سست ولاغراند که هر کس سوار میشود خیال میکند که این مال بقدرِ یک فرسخ راه نخواعد رفت باوجودِ این لاغری	*Irānī.* Khub u bad darad. aksar-i shan Inqadr zaʿif va bad va sust va laghir and, ki har kas savar mishavad, kheyal mikunad ki In mal bi qadr-i yak farsakh rah nakhahad raft. ba vujud-i In	*Persian.* There are good ones and bad ones. Most of them are so weak, bad, tired and lean, that everyone who rides them thinks: this beast will not go one farsakhs' distance. Notwithstanding this leanness,

بعضی این اسپها که مثلِ چار چوبه میمانند سوار را با بار بمنزل میرسانند گاهی اسپِ چاپاری دیدم که نهایت خوب و تندرو بود و مثلِ آهو میدویدند قریب اصفهان سوارِ یك اسپی شدم که اسبهای شاه هم از او بهتر نیستند اسپ عربی بود صاحبش یعنی نایب چاپار معیار از عربها پانزده تومان خریده بود برای چاپار اسپهای بزرك ترکمنی از یابوهای کوچك بهتراند	lāghirī baʿzī īn asphā, ki misl-i chahārchūba mīmānand, savār-rā bā bār bi manzil mīrasānand. gāhī asp-i chaparī dīdam, ki nihāyat khūb va tandrou būd va misl-i āhū mīdavīd. qarīb-i *Isfahān* savār-i yak aspī shudam, ki asphā-yi Shāh ham az ū bihtar nīstand. asp-i ʿarabī būd. sāhib-ash, yaʿnī nāyib chapar-i *Maʿyār* az Arabhā punzdah tuman kharīda būd. barā-yi chapar asphā-yi buzurg-i turkmanī az yābūhā-yi kūchik bihtar and.	some of these horses, which look like frames, can carry a rider with a load to the station. Sometimes I have seen post-horses, that were very good and swift, and they ran like gazelles. Near *Isfahan* I rode a horse, that was as good as the Shah's horses. It was an Arab. Its master, namely the Post-master of *Maʿyār*, had bought it from Arabs for fifteen tumans. As posthorses, tall Turkoman horses are better than small ponies.
فرنگی زین و دهنه خودم همراه ببرم یا از نایب چاپار	*Farangī.* Zīn va dahana khudam hamrāh bibaram, yā	*European.* Must I take my own saddle and bridle, or cannot

امانت بگیرم	az nāyib-chapar amānat bigīram?	I borrow that from the Post-master.
ایرانی دهنه و زین و عرقگیر و خرجین و دو تا تنك برای بستنِ بار باید از خودِ تان باشد	*Irānī*. Dahana va zīn va ʿaraqgīr va khurjīn va du tā tang barāyi bastan-i bār bāyad az khud-i tun bāshad.	*Persian*. You must have your own bridle, saddle, saddle-cloth, saddle bags, and two girths for fastening the loads.
فرنگی نزدیك چاپار خانه‌ها کاروانسرا یا مهمانخانه یا جای دیگری پیدا میشود که شب‌را بگذرانم	*Farangī*. Nazdīk-i chaparkhānahā kārvānsarā yā mihmān-khāna yā jā-yi dīgarī peidā mīshavad, ki shab-rī bugzarānam?	*European*. Near the post-houses are there caravanseries, inns, or such places, where one can spend the night?
ایرانی توی خودِ چاپار خانه باید ماند برای سیاحهای معتبر در بالا خانه خوابگاه موجود است رختِ خواب هم در بیشترِ جاهاپیدا میشود	*Irānī*. Tūyi khud-i chapar-khāna bāyad mund. barāyi seiyāhhā-yi muʿtabar dar bālākhāna khābgāh moujūd ast. rakht-i khāb ham dar bīshtar-i jāhā peidā mīshavad.	*Persian*. You must stay in the post-house itself. For distinguished travellers there is, in the upper storey, a sleeping-room. Bed-covers too are to be found in most places.
فرنگی پس خوراك هم شاید	*Farangī*. Pas khurāk ham shā-	*European*. Perhaps food is also

در چاپار خانه‌ها حاضر میشود	yad dar chaparkhānahā hāzir mī-shavad?	to be found at the post-houses?
ایرانی بلی جزوی نان و ماست و تخم مرغ و چای و قلیان همه جا پیدا میشود اگر چیز دیگر خواسته باشید از ده یا بازار میآرند اما هر کسیکه بزودی میخواهد حرکت کند بغیر از نان و ماست و تخم چیزی نمیخورد که اسباب معطلی نشود در چاپار خانهای شهرها و قصبه ها هر چیزی که میل داشته باشید موجود است	*Irānī.* Balī, juzvī. nān u māst u tukhm-i murgh u chāī u qalyān hama jā peidā mī-shavad. agar chīz-i dīgar khāsta bāshīd, az dih yā bāzar mīārand, ammā har kasī-ki bi zūdī mīkhāhad harakat kunad, bi gheir az nān u māst u tukhm chīzī na-mī-khurad, ki asbāb-i muʿattalī na-shavad. dar chaparkhānahā-yi shahrhā va qasaba-hā har chīzī ki meil dāshta bāshīd moujūd ast.	*Persian.* Yes, but it is scanty. Bread, sour milk, eggs, tea, and galyans are to be found everywhere. If you order anything else from the village or the bazaar, they bring it; but those who wish to move on quickly, do not eat anything except bread, sour milk, or eggs, so as not to be kept waiting. In the post-houses of towns and villages, there is everything that you can wish for.
فرنگی التفات بفرمائید طول و اسم منزلهارا بیان کنید بدانم منزل بمنزل چه قدر راه است	*Farangī.* Iltifāt bifarmāyīd tūl va ism-i manzilhārā beiān kunīd, bidānam manzil bi manzil chi qadr rāh ast va	*European.* Have the kindness to make me acquainted with the distances and names of the stations, so that I know

و کرایه اسپها چند باید بدهم	kirāya-yi asphā chand bāyad bidaham.	how far each station is, and how much I must give for horses' hire.
ایرانی خیلی خوب منازلِ راه را از شیراز گذشته تا بطهران و از آنجا تا لبِ دریای خزر عرض خواهم نمود	*Irānī.* Kheilī khūb, manāzil-i rāh-rā az *Shīrāz* guzashta tā bi *Tahrān* va az unjā tā lab-i *Daryā-yi Khazir* ʿarz khāham namūd.	*Persian.* Very well. I will name the stations on the road from *Shiraz* to *Tehran*, and from there to the coast of the *Caspian Sea.*
از شیراز تا زرغان ٥ فرسخ	az *Shīrāz* ta *Zarghān* panj fars.	From *Shiraz* to *Zarghan* 5 fars.
پوزه ٥	*Pūza* panj „	*Pūza* 5 „
قوام‌آباد ٦	*Qavāmābād* shish „	*Qavamabad* 6 „
مشهد مرغاب ٧	*Mashhad-i Murghāb* haft „	*Mashhad-i Murghab* 7 „
دهبید ٧	*Dahbīd* haft „	*Dahbīd* 7 „
خان خوره ٥	*Khān-i Khura* panj „	*Khan-i Khura* 5 „
سرمك ٧	*Surmak* haft „	*Surmak* 7 „
آباده ۴	*Abāda* shish „	*Abada* 6 „
شلکستان ٥	*Shulgistān* panj „	*Shulgistan* 5 „
یزدخاست ٦	*Yazdikhāst* shish „	*Yazdikhast* 6 „
مقصودبگی ٦	*Maqsūd Begī* shish „	*Maqsud Begi* 6 „

از شیراز تا قمشه ٥ فرسخ
معیار ٥
مرغ ٥
اصفهان (جلفا) ٣

میانِ زرقان و پوزه قبرهای شاهانِ ایامِ قدیم و خرابه های بیوتات و عمارات عظیم و آتشکده‌های بزرك است كه اسمِ آنجا تخت جمشید است از راهِ چاپاری طرف مشرق بفاصلهٔ یك فرسخ واقع است باید بروید خوب تماشا بکنید نزدیكِ پوزه هم آثارِ زمانِ قدیم موجود است و آنجارا نقش

az *Shīrāz* ta *Qumishah* panj fars.
Maᶜyār panj „
Margh panj „
Isfahān (Julfā) si „

Mīān-i *Zarghūn* va *Pūza* qabr-hā-yi Shāhān-i ayyām-i qadīm va kharābahā-yi buyūtāt va ᶜimārāt-i ᶜazīm va ātashkadahā-yi buzurg ast, ki ism-i ān jā *Takht-i Jamshīd* ast. az rāh-i chaparī taraf-i mashriq bi fāsila-yi yak farsakh vāqiᶜ ast. bāyad biravīd khūb tamāshā bikunīd. nazdīk-i *Pūza* ham āsār-i zamān-i qadīm moujūd ast va unjārā *Naqsh-i Rustam* mīgūyand. sūrat-i pādishāhān va pahla-

From *Shiraz* to *Qumishah* 5 fars.
Mayar 5
Margh 5
Isfahan (Julfa) 3

Between *Zarghūn* and *Puza* are tombs of kings of olden times, and ruins of buildings, fine palaces, and great fire-temples. The name of this place is *Takht-i Jamshid* [1]). It lies east of the road at a distance of one farsakh. You must go there and see it all. Near *Puza* there are also remains from olden times; these they call: *The Picture of Rustam.* Portraits of kings and heroes, and very old inscrip-

1) The throne of [the Persian King] Jamshid is the name which the Persians have given to the ruins of *Persepolis.*

رستم میگویند صورتِ پادشاهان و پهلوان‌ها و خطوط بسیار قدیم هم میخی و هم پهلوی بر کمرکشِ کوهِ بلندِ سنگی نمایان است خیلی جای دلچسپِ قابل دیدن است	vanhā va khutut-i bisyār qadīm, ham mīkhī va ham pahlavī bar kamarkash-i kūh-i buland-i sangī namāyān ast. kheilī jā-yi dilchasp-i qābil-i dīdan ast.	tions, cuneiform and pahlavi[1]) are visible on the side of the high mountain. It is a very interesting spot, and well worth seeing.
از چاپارخانهٔ پوزه تا نقش رستم یك فرسخ راه است	Az chaparkhāna-yi *Pūza* tā *Naqsh-i Rustam* yak farsakh rāh ast.	From the post-house of *Puza* to *Naqsh-i Rustam* is a distance of one farsakh.
اینطرف قوام‌آباد میرسید بقصبهٔ سیوند تلگرافخانهٔ دارد که تلگرافچی انکلیس آنجا ساکن است جای با صفائی است و انکورستانِ زیاد دارد در صحرای مشهد مرغاب ستونها	Intaraf-i *Qavāmābūd* mīrasīd bi qasaba-yi *Sīvand.* talagrāfkhānayī dārad, ki talagrāfchī-yi inglīs unjā sākin ast. jā-yi bā-safā-yī-st va angūristān-i zīād dārad. dar sahrā-yi *Mashhad-i Murghāb* sutūnhā dīda mīshavad, ki unhā ham	On this side of *Qavamabad*, you reach the village of *Sivand.* It has a telegraph-office, and an English telegraph-clerk lives there. It is a pretty place and has many vineyards. In the plain of *Mashhad-i Murghab* columns are to be

1) The Persian language at the period which proceded the muhammedan conquest.

دیده میشود که آنها هم از آثار زمان قدیم است و عمارتِ سنگی سرِ راه است که اهلِ اسلام میگویند قبر مادر سلیمان است و فرنگیها میگویند قبر کیخسرو است	az āsār-i zamān-i qadīm ast, va ᶜimārat-i sangī sar-i rāh ast ki ahl-i islām mīgūyand *qabr-i Mādar-i Suleimān* ast va Farangīhā mīgūyand *qabr-i Kei Khusrou* ast.	seen; they also are remains of former days. A stone building lies near the road. The Mohammedans say that it is the *Tomb of Solomon's Mother*, and the Europeans say that it is the *Tomb of Cyrus*.
در دهبید تلگرافچی انکلیس سکنا دارد	dar *Dihbīd* talagrāfchī-yi inglīs suknā dārad.	An English telegraph-clerk lives at *Dihbid*.
آباده قصبهٔ بزرگی است قلعه و بازار و تلگرافخانه دارد قاشوق و کشکول مالِ آباده که از چوب کلابی بسیار خوب و با سلیقه درست میکنند مشهور است	*Abāda* qasaba-yi buzurgī-st qalᶜa va bāzār va talagrāf-khāna dārad. qāshuq va kashkūl māl-i *Abāda*, ki az chūb-i gulābī bisyār khūb va bā salīqa durust mīkunand, mashhūr ast.	*Abada* is a large village. It has a fort, a bazar, and a telegraph-office. The spoons and beggars' bowls of Abada, which are beautifully and tastefully carved in pear-wood, are celebrated.
یزدخاست هم قصبهٔ معتبریست روی کوهِ سنگیِ پست وبلندی	*Yazdikhāst* ham qasaba-yi muᶜtabarī-st. rū-yi kūh-i	*Yazdikhast* is also an important village. It has been built

که در وسطِ درّهٔ ایستاده است بنا شده است یك طرف قصبه پلی است که از او عبور میشود غیر از آن هیچ جا دروازهٔ ندارد کاروانسرا و چاپار خانه در خارج قصبه است	sangī-yi past u bulandī, ki dar vasat-i darra-yi īstāda ast, binā shuda ast. yak taraf-i qasaba pulī-st, ki az ū ʿubūr mīshavad. gheir az ān hīch jā darvāzayī na-dārad. kār-vānsarā va chapar-khāna dar khārij-i qasaba ast.	on a steep and high rocky hill which stands in the centre of a valley. On one side of the village is a bridge, over which one can pass. Except at this place, there is no other gate. The caravansery and the post-house are outside the village.
قمشه شهر کوچکی است که اطرافش زراعت بسیار است	*Qumishah* shahr-i kūchikī-st, ki atrāf-ash zarāʿat-i bisyār ast.	*Qumishah* is a small town, the environs of which are very well cultivated.
اصفهان چنانچه معروف است در زمانِ سابق پای تختِ ایران بوده است اگرچه شهر	*Isfahān*, chunānchi maʿrūf ast dar zamān-i sābiq pāyitakht-i Irān būda ast. agarchi shahr hālā bi buzurgī-yi zamān-ī	*Isfahan*, as every one knows, was formerly the capital of Persia. Although the town is not as large now as it used to be,

حالا بزرگی زمان گذشته نیست و جمعیّتش بیشتر از دویست هزار نفر نباشد باز از شهرهای درجهٔ اوّل محسوب وبدار السلطنه معروف است بازارهای بارونق و میدانهای وسیع و چهار باغ جنّت طراز و پلهای ممتاز رود خانه زنده رود و عمارات و مساجد و مدارس عظیم دارد که باقی ماندهٔ ایام دولتِ سلاطینِ صفویه است	guzashta nīst va jam^cyyat-ash bīshtar az davīst hazār nafar na-bāshad, bāz az shahrhā-yi daraja-yi avval mahsūb va bi *Dār as Saltana* ma^crūf ast. bāzārhā-yi bā rounaq va meidānhā-yi vasī^c va chahārbāgh-i jannat tarāz va pulhā-yi mumtāz-i rūdkhāna-yi *Zandarūd* va ^cimārāt va masājid va madāris-i ^cazīm dārad, ki bāqī munda-yi ayyām-i doulat-i salātīn-i *Safaviyya* ast.	and although it has a population of not more than 200,000 people, yet it is considered one of the towns of first degree, and is known as *Dār as Saltana* (House of the Kingdom). It has splendid bazaars, large squares, heavenly avenues, magnificent bridges over the river *Zandarūd*, buildings, mosques, and excellent schools, which have remained from the days of the *Safavi* kings.
قصبهٔ جلفا پهلوی شهر اصفهان واقع است اهل جلفا همهٔ شان ارمنی اند چاپار خانه و خانهای	qasaba-yi *Julfā* pahlū-yi shahr-i *Isfahān* vāqi^c ast. ahl-i *Julfā* hama-yi shān *Armanī* and, chaparkhāna va khā-	The village of *Julfa* is situated near the town of *Isfahan*. The inhabitants of *Julfa* are all *Armenians*. The post-house

فرنگیها هم در جلفا است	nahā-yi *Farangīhā* ham dar Julfā-st.	and the houses of *Europeans* are also at Julfa.
منزلهای راهِ طهران از این قرار است	manzilhā-yi rāh-i *Tahrān* az in qarār ast:	The stations on the way to *Tehran* are the following:
از اصفهان (جلفا) تا گز ۳ فرسخ	az *Isfahān* tā *Gaz* si farsakh	From *Isfahan* to *Gaz* 3 fars.
مورچه‌خوار ۶	*Mūrchakhār* shish „	*Murchakhar* 6 „
بیداشك ۶	*Bīdashk* shish „	*Bidashk* 6 „
قهرود ۶	*Quhrūd* shish „	*Quhrud* 6 „
کاشان ۷	*Kāshān* haft „	*Kashan* 7 „
سن‌سن ۶	*Sinsin* shish „	*Sinsin* 6 „
پاسنکان ۷	*Parsangān* haft „	*Pāisangan* 7 „
قم ۴	*Qum* chahār „	*Qum* 4 „
منظریه ۴	*Manzaria* „ „	*Marzaria* 4 „
کوشك نصرت ۴	*Kūshk-i Nusrat* „ „	*Kushk-i Nusrat* 4 „
قلعه محمد علی خان ۴	*Qalᶜa-yi Muham-mad Ali Khān* „ „	*Qalᶜa-yi Muhammad Ali Khān* 4 „
حسن‌آباد ۴	*Hasanābād* „ „	*Hasanābad* 4 „
کهریزك ۴	*Kahrīzak* „ „	*Kahrīzak* 4 „
طهران ۴	*Tahrān* „ „	*Tahrān* 4 „

کوتل قهرود بقدری مرتفع است که تا وسطِ تابستان برف در آنجا باقی میماند خودِ دهِ قهرود مثلِ بهشت است آبِ بسیار دارد در زیرِ آبادیِ قریه بندِ قدیمی است از چشم اندازی که از سرِگردنه خواهید داشت حیران خواهید شد تمامِ افقِ شمالی را رشتهٔ کوهستانِ البرز کرفته است در بهاری که کذشتم همهٔ این کوهها برف داشتند واز همه بالاتر و بلند تر کوه دماوند نمایان بود	Kūtal-i *Quhrūd* bi qadrī murtafiᶜ ast, ki tā vasat-i tābistān barf dar ānjā bāqī mīmānad. khud-i dih-i Quhrūd misl-i bihisht ast. āb-i bisyār dārad. dar zīr-i ābādī-yi qarya band-i qadīmī-st az. chashmandāzī ki az sar-i gardana khāhīd dāsht heirān khāhīd shud. tamām-i ufuq-i shamālī-rā rishta-yi kūhistān-i *Alburz* girifta ast. dar bahārī ki guzashtam hama-yi īn kūhhā barf dāshtand va az hama bālātar va bulandtar kūh-i *Damāvand* namāyān būd.	The pass of *Quhrud* is so elevated, that the snow lies there till mid-summer [1]). The village of *guhrud* itself is like Paradise. It has much water. Beneath the cultivated land of the village is an ancient dyke. You will be astounded at the view, which you have from the top of the Pass. The whole northern horizon is bound in by the line of the *Alburz* mountains. When I passed there in the spring, all these mountains had snow, and the highest and tallest of them, the mountain *Damavand* was visible.
کاشان شهر بزرکی است بازارها و کاروانسراهای معتبر دارد و	*Kāshān* shahr-i buzurgī-st bāzārhā va kārvānsarāhā-yi muᶜ-	*Kashan* is a large town. It has important bazaars and

1) This pass is about 9000 feet high.

تلگرافخانهٔ هم دارد در کاشان عقرب و پشه بقدری فراوانست که مثلشرا هیچ جای دیکر ندیده ام وقتِ خوابیدن خوب نکاه باید کرد توی رختِ خوابتانِ عقربی نباشد	tabar dᴀrad va talagrᴀf khᴀnayɪ ham dᴀrad. dar *Kāshān* ʿaqrab va pasha bi qadrɪ farᴀvᴀn ast, ki misl-ash-rᴀ hɪch jᴀɪ dɪgar na dɪda am. vakht-i khᴀbɪdan khᴜb nigᴀh bᴀyad kard tuyi rakht-i khᴀb-i tun aqrabɪ na-bᴀshad.	caravanseries, and it also has a telegraph-office. In *Kashan* scorpions and mosquitoes are so plentiful, that I have never seen the like in any other place. At the time of going to rest, you must search your bed-clothes to see that no scorpion is in them.
قم هم مثلِ کاشان شهری ست که جمعیت اش بقدر پنجاه هزار نفر است کاشی‌کاری مساجد قم نهایت خوش رنك و قشنك است	*Qum* ham misl-i *Kāshān* shahrɪst, ki jamʿiyyat-ash bi qadr-i panjᴀh hazᴀr nafar ast. kashɪkᴀrɪ-yi masᴀjid-i Qum nihᴀyat khushrang va qashang ast.	*Qum* is also a town like *Kashan*, having a population of 50,000 people. The tiles on the mosques of Qum are exceedingly fine in colour and very beautiful.
میان قم و حوض سلطان دشت کویراست که آب آن همهٔ اش	mɪan-i *Qum* va *Houz-i Sultān* *Dasht-i Kavīr* ast, ki ᴀb-i un hama-yash shᴜr ast. bᴀyad	Between *Qum* and *Houz-i Sultan* is a *Salt-Desert*, the water of which is brackish.

شور است باید مطارهٔ بلغاری پر از آب خوردن همراه داشته باشید و حال در اینقطه ده سال است که دریاچهٔ تشکیل یافته است	matāra-yi bulghārī pur az āb-i khurdan hamrāh dāshta bāshīd. va hāl dar īn nuqta dah sāl ast ki daryāchayī tashkīl yāfta ast.	You must have a leather bottle full of drinking-water with you. It is now 10 years ago that a lake formed itself at this place.
از قم تا طهران راهِ ساخته است که از روی آن کالسکه میتواند کار بکند	Az *Qum* tā *Tahrān* rāh-i sākhta ast, ki az rūyi un kālaska mītavānad kār bikunad.	From *Qum* to *Tehran* there is a made road, on which carriages can go.
در طهران خانهٔ کی میخواهید منزل بکنید	Dar *Tahrān* khāna-yi kī mī-khāhīd manzil bikunīd?	At whose house do you nean to stay at *Tehran*?
فرنگی نمیدانم با هیچ کس آشنا نیستم	*Farangī*. Na-mīdānam, bā hīch kas āshnā nīstam.	*European*. I do not know, I am not acquainted with any one.
ایرانی بنده میدانم که شما حکمًا جائی مهمان خواهید شد و کرنه مهمانخانهٔ خوبی دارد	*Irānī*. Banda mīdānam ki shumā hukman jāī mihmān khāhīd shud, vagarna mihmānkhāna-yi khūbī dārad.	*Persian*. I know for certain that you will be some one's guest, but if not, there is a good hotel.

تعریفِ پای تختِ ممالکِ محروسه را نخواهم کرد احوالات دار الخلافهٔ طهران در سفر نامجات سیاحهای فرنگی بقدر کفایت نوشته شده است بغیر از شرح خود سفر دیکر هیچ زحمتی نمیدهم از طهران تاقزوین راه ساختهٔ خوبیست که کالسکه و ترمتاس کار میکند اکر میل داشته باشید با کالسکه میتوانید بروید و منازل راه تا بقزوین از این قرار است	Taᶜrīf-i pāyitakht-i *mamālik-i mahrūsa-rā* [1]) na-khāham kard. ahvālāt-i *Dār ul Kkilāfa-yi Tahrān* dar safarnāmajāt-i seiyāhhā-yi Farangī bi qadr-i kafāyat navishta shuda ast. bi gheir az sharh-i khud-i safar dīgar hīch zahmatī na-mīdaham. az *Tahrān* tā *Qazvīn* rāh-i sākhta-yi khūbī-st, kālaska va turumtās kār mīkunad. agar meil dāshta bāshīd, bā kālaska mītavānīd biravīd va manāzil-i rāh tā bi *Qazvīn* az īn qarār ast:	I will not describe the capital of the "*Protected Provinces*". The "*House of the Chalifate*, *Tehran*", has been often enough described in the European Books of Travel. I will not trouble you with anything but an account of the journey itself. From *Tehran* to *Qazvin* there is a good, made road, over which carriages and tarantas can go. If you like, you can drive in a carriage. The stations on the way to *Qazvin* are the following:

1) ممالک محروسه mamālik-i mahrūsa i. e. the "protected provinces" is the official title of the Persian Empire.

از طهران تا شاه اباد چهار فرسخ	az *Tahrān* ta *Shāhābād* chah. f.	From *Tehran* to *Shahabad* 4 fars.
حصارك چهار „	*Hisārak* chahār farsakh	*Hisarak* 4 „
ینکی امام چهار „	*Yangī Imām* „ „	*Yangi Imam* 4 „
کونده چهار „	*Kavanda* „ „	*Kavanda* 4 „
قزوین چهار „	*Qazvīn* „ „	*Qazvin* 4 „
در قزوین مهمانخانهٔ خوبِ بزرکی است بامبل و اسباب و خوراکی	Dar *Qazvīn* mihmānkhāna-yi khubī buzurgī-st, bā mubl [1]) u asbāb, va khurākī hama	In *Qazvin* there is a good, big Hotel, with furniture and other things, and you can
همه چیز در آنجا پیدا میشود	chīz dar unjā peidā mīshavad.	get any kind of food there.
و خود قزوین از بلادِ معظمهٔ ایران است و سابقًا هم پای تخت بوده است میکویند اهل قزوین بسیار بد ذات و نادرست اند و این بیت مشهور است	Va khud-i *Qazvīn* az balād-i muᶜzama-yi Irān ast va sābiqan *pāyitakht* būda ast. mīgūyand ahl-i *Qazvīn* bisyār bad zāt va nā-durust and va īn beit mashhūr ast:	*Qazvin* itself is an important Persian town, and was formerly the *capital* of Persia. They say that the inhabitants of *Qazvin* are great ruffians and rascals, and the following verse is well known:
مار و قزوینی چو بینی مرد هش	»Mār u Qazvīnī chu bīnī mard-i hush,	«If you see a serpent and an inhabitant of Qazvin, oh wise man!

1) مبل mubl furniture is the French word meubles.

مار را بکذار و قزوینی بکش	»Mār-rā bugzār u Qazvīnī bi kush."	»Leave the serpent alone, but kill the inhabitant of Qazvin."
از قزوین تارشت بجهت ارتفاع کوهها عبور و مرور ترمتاس نقدًا غیر ممکن است خصوصًا میان مزرعه و پای چنار کوتل بلندی است موسوم به خرزان که عبور از آن بمال و مردم خیلی صدمه میزند	Az *Qazvīn* tā *Rasht* bi jihat-i irtifāᶜ-i kūhhā ᶜubūr u murūr-i turumtās naqdan gheir mumkin ast, khusūsan mīān-i *Mazraᶜa* va *Pāīchinār* kūtal-i bulandī-st mousūm bi *Kharzān* ki ᶜubūr az ān bi māl va mardum kheilī sadama mīzanad.	From *Qazvin* to *Resht*, on account of the height of the mountains, the going to and fro of carriages and tarantasses is at present impossible; especially between *Mazraᶜa* and *Paichinar*, where there is a high pass called *Kharzan*, the crossing of which causes great discomfort to man and beast.
منزلهای راه رشت از این قرار است	Manzilhā-yi rāh-i *Rasht* az īn qarār ast.	The stations on the *Resht* road are the following:
از قزوین تا مزرعه پنج فرسخ	az *Qazvīn* tā *Mazraᶜa* panj fars.	From *Qazvin* to *Mazraᶜa* 5 fars.
پاچنار پنج "	*Pāchinar* " "	*Pachiniar* 5 "
منجیل چهار "	*Manjīl* chahār "	*Manjil* 4 "
رستم‌اباد پنج "	*Rustamābād* panj "	*Rustamabad* 5 "

کهدم پنج فرسخ رشت شش فرسخ	*Kuhdum* panj fars. *Rasht* shish „	*Kuhdum* 5 fars. *Rasht* 6 „
در منزل مزرعه یك جانوری پیدا میشود مشهور به مله یاکنه از جنس سلس است و هم اورا غریب‌گز میگویند بجهت اینکه یك نوع سمی دارد که اگر بومی‌ها را بگزد اصلا اثر نمیکند امّا اگر غربارا گزید اثرِ سختی مینماید و گاهی منجر بهلاکت میشود بهیچ وجه آنجا نخوابید	Dar manzil-i *Mazra^ca* yak jānvarī peidā mīshavad, mashhūr bi *malla* yā *gana.* az jins-i *sās* ast va ham ūrā *gharībgaz* mīgūyand, bi jihat-i īnki yak nou^c sammī dārad, ki agar būmīhā-rā bigazad, aslā asar na-mīkunad, ammā agar ghurabā-rā gazīd, asar-i sakhtī mīnamāyad va gāhī munjar bi halākat mīshavad. bi hīch vajh unjā na-khābīd!	In the station of *Mazraa* an insect is found, known as "*malla*" or "*gana*". It is a kind of bug, which is also called "*gharib gaz*", (biter of strangers), because it has a kind of poison, which never harms the natives, if they get bitten. But if this insect bites a stranger, it does much harm, and is sometimes the cause of death. Do not on any acoount stay the night there!
قریب بقریهٔ منجیل بکنار سفید رود میرسید رود خانهٔ خیلی عریضِ عمیقی است پلی سنگی	Qarīb bi qarya-yi *Manjīl* bi kanār-i *Safīdrūd* mīrasīd rūd-khāna-yi kheilī ^carīz-i ^camī-	Near the village of *Manjil* you reach the banks of the *Safidrud* river. The river is

که در آنجا روی آب بسته بودند چند سال قبل از شدّت سیلاب تماماً خراب شده بود حالا درست کرده‌اند بنده در آن سفر با کرجی عبور کرده بودم بواسطهٔ کثرت آب و شدّت باد بیم غرق شدن بود	qī-st. pul-i sangī, ki dar unjā rū-yi āb basta būdand, chand sāl qabl az shiddat-i seilāb tamāman kharāb shuda būd. hālā durust karda and. banda dar ān safar bā karajī ʿubūr karda būdam. bi vāsita-yi kasrat-i āb va shiddat-i bād bīm-i gharq shudan būd.	very broad and deep. The stone bridge, which had been built across the water several years before, had been completely destroyed by the violence of a flood. Now it has been re-built. I (the slave) at that time crossed in a boat. On account of the quantity of water, and the strength of the wind, we were in danger of being drowned.
درباب باد که در منجیل میوزد اعلیحضرت ناصر الدّین شاه در مسافرت نامهٔ اوّل فرنگستان چنین تحریر فرموده اند که از عجایب و بدایع اینکه در این منزل در هر فصل که باشد نزدیک بعصر باد شدیدی	Dar bāb-i bād ki dar *Manjīl* mīvazad, Aʿlāhazrat-i *Nāsir ad dīn Shāh* dar musāfarat nāma-yi avval-i *Farangistān* chunīn tahrīr farmūda and, ki az ʿajāyib va badāyiʿ īnki dar īn manzil, dar har fasl ki bāshad, nazdīk bi ʿasr	Concerning the wind which blows at *Manjil*, His Majesty *Nasir ud din Shah*, in the description of his first journey to Europe, has written: Among the marvels and wonders of this place, is this: that at whatever season it may be,

میوزد بطوری سخت و شدید است که درختهای زیتون که در اینجا رسته است یك سر بطرفی که باد میوزد کج و متمایل گشته است	bād-i shadīdī mīvazad, bi tourī sakht va shadīd ast, ki dirakhthā-yi zeitūn, ki dar īnjā rusta ast, yak sar bi tarafī ki bād mīvazad, kaj va mutamāyil gashta ast.	a strong wind blows every afternoon; it is so strong and violent that the olive-trees which grow there, are all of them crooked and bent over towards the direction in which the wind blows."
از منجیل که اولِ خاكِ گیلان است همه جا رو بشمال میروید تا قریبِ کهدم دستِ چپ کوه و دستِ راست رود خانه است کوههای سنگی و خاکیِ مرتفعِ بسیار مهیب و سراشیب طرفین راه است	Az *Manjīl*, ki avval-i khāk-i *Gīlān* ast hama jā rū bi shamāl mīravīd. tā qarīb-i *Kuhdum* dast-i chap kūh va dast-i rāst rūdkhāna ast. kūhhā-yi sangī va khākī-yi murtafiʿ-i bisyār muhīb va sarāshīb tarafein-i rāh ast.	From *Manjil*, which is the beginning of the province of *Gilan*, you go all the way in a northerly direction. Till you approach *Kuhdum* you have the mountains on your left, and the river on your right. Rocky, sandy, high, imposing and steep over-hanging hills are on both sides of the way.
بعد از گذشتن از قصبهٔ رودبار	Baʿd az guzashtan as qasaba-	After passing through the vil-

که مثلِ باغِ ارم سبز و خرّم
و آباد و پر درخت و پر گل
است راه بجنگل میافتد و
طرفینِ راه هم کوهها پوشیده از
جنگل است زغالسازها اغلبِ
اشجارِ جنگل را بریده زغال
کرده اند از چند سال قبل
الی حال که این راهرا دیده
بودم اشجار زیاد انداخته
جنگلرا خالی کرده اند اگرچه
بعضی جاها باطلاقِ سختی
است باز خیلی جای با
صفائی است درختهای موِ

yi *Rūdbār*, ki misl-i bāgh-i *Iram* [1]) sabz u khurram va ābād va pur dirakht va pur gul ast, rāh bi jangal mīuftad, va tarafein-i rāh ham kūhhā pūshīda az jangal ast. zughālsāzhā aghlab-i ashjār-i jangal-rā burrīda zughāl karda and. az chand sāl qabl ilā hāl, ki īn rāh-rā dīda būdam, ashjār-i zīād andākhta jangal-rā khālī karda and. agarchi baᶜzī jāhā bātlāq-i sakhtī-st, bāz kheilī jā-yi bā safāyī-st. dirakhthā-yi *mou-i*

lage of *Rudbar*, which, like the garden of *Iram*, is green, cheerful, cultivated, and full of trees and flowers, the road leads into the wood. On both sides of the way there are hills covered with forests. Coal-burners have cut down the forest-trees in many places, and have made char coal out of them. It is several years ago now since I saw this road; they must have cut down more trees by now and have made the forest bare. Although in many places there is deep morass, yet it is a lovely spot.

1) A fabulous garden much praised by Arabic and Persian poets.

جنکلی طبیعتًا روی درختهای نارون وغیره کشیده شده	*jangalī* tabīᶜatan rū-yi di-rakhthā-yi *nārvan* va gheira.	Wild vines have sprung up and covered the *elms* and
است از همه جا جوبها وآب شارهای بسیار صاف از بالای	kashīda shuda ast. az hama jā jūbhā va ābshārhā-yi bis-yār sāf az bālā-yi kūh mī-	other trees. Everywhere there are brooks, and very clear water-falls, which flow from
کوه میریزند همهٔ آبها بسفید رود ریخته منصبِ دریای خزر میشود	rīzand. hama-yi ābhā bi *Sa-fīdrūd* rīkhta munsabb-i *Da-ryā-yi Khazir* mīshavad.	the summit of the hills. All these waters flow into the *Safīdrud* and then into the *Caspian Sea.*
از جائی که کوهستان تمام میشود که اسم آن نقطه امام	Az jā-yī ki kūhistān tamām mīshavad, ki ism-i ān nuqta	Just where the mountains end, the spot being named »*Imam*
زاده هاشم است خیابانِ دولتیِ خیلی خوبی است اما	*Imāmzāda Hāshim* ast, khīā-bān-i doulatī-yi kheilī khūbī-st, ammā	*zada Hashim*, there is a very good state-road, but in some
بعضی جاها تعمیر لازم دارد اهل آن ولایت اکثر تختِ	baᶜzī jāhā taᶜmīr lāzim dārad. ahl-i un vilāyat aksar takht-i ravān nishasta	places it wants repairing. The inhabitants of this province mostly travel in a litter [1]).

1) The „*takht-i ravān*" (travelling-throne), is generally carried between two mules.

روان نشته سفر میکنند بنده هرکز از این جور مسافرت خوشم نمیاید تکانِ تختِ روان بمن خیلی صدمه میزند	safar mīkunand. banda har giz az īn jūr musāfirat khush-am na-mīāyad. takān-i takht-i ravān bi man kheilī sadama mīzanad.	I do not at all like this mode of travelling. The shaking of the litter causes me much discomfort.
آب وهوای کیلان مثل هند کرم و تر و خفه است و مورث امراض سخت است چند نفر از دوستهای من در رشت ناخوش شده تب کرده اند	Ab u havā-yi *Gīlān* misl-i Hind garm u tar u khafa ast, va mūris-i amrāz-i sakht ast. chand nafar az dūsthā-yi man dar *Rasht* nākhush shuda tap karda and.	The climate (water and air) of *Gilan*, like the Indian climate, is warm, damp and oppressive, and is the cause of many severe illnesses. Several friends of mine became ill at *Resht* and had fever.
فرنکی مکر خود شهر رشت لب دریای طبرستان واقع است	*Farangī*. Magar khud-i shahr-i *Rasht* lab-i *Daryā-yi Tabaristān* vāqi^c ast?	*European*. Is the town of *Resht* itself situated on the shores of the *Caspian Sea*?
ایرانی خیر از رشت تا پیره بازار یك فرسخ بیشتر راه است از آنجا سوار کرجی شده میروید تا انزلی	*Irānī*. Kheir, az *Rasht* tā *Pīra Bāzār* yak farsakh bīshtar rāh ast. az unjā savār-i karajī shuda mīravīd tā *Anzalī*.	*Persian*. No, from *Resht* to *Pira Bazaar* it is more than one farsakh. From there you go by boat to *Anzeli*.

شهر انزلی سرِ نیم جزیرهٔ در دهنهٔ مرداب افتاده است که یک طرف دریای بزرک و طرف دیگرش دریای کوچک است	Shahr-i *Anzalī* sar-i nīm jazīra-yī, dar dahana-yi *Murdāb* aftāda ast, ki yak taraf daryā-yi buzurg va taraf-i dīgar-ash daryā-yi kūchik ast.	The town of *Anzeli* is situated on a peninsula at the mouth of the *Lagoon*. On one side is the open sea, on the other the lagoon.
کشتی های بخار مالِ روسیه نزدیک انزلی لنکر میاندازند و به استرا که سرحد ایران و روس است رفته از آنجا به لنکران و به بادکوبه میرود	kashtīhā-yi bukhār māl-i *Rūsīa* nazdīk-i *Anzalī* langar mī-andāzand va bi *Astarā*, ki sarhadd-i *Irān* va *Rūs* ast rafta az unjā bi *Lankurān* va bi *Bādkūba* mīravad.	Steamers belonging to *Russia* anchor in *Anzali*, then go to *Astara*, which is the Russo-Persian frontier. From there they go to *Lankuran* and to *Baku*.
از بادکوبه میتوانید سوار کالسکهٔ بخار شده به تفلیس و بباطوم بروید از باطوم تا اودیسه یا اسلامبول کشتی بخار کار میکند و از اودیسه و اسلامبول راه اهن است تا ولایت شما	Az *Bādkūba* mītavānīd savār-i kālaska-yi bukhār shuda bi *Tiflīs* va bi *Bātūm* biravīd. Az *Bātūm* tā *Udīsa* yā *Islāmbūl* kashtī-yi bukhār kār mīkunad va az *Udīsa* va *Islāmbūl* rāh-i āhan ast tā vilāyat-i shumā.	From *Baku* you can take the train and go to *Tiflis* and to *Batum*. Ships sail from *Batum* to *Odessa* or to *Constantinople*. From *Odessa* or *Constantinople* there are trains to your country.

از تفلیس هم سوار کالسکه اسپی تا ولادی قفقاز میتوانید بروید و از آنجا بهمه جا تا فرنکستان	Az *Tiflīs* ham savār-i kālaska-yi aspi tā *Vlādī qafqāz* mi-tavānid biravīd va az unjā bi hama jā tā *Farangistān.*	From *Tiflis* you can also go by carriage to *Vladikavkas*, and from there to any place in *Europe.*
راه دیکری هم از بادکوبه هست سوار همان کشتی که از انزلی آمدید بشهر حاجی ترخان دهنه رودخانهٔ ولکا میرسید کشتی دیکر شمارا به تساریتسین که استاسیونِ راهِ آهن است میرساند راهِ آهن مالِ روسیه از راهِ مسکو و پطر تا همه جای فرنکستان میرود	Rāh-i digar ham az *Bādkūba* hast. savār-i hamun kashti, ki az *Anzalī* āmadid bi shahr-i *Hājī Tarkhān*, dahana-yi rūdkhāna-yi *Vulgā* mirasid. kashti-yi digar shumā-ra bi *Tsārītsīn* ki istāsiūn-i rāh-i āhan ast, mirasānad. rāh-i āhan māl-i *Rūsīa* az rāh-i *Muskū* va *Pitr* tā hama jā-yi Farangistān miravad.	There is yet another way from *Baku.* With the same ship, with which you sailed from *Anzali*, you can reach the town of *Astrakhan*, at the mouth of the *Volga.* Another ship brings you to *Tsaritsin*, which is a railway-station. The *Russian* railway takes you via *Moscow* and *St. Petersburg* to any place in Europe.

حکایت ۱

روزی کسی ده تا کوسفند با یک کاغذ بتوسطِ نوکر برای دوستِ خودش تعارف فرستاد آن نوکر یکی از آن کوسفندهارا در بین راه دزدید و نه تای آن را با کاغذ پیش دوست آقایش آورد وقتی که آن پاکت را واز کرده خواند دید که ده کوسفند نوشته شده است کوسفندهارا که شمرد دید نُه تا است از حاملِ کوسفند پرسید اینها نه کوسفند است حامل جواب داد چه

Hikāyat 1.

Rūzɪ kasɪ dah tā gūsfand bā yak kāghaz bi tavassut-i noukar barāyi dūst-i khud-ash taʿāruf faristād. An noukar yakɪ az ān gūsfandhārā dar bein-i rāh duzdɪd va nuh tā-yi un-rā bā kāghaz pɪsh-i dūst-i āgha-y-ash āvurd. Vakhtɪ-ki ān pākat-rā vāz karda khund, dɪd ki dah gusfand navishta shuda ast. Gūsfandhārā ki shumurd, dɪd nuh tā-st. Az hāmil-i gusfand pursɪd: «ɪnhā nuh gusfand ast?" hāmil javāb dād: «chi ʿarz kunam? nuh tā bāshad". Guft: ‹dar kāghaz dah tā

Anecdote No. 1.

Once somebody sent ten sheep with a note by a servant as a present to his friend. This servant stole one of those sheep on the way and brought nine of them with the note to his master's friend. When that (friend) opened the envelope and read it, he saw that *ten* sheep had been written. When he counted the sheep he saw there were *nine*. He asked the man who brought the sheep: «Are these (only) *nine* sheep?" The bearer answered: «What can I say? there may be (only) *nine*".

عرض کنم نه‌تا باشد کفت در
کاغذ ده تا نوشته شده است
باز حامل جواب داد چه عرض
کنم ده تا باشد آن شخص
پیش خود خیال کرد که این
نوکر شاید آدمِ خری است
میان نه تا و ده تا فرق
نمیدهد پس برایِ اینکه خوب
نوکر حالی کند که نه تا
غیر از ده تا است ده نفر از
آدمهای خودش‌را صدا کرده
بان مرد که کفت این‌هارا بشمار
نوکر شمرد پرسید چند نفر
هستند کفت ده تا کفت
بسیار خوب حالا این‌ها هر
کدام یک یک بروند یک
کوسفند بکیرند ببینی چند
تا از کوسفندها کم است

navishta shuda ast". Bāz hāmil javāb dād: "chi 'arz kunam? dah tā bāshad". Un shakhs pīsh-i khud kheyāl kard, ki īn noukar shāyad ādam-i kharī-st mīan-i nuh tā va dah tā farq na-mīdahad. Pas, barāyi īnki khūb bi noukar hālī kunad, ki nuh tā gheir az dah tā-st, dah nafar az ādamhā-yi khudash-rā sadā karda bi un mardaka guft: "īnhāra bishumār"! noukar shumurd. Pursīd chand nafar hastand"? guft: "dah tā" guft: "bisyār khūb! hālā īnhā har kudām yak yak biravand, yak gūsfand bigīrand, bi-bīnī chand tā az gūsfandhā kam ast". pas

(The other) said: "In the letter is written *ten* sheep". Again the bearer answered. "What can I say? There may be *ten*". That man thought to himself: "This servant is perhaps an idiot (lit: ass-man) and does not distinguish between *nine* and *ten*. Therefore, in order to make the servant well understand that *nine* is different from *ten*, he called ten of his people and said to that man: "Count these". The servant counted them. He then ashed: "How many are they"? He answered; "ten". He said: "Very well! now let every one of these singly go and lay hold of one sheep, so that

پس آن ده نفر یك یك رفته
یك کوسفند کرفتند دهمی
کوسفند نداشت آن شخص
بنوکر کفت ببین آدمها ده
تا هستند همین طور که خودت
شمردی اکر کوسفندها ده تا
باشد باید هر کدام یك کوسفند
داشته باشند پس از این قرار
کوسفندها نه تا است نوکر
باز کفت چه عرض کنم نه
تا باشد کفت پس چرا آدمِ
دهمی بی کوسفند ماند کفت
انها که هرکدام کوسفند
کرفتند زرنك بودند آن دهمی

ān dah nafar yak yak rafta yak gūsfand giriftand. dahumī gūsfand na-dāsht. Un shakhs bi noukar guft: «Bibīn ādamhā dah ta hastand, hamintour ki khudat shumurdī. Agar gūsfandhā dah tā bāshad, bāyad har kudām yak gūsfand dāshta bāshand; pas az īn qarār gūsfandhā nuh tā-st". Noukar bāz guft: «chi ʿarz kunam? nuh tā bāshad". guft pas chirā ādam-i dahumī bī gusfand mund? guft: «unhā ki har kudām gūsfand giraftand, zarang būdand. un dahumī tambal

you may see how many sheep are missing". So these ten men went and each one caught hold of a sheep, (only) the tenth had no sheep. That man said to the servant: «Look here, there are ten men, as you have counted them yourself. If there were ten sheep, each one of the men ought to have one sheep. Now, according to this there are *nine* sheep". The servant again said: «What can I say? Let them be *nine*". (The other) said: «Then why has the tenth man remained without a sheep?" He answered: «Each of those who caught a sheep was quick, the tenth

تنبل بود اگر تنبل نبود او هم یك گوسفند گیرش می آمد این تقصیر بنده نیست تقصیر تنبلی خودش است	būd; agar tambal na-būd, ū ham yak gūsfand gīr-ash mīāmad. In taqsīr-i banda nīst, taqsīr-i tambalī-yi khudash ast.	man was slow; if he had not been slow, he too would have caught hold of a sheep. This is not the slave's (my) fault, it is the fault of his own laziness.
حکایت ۲	*Hikāyat-i duyum.*	*Anecdote N°. 2.*
ترکی شتر خودشرا سوار شده بشهری رفت و در انجا قدری گندم خرید	Turkī shutur-i khudashrā savār shuda bi shahrī raft va dar unjā qadrī gandum kharīd.	A Turk, having mounted his own camel, went to town and there bought some wheat.
چون آن گندم بقدر یك بار نبود گندم هارا در یك لنگه ریخت و در لنگهٔ دیگر هموزنِ گندم سنگ گذاشت	Chun ān gandum bi qadr-i yak bār na-būd, gandumhārā dar yak linga rīkht va dar linga-yi dīgar, hamvazn-i gandum, sang guzāsht	As the wheat was not enough to make up one load, he put all the wheat in one saddle-bag, and in the other he put stones of the same weight as the wheat.
و هر دو لنگهرا بارِ شتر کرده مهارِ شتر را گرفته پیاده از شهر بیرون آمد	va har du linga-rā bār-i shutur karda mahār shutur rā girifta pīada az shahr bīrūn	Having placed both loads on the camel's back, he took the

	āmad.	camel's rope and walked out of the town.
قدری راه که طیّ کرد یک نفر پیادهٔ دیکر باو رسید	Qadrī rāh ki tei kard, yak nafar pīāda-yi dīgar bi ū rasīd.	Having gone a little way, he met a man on foot.
از او پرسید که بارِ شترت چه چیز است	Az ū pursīd, ki: «bār-i shutur-at chi chīz ast"?	This man asked him: «What is your camel's load"?
ترك جواب داد که یك لنکهٔ بار شتر کندم است و لنکهٔ دیکر سنك	Turk javāb dād ki «yak linga-yi bār-i shutur gandum ast va linga-yi dīgar sang".	The Turk answered «On one side is wheat and on the other side are stones".
آن شخص پیاده به آن شتردار کفت شترت را بخوابان یك کاری با این بارِ شتر بکنم که هم بارِ شترت سبك بشود و هم خودت سوار بشوی و پیاده راه نروی	An shakhs-i pīāda bi un shutur-dār guft: «Shutur-rā bi-khābān! yak kārī bā īn bār-i shutur bikunam, ki ham bār-i shutur-at sabuk bishavad, va ham khud-at savār bishavī va pīāda rāh na-ravī".	The man on foot said to the owner of the camel: «Make your camel lie down! Let me arrange this load in such a way, that not only your camels' burden should become light, but that at the same time you should be able to ride and not go on foot".
شتربانِ ترك شتررا خوابانید	Shuturbān-i Turk shutur-rā khābānīd.	The turkish camel-driver made the camel lie down.
آن پیاده تمامِ آن سنك ها	An pīāda tamām-i	The tra-

را بیرون ریخت نصف ان
کندم را در لنکهٔ دیکر ریخت
و ثانیًا بارِ شتر کرده بشتربان
کفت حالا خودت هم سوار شو
شتربان باخوشحالی سوار شد و
از هوش و عقلِ آن پیاده
متحیّر بود بعد از اینکه
قدری راه رفت از پیاده
پرسید شما با این هوش و
کمال چقدر شتر دارید جواب
داد هیچ شتربان خیال کرد
که شاید کوسفند زیاد دارد
پرسید چه قدر کوسفند داری
باز جواب داد هیچ پس
پرسید چه قدر پول و دولت

ān sang-hā-rā bīrūn rīkht, nisf-i ān gandum-rā dar linga-yi dīgar rīkht va sānīan bār-i shutur karda bi shuturbān guft: «Hālā khudat ham savār shou». Shuturbān bā khushhālī savār shud va az hūsh u ʿaql-i ān pīāda mutaheyyir būd. Baʿd az īnki qadrī rāh raft, az pīāda pursīd: «Shumā bā īn hūsh u kamāl chi qadr shutur dārīd»? javāb dād: «hīch». Shuturbān kheyāl kard ki shāyad gūsfand-ī zīād dārad; pursīd: «chi qadr gūsfand dārī»? bāz javāb dād: «hīch». Pas pursīd: «Chi qadr pūl u doulat

veller threw out all the stones, and put half of the wheat into the other saddle-bag. Secondly having put up the loads, he said to the camel-driver: «Now you can also ride».

The camel-driver joyfully mounted and was astounded at the cleverness and intelligence of the traveller. After having gone a short way, he asked him: «You who are so clever and wise, how many camels have you»?

He answered: «None». The camel-driver thought that he must have many sheep, and asked: «How many sheep have you?» Again he answered:

داری جواب داد هیچ ندارم
و مرد فقیری هستم شتربان
بشنیدن این حرف زود از
شتر پیاده شده شتر را
خوابانید و کندم را در یک
لنکه ریخت باز لنکهٔ دیکر را
از سنک پر کرده خودش پیاده
با شتر میرفت پیاده کفت چرا
اینطور کردی جواب داد که
علم و دانائی مشئوم است
و سبب بد بختی است اکر
مشئوم نبود تو باید با این
هوش خیلی شتر و رمه داشته
باشی وبار شترم را بصورت اول

dārī"? Javāb dād: "Hīch nadāram va mard-i faqīrī hastam". Shuturbān bi shanīdan-i īn harf zūd az shutur pīāda shuda shutur-rā khābānīd va gandum-rā dar yak linga rīkht; bāz linga-yi dīgar-rā az sang pur karda, khudash pīāda bā shutur mīraft. Pīāda guft: "chirā īntour kardī"? Javāb dād ki: "ʿilm u dānāī mashʿūm ast" va sabab-i badbakhtī-st. Agar mashʿūm nabūd, tu bāyad bā īn hūsh kheilī shutur va rama dāshta bāshī, va bār-i shutur-am rā

"None". Then the other asked. "How much money and wealth do you possess"? The wanderer answered "I have nothing, I am a poor man". The camel-driver, having heard these words, quickly got off the camel, and made him lie down. He then put back all the wheat into one saddle-bag, filled the other bag with stones and went on walking by his camel's side. The other traveller said: "Why did you do this"? He answered: Science and wisdom are of bad omen and bring ill-luck. If they did not cause ill-luck, you would, with your cleverness, possess

کردم ترسیدم که مبادا از نکبت علم تو یك بد بختی و بلائی بمن و شتر من برسد	bi sūrat-i avval kardam, tarsīdam ki mabādā az nikbat-i ʿilm-i tū yak badbakhtī va balāī bi man va shutur-i man birasad.	many camels and flocks. So I have replaced my camel-load as it was, for I fear that through the misfortune of your cleverness an adversity or calamity will befall me and my camel.
حکایت ۳	*Hikāyat* 3.	*Anecdote* №. 3.
یك شیرازی باصفهان آمده شنیده بود که در آنجا جیب بر بسیار هستند قدری چینی شکسته بصورت پول درست کرده در جیب خودش ریخت و هر روز در بازار اصفهان راه میرفت منتظر بود که یك جیب بر جیب او را ببرّد تا گول بخورد لیکن جیب	Yak Shīrāzī bi Isfahān āmada shanīda būd ki dar ānjā jīb-burr bisyār hastand. Qadrī chīnī-yi shikasta bi sūrat-i pūl durust karda dar jīb-i khudash rīkht va har rūz dar bāzār-i Isfahān rāh mīraft; muntazir būd, ki yak jībburr jīb-i ūrā biburrad, tā gūl bikhurad. Līkan jīb-i ūrā	A man from *Shīrāz* had come to *Isfahān* and had heard that there were many pickpockets there. He made some broken china into something resembling money, put it into his pocket and walked about every day in the bazaars of Isfahan; waiting for a pickpocket to pick his pocket and be deceived.

اورا هیچ نبریدند روزی در جائی با چند نفر اصفهانی نشسته بود کفت من شنیده بودم که در اصفهان جیب‌بر فراوان است وحالا مدّتی است که پول زیاد در جیب دارم و همه جا هم کردش کرده ام هنوز نتوانسته اند جیب مرا ببرّند یکی از آن اصفهانیها کفت ای بیچاره ده دفعه آنچه در جیب تو بود در آوردم دیدم که همه چینی شکسته است باز تویش کذاشتم و تو نفهمیدی

hīch na-burrīdand. Rūzī dar jāī bā chand nafar Isfahānī nishasta būd. Guft: “Man shanīda būdam, ki dar Isfahān jībburr farāvān ast va hālā muddatī-st ki pūl-i zīād dar jīb dāram va hama jā ham gardish karda am; hanūz na tavānista and, jīb-i marā biburrand. Yakī az ān Isfahānīhā guft: “ei bīchāra! dah dafʿa unchi dar jīb-i tu būd dar āvurdam; dīdam ki hama chīnī-yi shikasta ast, bāz tū-yash guzāshtam va tu na-fahmīdī.

But his pocket was not picked. One day he was sitting with some people of Isfahan and said: “I have heard that there are a great many pickpockets at Isfahan and now for some time past I have had much money in my pocket and have also walked about everywhere; as yet they have not been able to pick my pocket. One of those Isfahanis said: “My good fellow! ten times have I taken out what you had in your pocket; I saw it was only broken china and put it in again and you did not notice it”.

Extracts from Nāsir ed-Dīn Shāh's Diaries.

بیانِ راهِ اهن	*Beyān-i rah-i āhan.*	*Description of a train.*
کالسکه های راه آهن از کالسکه هـای مخصوص امپراطـور بـود	Kālaskahā-yi rāh-i āhan az kālaska-hā-yi makhsūs-i Imparātūr būd,	The railway carriages were a special train of saloons for the use of the Emperor,
بسیار خوب و وسیع و مزین	bisyār khūb va vasī' va muzeiyan;	very handsome, spacious, and beautifully fitted up.
و اطاقهای متعدد از سفره‌خانه و خوابگاه و اطاق پذیرائی همه	va utāqhā-yi muta^caddad az sufra-khāna va khābgāh va utāq-i pazīrāī	They contained many different apartments, dining-saloons, sleeping-carriages, reception-saloons,
مزین بچراغ و میز و صندلی و تخت و نیم تخت کالسکه‌ها همه بهم وصل بود بطوری که به جمیع کالسکه ها میشد	hama muzeiyan bi chirāgh va mīz va sandalī va tākht va nīm-takht. Kālaskahā hama bi ham vasl būd, tourī-ki bi jamī^c-i kālaskahā mīshud	all furnished with lamps, tables, chairs, sofas, and couches. They all communicated with one another, so that one could pass from end to end of the train.
رفت و آمد اشخاصی که در کشتی قسطنطین با ما بودند در کالسکه ما نشسته و شاهزاده‌گان و سایرین با یکدسته	raft u āmad. Ashkhāsī-ki dar kashtī-i "Qustantīn" bā mā būdand, dar kālaska-yi mā nishasta, va shāhzādagān va	Those of our suite who accompanied

کالسکهٔ دیگر از عقب میآمدند
اوّل مرتبهٔ است که بکالسکه
بخار می نشینیم بسیار خوب
و راحت است ساعتی پنج
فرسنگ راه میرود

sārīn bā yak dasta-yi kālaska-yi dīgar az 'aqab mīāmadand. Avval martabaī-st ki bi kālaska-i bukhār mīnishīnīm. Bisyār khūb va rāhat ast. Sā'atī panj farsang rāh mīravad.

us on board the "Constantine" were placed in the same saloon with ourselves; our princes and the rest following in a separate train. This is the first time we travel on a railway, and very nice and comfortable it is; it goes five leagues in an hour.

رود خانهٔ نوا

Rūdkhāna-yi Navā.

The river Neva.

رود خانه نوا از سمت شمال
پطر بطرف مابین جنوب و
مشرق جاری و خیلی رود
خانهٔ عظیمی است کشتی
بخار بزرك در آن كار میکنند
هر روز پارچیهای یخ زیاد
مانند کوه از شمال میآرد که

Rūdkhāna-yi *Navā* az samt-i shamāl-i *Pitr* bi taraf-i mābein-i junūb va mashriq jārī va kheilī rūdkhāna-yi ʿazīmī-st. Kashtī-yi bukhār-i buzurg dar un kār mīkunand. Har rūz pārchahā-yi yakh-i zīād, mānand-i kūh az shamāl mīā-

The river *Neva* flows from the north of St Petersburg in a south easterly direction; and is a very large river. Large steamers navigate it. Every day many pieces of ice like mountains are brought down by it from the north, which are extremely pure and beautiful, like the ice on the mountain Tuchal in the Elburz. It is said that the water of the Neva is not wholesome, and the Emperor cautioned us against drinking it. On one side of the stream is the palace in which we have our quarters, and on the other side is the old fort built in the time of Peter the Great, within which there is a church with a high tower and spire of gold. The tombs of the sovereigns of Russia are in that church. The mint of the Government is also within the fort. — The streets of St. Petersburg are lighted with gas.

rad, ki bisyār sāf u khūb misl-i yakh-i Tūchāl-i Alburz ast. Mīgūyand āb-i Navā sālim nīst. Imparātūr ham mārā az khurdan-i un man[c] mīkard. Yak taraf-i rūdkhāna [c]imāratī-st ki manzil-i māst, va taraf-i muqābil qal[c]a-i kuhnaī-st ki dar ayyām-i *Patar Kabīr* sākhta and. Kalīsāyī dar vasat-i qal[c]a ast; manāra va mīl-i bulandī az tilā dārad, va maqbara-yi salātīn-i *Rūs* dar un jā-st. Zarrāb-khāna yi doulatī ham dar qal[c]a ast. — Kūchahā-yi *Patarburgh* bā gāz roushan mīshavad.

بسیار صاف و خوب مثل یخ
توچال البرز است میکویند
آب نوا سالم نیست امپراطور
هم مارا از آشامیدن آن منع
میکرد یکطرف رود خانه عمارتی
است که منزل ما است و طرف
مقابل قلعهٔ کهنهٔ است که در
ایّام پطر کبیر ساخته اند
کلیسائی در وسط قلعه است
مناره و میل بلندی از طلا دارد
مقبرهٔ سلاطین روس در آنجا است
ضرابخانه دولتی هم در قلعه
است کوچهای پطر بورغ با
کاز روشن میشود

سرحد روس و آلمان

در این سر حدّ وضع همه چیز
از آدم و زمین و کالسکه و
خوراکی وغیره تغییر کرد آبادی
خاك پروس از روسیّه بیشتر
است هرچه نگاه میکردیم ده
خانه آدم اسپ مادیان گاو
گوسفند چمن زراعت آب
گلهای الوان بود از رودخانهٔ
زیادی گذشتیم آبادیهای بسیار
پاکیزه از دور و نزدیك پیدا
بود تا رسیدیم بیك استاسیون
ایستادیم صدر اعظم بکالسکه
ما آمد تلگرافچی پروس

Sarhadd-i Rūs u Almān.

Dar īn sarhadd vazᶜ-i hama chīz az ādam va zamīn va kālaska va khurākī va gheira taghyīr kard: Abādī-yi khāk-i *Prūs* az *Rūsīa* bīshtar ast. Har chi nigāh mīkardīm dih, khāna, ādam, asp, mādīān, gāv, gūsfand, chaman, zarāᶜat, āb, gulhā-yi alvān būd. Az rūdkhāna-yi zīādī guzashtīm. Abādīhā-yi bisyār pākīza az dūr u nazdīk peidā būd tā rasīdīm bi yak *istāsyūn*, īstādīm. Sadr aᶜzam bi kālaska-yi mā

The Russian and German frontier.

In these regions everything became changed, — the men, the country, the carriages, the food, etc. The populousness and cultivation in the land of the Prussian are greater than in Russia. Whenever I looked out there were villages, houses, men, horses, oxen, mares, sheep, meadows, sown-fields, water, and flowers of all colours. We crossed many rivers. Human improvements of charming aspect came in sight, near and afar. And so we came to a station. The train stopped; the Grand-

Vazīr came to our carriage. The Prussian Telegraph-Officer handed in a number of telegrams from Tehrān, and these were perused. Thanks be to God, they the conveyed good tidings. Again we started.	āmad; talagrāfchī-yi Prūs talagrāf-i zīādī az Tahrān dād. Khunda shud; alhamdu lillāh akhbār-i khūb dāsht. Bāz bi rāh uftādīm.	تلگراف زیادی از طهران داد خوانده شد الحمد لله اخبار خوب داشت باز براه افتادیم
As the Prussian train travelled very fast, within two hours and a half of our leaving the Russian frontier we arrived at *Königsberg*, a city of Prussia, and very near to the *Baltic Sea.* A large river passes through this city, which is named the *Pregel.* Merchant-steamers come up from the sea to the interior of the city, and return	Chun kālaska-yi bukhār bisyār tund mīraft, az sarhadd-i Rūs du sāʿat u nīm kashīd, tā rasīdīm bi shahr-i *Kunigsbarg*, ki yakī az shahrhā-yi Prūs, va bi *Daryā-yi Bāltik* bisyār nazdīk ast. Rūdkhāna-yi ʿazīmī az vasat-i īn shahr mīguzarad, ki ismash *Prajal* ast. Kashtī-yi bukhār-i tijāratī az daryā tā vasat-i shahr mīāyad va mīravad. Shahr i	چون کالسکهٔ بخار بسیار تند میرفت از سر حدّ روس دو ساعت و نیم کشید تا رسیدیم بشهر کنیکس برك که یکی از شهرهای پروس وبدریای بالتك بسیار نزدیك است رود خانهٔ عظیمی از وسط این شهر میگذرد که اسمش پرژل است کشتی بخار تجارتی از دریا تا وسط شهر میآید و میرود شهر

کوچکی است اما قشنك جمعیتش نود و پنج هزار نفر است	kūchikī-st ammā qashang. Jamᶜīat-ash navad u panj hazār nafar ast.	in like manner. It is a small city, but pretty; its population is 95,000 souls.
یکنوع زراعتی که اسمش راپ است در صحرای خاك پروس امروز دیده شد که کل زرد بسیار خوش رنکی داشت برای روغنش میکارند که بجهت چرب کردن آلات ماشین راه آهن و غیره خیلی بکار میرود بسیار کاشته بودند و صفای زیادی بصحراها داده بود طبیعتًا تمام صحرا چمن است و جنکلهای سرو و کاج اما در خاك پروس بسیار کمتر از خاك روس است	Yak nouᶜ-i zarāᶜatī ki ism-ash "*rāp*" ast, dar sahrāhā-yi khāk-i Prūs imrūz dīda shud, ki gul-i zard-i bisyār khush-rangī dāsht. Barāyi roughan-ash mīkārand, ki bi jihat-i charb kardan-i ālāt-i māshīn-i rāh-i āhan va gheira kheilī bi kār mīravad. Bisyār kāshta būdand, va safā-yi zīādī bi sahrāhā dāda būd. Tabīᶜatan tamām-i sahrā chaman ast va jangalhā-yi sarv u kāj, ammā dar khāk-i Prūs bisyār kamtar az khāk-i Rūs ast.	We have to-day seen in the Prussian territory the cultivation of rape-seed, which has a yellow flower of a very charming tint. It is sown for its oil (colza oil), which is much used for the lubrication of locòmotives, and the like. It was very extensively cultivated, and it gave a peculiar charm to the landscape. Naturally, the country is all meadowland interspersed with forests of fir and yews, though these latter an far less common than in Russia.
خلاصه وارد کار شدیم صاحب	Khulāsa vārid-i gār shudīm.	*In* fine, we reached the station,

منصب و سرباز زیادی بودند همه جوانهای بسیار خوب کلاه خود بر سر لباسهای خوب در تن خیلی قشون خوبی بودند مملکت پروس همه قشون است موزیکانچیان اینجا مثل افواج طهران همه بالابان و نی دارند اما در روس این قسم نی نبود	Sāhibmansab va sarbāz-izīādī būdand. Hama javānhā-yi bisyār khūb, kulāh-i khūd bar sar, libāshā-yi khūb dar tan, kheilī qushūn-i khūbī būdand. — Mamlikat-i Prūs hama qushūn ast. — Mūzīkānchīān-i īnjā, misl-i afvāj-i Tahrān, hama bālābān va nei dārand, ammā dar Rūs īn qism-i nei na būd.	where there was a large body of troops and officiers, all very handsome young men, with helmets on their heads, and beautiful clothing on their bodies. They were a very pretty soldiery. The Prussian Kingdom is all soldiery. The bands here, like those in Tehrān, have all drums and fifes, whereas in Russia they have not this kind of fife.
مرد و زن الی غیر النهایة همه جا در دو طرف راه صف کشیده بودند من سوار کالسکهٔ رو باری شده راندم اطفال زیادی دور کالسکه میدویدند یک هنگامهٔ	Mard u zan ilā gheir annihāyat hama jā dar du taraf-i rāh saff kashīda būdand. Man savār i kālaska-yi rūbāzī shuda rāndam. Atfāl-i zīādī dour-i kālaska mīdavīdand; yak hangāma-yi gharībī būd. Kūcha-yi tūlānī tei shud.	Infinite numbers of men and women lined both sides of the streets everywhere. I mounted an open carriage and drove off. Crowds of children ran by its side. It was a curious hubbub. We passed down a long street. The hou-

غریبی بود کوچهٔ طولانی طی شد خانها همه سه چهار طبقه و کوچك و تنکست بعمارت دولتی قدیم که پانصد سال است بنا شده رسیده در عمارت پیاده شده از پله زیادی بالا رفتیم عمارت کهنه است همکی همراهان هم از شاهزادکان و عمله خلوت و غیره آمدند

Khānahā hama sih, chahār tabaqa va kūchik u tang ast. Bi ʿimārat-i doulatī-yi qadīm, ki punsad sāl ast binā shuda, rasīda, dar ʿimārat pīāda shuda, az palla-yi zīādī bālā raftīm. ʿImārat-i kuhna ast. Hamagī-yi hamrāhān ham az shāhzādagān va ʿamala-yi khalvat va gheira āmadand.

...ses are all of three or four stories, small, and narrow. We arrived at an ancient palace, built five hundred years ago, dismounted at its gate, and went up many stairs. It is an old structure. The whole of our suite, princes, household officials, etc., all came there.

چون اهل این شهر هرکز ایرانی ندیده بودند از ملاقات ما خیلی متعجب بودند

Chun ahl-i īn shahr har giz Īrānī na dīda būdand, az mulāqāt-i mā kheilī mutaʿajjib būdand.

As the people of this city had never seen a Persian, they were much surprised at the sight of us.

اسم حاکم شهر و یوکلر است کالسکه های این شهر واسپهای کالسکه ها بزیادی و خوبی کالسکه های روس و اسپهای آنجا نیست

Ism-i hākim-i shahr *vivaklar* ast. — Kālaskahā-yi īn shahr va asphā-yi kālaskahā bi zīādī va khūbī-yi kālāskahā-yi Rūs va asphā-yi ūnjā nīst.

The name of the Governor of the city is Vivekler. The carriages of this place, and the horses in the carriages, are not so numerous nor so beautiful as those in Russia.

کبوتر بازی‌کن دم سیاه و غیره ابابیل سیاه لقلق وکلاغ ابلق در اینولایت زیاد دیده شد	Kabūtar-i bāzīkun-i dumsīāh va gheira, abābīl-i sīāh, laqlaq va kalāgh-i ablaq dar īn vilāyat zīād dīda shud.	Black-tailed tumbler pigeons, and others, swifts, storks, and magpies, appeared very numerous in this country;
آسیای بادی هم بسیار است	Asyā-yi bādī ham bisyār ast.	windmills are in great plenty.
خلاصه شب‌را چند دسته موزیکانچی زیر عمارت ایستاده بسیار زدند یعنی طبل شب‌را میزدند	Khulāsa shabrā chand dasta mūzīkānchī, zīr-i ʿimārat īstāda, bisyār zadand, yaʿnī tabl-i shabrā mīzadand.	In the night several military-outside bands stood in front the palace and played a long time, i. e., they beat the night-roll on the drums.
آهنك شیپور های موزیکان و وضع آنها خیلی خوب بود	Ahang-i sheipūrhā-yi mūzīkān va vazʿ-i unhā kheilī khūb būd.	The harmony of the fifes of these bands, and the tenue of the men, were excellent.
طبل بزرك سربازی را هم بیك سك بزرکی بسته بودند	Tabl-i buzurg-i sarbāzīrā ham bi yak sag-i buzurgī basta būdand.	A great military drum, too, was fastened to a large dog,
زیر طبل عرّاده بود که سك میکشید	Zīr i tabl ʿarrāda būd, ki sag mīkashīd.	with a truck beneath it, which the dog drew.

ورود برلن

بآبادی اطراف شهر رسیدیم کالسکهٔ راه آهن را گاهی روی پل گاهی بالاگاهی پائین میبردند و گاهی بر میگردانددند مثل اسبی که دهنهٔ آن دست آدم باشد خیلی جای تعجب بود و راه آهن بسیار در هر طرف کشیده است واگون و لوکوموتیو زیاده از حدّ در راه دیده شد کالسکهٔ بخار زیادی امروز با ما تلاق کرد خلاصه وارد گار شده پیاده شدیم

Vurūd-i Barlin.

Bi ābādī-i atrāf-i shahr rasīdīm. Kālaska-yi rāh-i āhanrā gāhī rū-yi pul, gāhī bālā, gāhī pāīn mīburdand, gāhī bar mīgardānd and misl-i aspī, ki dahana-yi un dast-i ādam bāshad. Kheilī jā-yi taʿajjub būd; va rāh-i āhan bisyār dar har taraf kashīda ast; vāgūn va lūkūmūtīv zīāda az hadd dar rāh dīda shud. Kālaska-yi bukhār-i zīādī imrūz bā mā talāqī kard. Khulāsa vārid-i *gār* shuda, pīāda shudīm.

Arrival at Berlin.

We reached the outskirts of the town. Our train was taken sometimes over a bridge, sometimes up and sometimes down, and then again turned back, like a horse, whose bit is in a man's hand. This was to us a source of wonder. Many lines of railway are laid down in every direction. Carriages and engines without number were seen on the lines, and many trains passed us on the road to-day. At last we reached the station and alighted.

اعلیحضرت امپراطور المان کیوم
و نوّاب ولیعهد پسر ایشان
و نوّاب پرنس شارل برادر
ایشان و فردریك شارل پسر
برادر امپراطور که فاتح متز
است و شاهزادهای دیگر از
خانوادهٔ سلطنت مثل پرنس
هوهن‌زولرن که جوانکی است و
جنك آلمان و فرانسه در سر
همین شاهزاده شد که فرانسویان
راضی نبودند پادشاه اسپانیول
شود پرنس بیزمارك وزیر مشهور
معروف دولت آلمان و مارشال

Aʿlāhazrat-i Imparātūr-i Almān Gīyūm[1]) va *Navvāb Valīʿahd*, pisar-i īshān, va *Navvab Prins Shārl*, birādar-i īshān, va *Fradarīk Shārl*, pisar-i barādar-i Imparātūr, ki fātih-i *Matz* ast, va Shāhzādahā-yi dīgar az khānvāda-yi saltanat, misl-i *Prins Hūhanzūlarn*, ki javānakī-st, va jang-i *Almān* u *Farānsa* dar sar-i hamīn shahzāda shud, ki *Farānsavīān* rāzī na būdand pādishāh-i *Ispānyūl* shavad, *Prins Bīzmārk*, vazīr-i mashūr-i maʿrūf-i dou-

His Most Exalted Majesty, the Emperor of Germany, William, the Nawwāb the Heir-Apparent, his son, *the Nawwāb Prince Charles*, his brother, *Frederīck Charles*, son of a brother of the Emperor and captor of *Metz*, together with other princes of the royal family, such as *Prince Hohenzollern*, a mere boy, and the very prince respecting whom the war between *Germany* and *France* occured, as the *French* were not willing that he should become king of *Spain*; also *Prince Bismarck*, — the

1) Guillaume. Most European names are adopted by the Persians in their French form.

رون وزیر جنك و صدر اعظم
پروس و جنرال مورك كه حالا
مارشال و سپهسالار و بسیار
معروف و مشهور است با سایر
جنرالها و صاحبمنصبان و فوج
خاصه موزیكانچی سواره نظام
وغیره و جمعیت زیاده از حدّ
همه سر راه آهن بودند پزیرائی
بسیار خوبی كردند دست
اعلیحضرت امپراطوررا كرفته سوار
كالسكهٔ روبازی شده از كوچهٔ
وسیعی كه طرفین آن همه
از درختهای كهن و كلسفید
خوشه بسته و همه جا سنك

lat-i Almān, va *Mārshāl Rūn*, vazīr-i jang va sadr aʿzam-i Prūs, va *janarāl Mūrk*, ki hālā mārshāl va sipahsālār va bisyār maʿrūf u mashhūr ast, ba sāʿir-i janarālhā va sāhib-mansabān va fouj-i khāssa, mūzīkānchī, savāra yi nizām va gheira va jamʿīat zīāda az hadd hama sar-i rāh-i āhan būdand, pazīrāī-i bisyār khūbī kardand. Dast-i aʿlāhazrat Imparātūrrā girifta, savar-i kālaska-yi rūbāzī shuda, az kūcha-yi vasīʿī, ki tarafein-i un hama az dirakhthā-yi kuhan va gulsafīd khūsha

famous Chancellor of Germany, *Marshal Roon*, the Minister of War and Premier of Prussia, and *General Moltke*, now Marshal and Generalissimo, very celebrated, and much spoken of, and other generals and officials, with a battalion of the Guards, a band, a cavalry regiment, and the like, a vast concourse of people moreover there was at the station who gave us a hearty reception. Taking the hand of His Most Exalted Majesty, we mounted an open carriage; and drove along a wide street, bordered on either side with ancient trees and

فرش و وسیع و اطراف همه خانه بود گذشتیم	basta, va hama jā sangfarsh va vasī' va atrāf hama khāna būd, guzashtīm.	white cluster roses in flower, everywhere paved with stones, and spacious, with houses the whole way.
جمعیت زیادی بود هورا میکشیدند من هم بهمه تعارف میکردم	Jam'īat-i zīādī būd, hūrā mīkashīdand. Man ham bi hama ta'āruf mīkardam.	The crowds were great. They all shouted hurrahs while I saluted them.
با امپراطور بزبان فرانسه حرف میزدم تاجائی رسیدیم دروازه مانند درختها تمام شد کوچهٔ وسیعی بود طرفین عمارت عالیِ چند مرتبه یك ستونی دیده شد که تازه بیادگار فتح فرانسه میسازند و هنوز ناتمام است	Bā Imparātūr bi zabān-i Farānsa harf mīzadam, tā bi jā-yī rasīdīm darvāzamānand. Dirakhthā tamām shud; kūcha-yi vasī'ī būd, tarafein 'imārat-i 'ālī-yi chand martaba. Yak sutūnī dīda shud, ki tāza bi yādgār-i fath-i Farānsa mīsāzand, va hanūz nātamām ast.	I conversed with the Emperor in French, until we reached a place like a gateway, where the trees ended. It was a wide street, with sumptuous palaces on either side, of several stories. We noticed a column recently erected in commemoration of the victory over France, and not yet completed.
یك صورت فردریك اوّل یعنی فردریك بزرك که بامفرغ	Yak sūrat-i *Fradarīk-i Avval*, ya'nī *Fradarīk-i Buzurg*, ki	A statue of *Frederick I.*, i. e. of *Frederick the Great*, cast

ریخته‌اند سر راه بود از	bā mufarrigh rīkhta and, sar-i rāh būd.	in metal, lay on our road.
اونیورسیته گذشتیم مدرسهٔ بسیار عالیست دو هزار نفر شاگرد در انجا تحصیل میکنند	Az Univarsita guzashtīm. Madrasa-yi bisyār ʿālī-st, du hazār nafar shāgird dar unjā tahsīl mīkunad.	We passed the University, a great place of instruction where two thousand students study; we passed the Arsenal,
از ارسنال که طرف چپ بود و دست راست از عمارت مخصوص امپراطور که از زمان ولیعهدی تابحال همان جا می‌نشیند	Az *Arsanāl*, ki taraf-i chap būd, va dāst-i rāst az ʿimārat-i makhsūs-i Imparātūr, ki az zamān-i valīʿahdī tā bi hāl hamun jā mīnishīnad,	on our left hand; while on our right was the Emperor's own palace, in which he has resided from the days when he was Heir-Presumptive until now.
و بعد از خانهٔ ولیعهد گذشته رسیدیم بمیدانیکه دو حوض داشت و از هر یك فوّارهٔ بلندی میجست	va baʿd az khāna-i *Valīʿahd* guzashta rasīdīm bi meidānī, ki du houz dāsht, va az har yak favvāra-yi bulandī mījast.	Next we passed the palace of the Heir-Apparent, and so reached a square with two basins of water, from which sprang lofty jets d'eau.
دست راست قصر سلطنتی است که برای ما معیّن کرده بودند تا دم قصر جمعیت بود	Dast-i rāst *qasr-i saltanatī* ast, ki barāyi mā muʿeyyan karda būdand. Tā dam-i qasr jamʿīat būd.	On our right was a royal residence, that was assigned to us. The crowd extended right up to this building.

پیاده شدیم سربازان قدیمی بالباسهای خوب که قراول عمارت بودند توی اطاقها قراولان از سواره که جوانهای بسیار خوب خوشکل خوش لباس بودند دم درها با پیشخدمتان و غیره همه ایستاده بودند	Pīada shudīm. Sarbāzān-i qadīmī bā libāshā-yi khūb, ki qarāvul-i ʿimārat būdand, tūyi utāqhā; qarāvulān, az savāra, ki javānhā-yi bisyār khūb-i khushgil-i khushlibās būdand, dam-i darhā, bā pīshkhidmetān va gheira hama istāda būdand.	We alighted. Veteran troops in beautiful uniforms, who are the guards of the palace, were in the rooms; patrols of cavalry, all handsome young men, with good figures, and fine uniforms, were at the gate, with officers of the household, etc., all stationed.
از پله ها بالا رفتیم وسط میدان جلو عمارت باغچهای بسیار قشنک است که اقسام کلها از یاس شیروانی و غیره کاشته اند دو مجسمهٔ اسپ هم که دهنهٔ هریک دست آدمی است از چودن ریخته اند امپراطور همه اطاقهارا بما نشان دادند پردها و اشکال	Az pallahā bālā raftīm. Vasat-i meidān-i jilou-i ʿimārat bāghchahā-yi bisyār qashang ast, ki aqsām-i gulhā az yās-i Shīrvānī va gheira kāshta and. Du mujassama-yi asp ham, ki dahana-yi har yak dast-i ādamī ast, az chūdan rīkhta and. Imparātūr hama utāqhārā bi mā nishān dā-	We went upstairs. The middle of the square in front of the palace was laid out in beautiful beds of flowers and shrubs, lilacs, and the like. There were also two cast-metal statues of horses, each held by the bridle by a man. The Emperor showed me all the apartments. There are

خوب در ین عمارت بود

من صدر اعظم و شاهزادهها و غیرهرا معرّفی کردم و امپراطور هم سر راهِ آهن شاهزادکان و نوکرهای خودشانرا معرّفی کرده بودند بعد با ایشان باطاق خلوت رفته قدری صحبت کردیم صدر اعظم بود امپراطور که رفتند بعد از دقیقهٔ ما باز سوار کالسکه شده رفتیم خانهٔ ایشان تا پای پله استقبال کردند رفتیم نشستیم صحبت شد بعداز چند دقیقه مراجعت کردیم امپراطور هفتاد

dand. Pardahā va ashkāl-i khūb dar īn ʿimārat būd.

Man sadr aʿzam va shāhzādahā va gheirarā muʿarrafī kardam, va Imparātūr ham sar-i rāh-i āhan shāhzādagān va noukarhā-yi khud-i-shānrā muʿarrafī karda būdand.

Baʿd bā īshān bi utāq-i khalvat rafta, qadrī suhbat kardīm; sadr aʿzam būd. Imparātūr ki raftand, baʿd az daqīqa yi mā bāz savār-i kālaska shuda, raftīm khāna-yi īshān. Tā pā-yi palla istiqbāl kardand. Raftīm, nishastīm, suhbat shud. Baʿd az chand daqīqa murājaʿat kardīm.

some beautiful paintings and portraits in this palace.

I presented the Grand Vazīr, the princes, and others; the Emperor also at the station had presented his princes and servants.

Next we went to a private apartment with him, and had some conversation, at which the Grand-Vazīr was present. When the Emperor left, I waited a short time, then entered my carriage, and drove to his residence. He came to the foot of the stairs to meet me; we went in; we sat down; a conversation ensued; and after a few minutes I returned.

و شش سال دارند برادر ایشان هفتاد و سه سال اما هر دو در کمال بنیه و قوت هستند پرنس بیزمارك پنجاه و هشت سال مارشال ملك هفتاد و پنج سال نوابِ ولیعهد چهل و دو سال دارند خلاصه شب را جائی نرفتیم	*Imparātūr* haftād u shish sāl dārand, *barādar-i īshān* haftād u sih sāl, ammā har du dar kamāl-i bunya va quvvat hastand. *Prins Bīzmārk* panjāh u hasht sāl, *Mārshāl Mulk* haftād u panj sāl, *Navvāb-i Valī ʿahd* chihil u du sāl dārand. Khulāsa shabrā jāī na raftīm.	The *Emperor* is seventy-six years of age; his brother seventy-three. Both of them, however, are in perfect bodily health and strength. *Prince Bismarck* is fifty-eight, *Marshal Moltke* seventy five. The *Nawwāb the Heir-Apparent* is forty-two. This evening I went nowhere.
شهر برلن باچراغ کاز روشن است چراغ اینجا بیش از پطر است	Shahr-i *Barlin* bā chirāgh-i gāz roushan ast. Chirāgh-i īnjā bīsh az *Pitr* ast.	The city of *Berlin* is lighted with gas; the lamps being more numerous here than in St Petersburg.
مقابل عمارت ما آن طرف میدان عمارت موزهٔ برلن است یک طرف هم کلیسا و طرف دیکر عمارت جبّه خانه است	Muqābil-i ʿimārat-i mā, un-taraf-i meidān, ʿimārat-i *Mūza-yi Barlin* ast; yak taraf ham kalīsā, va taraf-i dīgar ʿimārat-i jubbakhāna	Opposite our palace, on the other side of the square, is the building of the Berlin Museum. On one side is a church, and opposite it the Armoury. In the centre

وسط میدان سکوئی است از اطراف پله دار و مجسمهٔ فردریک کبیر را سواره از چودن ریخته اند	ast. Vasat-i meidān sakū-st az atrāf palladār va mujassama-yi *Fradarīk Kabīr*-rā savāra az chūdan rīkhta and.	of the square is a raised platform, with steps all round, on which is a cast-metal equestrian statue of *Frederick the Great.*
بر روی عمارات برلن رنگ خاکستری مالیده‌اند قدری شهررا از جلوه انداخته است بر خلاف پطر که عمارات بانواع رنگها ملوّن است	Bar rū-yi ʿimārāt-i Barlin rang-i khākistarī mālīda and. Qadrī shahrrā az jilva andākhta ast, bar khilāf-i Pitr ki ʿimārāt bi anvāʿ-yi ranghā mulavvan ast.	The exterior of the buildings of Berlin are coloured ash-colour, which takes away somewhat from the appearance of the city; on the contrary, at St Petersburg, the edifices are of all colours.
رودخانه که از کنار شهر برلن میگذرد واسمش اسپره است شعبه از آن هم از وسط شهر میگذرد اما کم عرض و آبش هم بسیار بد است	Rudkhāna-yi ki az kanār-i shahr-i Barlin mīguzarad, va ismash *Aspara* ast, shāʿba az un ham az vasat-i shahr mīguzarad, ammā kam ʿarz, va āb-ash ham bisyār bad ast.	The river that flows by Berlin is named the *Spree*: a branch of it runs through the middle of the town; but it is narrow, and its water is also very bad.

امروز ۸۰ فرسنگِ راه را در یازده ساعت طی کردیم	Imrūz hashtād farsang-i rāhra dar yāzdah sāʿat tei kardīm.	To-day we travelled eighty leagues distance in eleven hours.
رفتن به پوتسدام	*Raftan bi Putsdām.*	*Visit to Potsdam.*
روز پنج شنبه پنجم شهر ربیع الثانی امروز رفتیم پوتسدام که خارج برلن است سوار کالسکه شده از همان دروازه و کوچه که روز قبل وارد شدیم خیابانهای زیاد درختهای قوی جنکلی خانهای خوب جلو خانها باغچهای کلکاری بسیار خوب قشنك حوضهای	*Rūz-i panjshamba panjum-i shahr-i Rabīʿ assānī.* Imrūz raftīm Putsdām ki khārij-i Barlin ast, savār-i kālaska shuda, az hamun darvāza va kūcha ki rūz-i qabl vārid shudīm khīābānhā-yi zīād, dirakhthā-yi qavī-yi jangalī, khānahā-yi khūb, jilou-i khānahā bāghchahā-yi gulkārī-yi bisyār khūb-i qashang, houzhā-yi favvāradār gar-	*Thursday the 5th of the month of Rabīʿ assānī.* Today we went to the town of Potsdam, which is outside Berlin. Entering our carriage, we drove along the same track, and through the very gateway that we traversed yesterday, passed by many avenues, noble forest trees, beautiful houses with exquisitely pretty flower-gardens in front of them, and basins of water with fountains

فوارەدار گردش زیاد نمودیم و رفتیم بکار	dish-i zīād namūdīm va raftīm bi gār.	and jets-d'eau, so arriving at the station.
بکالسکه بخار نشسته راندیم نیم ساعت راه طی شده رسیدیم باین شهر	Bi kālaska-yi bukhār nishasta rāndīm. Nīm sāʿat-i rāh tei shuda, rasīdīm bi īn shahr.	We took our seats in the train, started, and after a journey of half an hour, arrived at this town.
شهر کوچکی است چهل و دو هزار نفر جمعیت دارد اغلب نظامی هستند حاکم شهر وغیره آمدند پیاده شدیم رودخانه عظیمی هم دارد که اسمش هاول است	Shahr-i kūchikī-st; chihil u du hazār nafar jamʿīat dārad, aghlab nizāmī hastand. Hākim-i shahr va gheira āmadand. Pīāda shudīm. Rūdkhāna-i ʿazīmī ham dārad, ki ism-ash *Hāval* ast.	It is a small place, with forty-two thousand inhabitants, for the most part regular troops. The Governor of the town came out to receive us. We alighted. There is also a large river here, named the *Havel*.
سوار کالسکه اسپی شده از خانهای شهری و غیره گذشته داخل خیابانها شدیم وضع خیابانها و باغها و غیره شبیه بباغات روسیه	Savār-i kālaska-yi aspī shuda, az khānahā-yi shahrī va gheira guzashta, dākhil-i khīābānhā shudīm. Vazʿ-i khīābānhā va bāghhā va gheira shabīh bi bāghāt-i	We entered a carriage (drawn by horses), and having passed houses and other buildings of the town, we entered an avenue. The parks, avenues, etc. in this place are similar to those in

بود عماراتیکه دارد یکی پتسدام و دیگر سانسوسی است هر دو از بناهای فردریک کبیر است منزل ولیعهد در پتسدام است با کالسکه رفتیم دم عمارت منزل نبودند	Rūsia būd. ʿImāratī ki dārad, yakī *Putsdām* va dīgar *Sānsūsī*-st. Har du az binahā-yi *Fradarīk Kabīr* ast. Manzil-i Valīʿahd dar *Putsdām* ast. Bā kālaska raftīm dam-i ʿimārat. Manzil na būdand.	Russia. Of the two palaces, one is called *Potsdam* and the other *Sans-Souci*; both built by *Frederick the Great*. The residence of the Heir-Apparent is in *Potsdam*. We drove in our carriage to that palace; he was not at home.
راندیم برای گردش از خیابانهای خوب و باغچهای مرغوب گذشتیم باغات اینجا جنگل بزرگیست مثل مازندران	Rāndīm barāyi gardish. Az khiābānhā-yi khūb va bāghchahā-yi marghūb guzashtīm. Bāghāt-i injā jangal-i buzurgī-st misl-i *Māzandarān*.	We then took a drive and passed through magnificent avenues in beautiful parks. The parks here are great forests, like those of *Māzandarān*.
امروز چون روز یکشنبه است کل مردم در گردش و جمعیت زیادی در خیابانها بودند رسیدیم بفوّاره بزرگی که سی	Imrūz chun rūz-i *yakshamba* ast, kull-i mardum dar gardish, va jamʿīat-i ziādī dar khiābānhā būdand. Rasīdīm	To-day being Sunday, (Whit-sunday), all the walking world was out, and the avenues were thronged. We came to a large fountain, the water of which shot

ذرع آب آن میجست	bi favvāra-yi buzurgī, ki sī zarᶜ āb-i un mījast.	thirty ells (105 feet) into the air.
مجسمهای مرمر بسیار خوبِ کارِ قدیم دورِ باغچها و حوضها زیاد بود خلاصه این فوّاره از عجایب دنیا است منبعش را با اسباب بخار تعبیه کرده اند که بزور بخار آب بالا میرود	Mujassamahā-yi marmar-i bisyār khūb-i kār-i qadīm dour-i bāghchahā va houzhā zīād būd. Khulāsa īn favvāra az ᶜajāīb-i dunyā-st. Mambaᶜash-rā bā asbāb-i bukhār taᶜbīa karda and, ki bi zūr-i bukhār āb bālā mīravad.	Statues of marble, very beautiful and antique, were to be seen around the gardens and the basins. In short, this fountain is one of the wonders of the world. Its head is due to steam power, by the force of which the water is raised.
ازدحام مردم قدری مانع از تماشا بود کل یاس شیروانی زیاد بود بلبل و هزار دستان در درختان میخواندند خوش عالمی داشت	Izdihām-i mardum qadrī māni' az tamāshā būd. — Gul-i yās-i Shīrvānī zīād būd. Bulbul va hazārdastān dar dirakhtān mīkhundand. Khush ᶜālamī dāsht.	Through the thronging of the people, we were somewhat impeded in going about. Lilacs abounded. Nightingales and other singing birds sang in the trees. It was delight ful.
بعد رفتیم به خیابان مقابل این فوّاره انتهای این حوض	Baᶜd raftīm bi khīābān-i muqābil-i īn favvāra. Intihā-yi īn houz-i dīgar būd. Fav-	We next went into an avenue opposite that fountain, at the end of which was another

دیگر بود فوّاره آنهم بلند میجست اما نه باین ارتفاع	vāra-yi un ham buland mī-jast, ammā na bi īn irtifā^c.	basin, the jet-d'eau of which was very lofty, but not equal to that of the first.
بعد سوار کالسکه شده رفتیم به عمارت سانسوسی دیدنِ ملکهٔ قدیم یعنی زنِ پادشاهِ سابقِ پروس که برادر امپراطورِ حالیّه بوده است پیشخدمت باشی و ایشیك آقاسی باشی ملکه و غیره جلو آمدند رفتیم به اطاق ملکه بر خاسته تا دم اطاق آمد زنی است مسنّ هفتاد سال بیشتر از عمرش میرود روی صندلی نشستیم	Ba^cd savār-i kālaska shuda raftīm bi ^cimārat-i *Sānsūsī*, dīdan-i Malika-yi qadīm, ya^cnī zan-i pādishāh-i sābiq-i Prūs, ki barādar-i Imparātūr-i hāliyya būda ast. Pīshkhidmat-bāshī va īshīkāghāsībāshī-yi Malika va gheira jilou āmadand. Raftīm bi utāq-i Malika; barkhāsta tā dam-i utāq āmad. zanī-st musinn; haftād sāl bīshtar az ^cumr-ash mīravad. Rū-yi sandalī nishastīm,	We then got into our carriage, and went to the palace of *Sans-Souci* to visit the Queen-Dowager, wife of the former Sovereign of Prussia, who was a brother of the reigning Emperor. The first Lord-in-Waiting and the Chief Usher of the Queen (Dowager) and others received us. We went to the apartment of the Queen (Dowager); she rose and came to the entrance of the apartment. She is a woman seventy years of age, or even more of her life may have elapsed. We sat down on chairs, and con-

صحبت شد بعد بر خاسته کشتیم	suhbat shud. Baᶜd barkhāsta gashtīm.	versation ensued. We then arose and walked about.
این عمارتِ مخصوصِ فردریك کبیر است اطاقی که همانجا مرده است دیده شد صندلی که روی آن فوت شده میز تحریر ساعت مجلسی سایرِ اسبابِ فردریك همه آنجا دیده شد چیزی محض احترام روی صندلی انداخته بودند وعقربك ساعت بعد از فوت در روی هر دقیقه بوده همانطور مانده است که دیگر تا بحال کوك نکرده اند پردهای اشکال بسیار خوب داشت که از همان زمان مانده است	In ᶜimārat-i makhsūs-i *Fradarīk-i Kabīr* ast. Utāqī ki hamunjā murda ast, dīda shud. Sandalī, ki rū-yi un fout shuda, mīz-i tahrīr, saᶜat-i majlisī, sāir-i asbāb-i Fradarīk hama unjā dīda shud. Chīzī mahz-i ihtirām rū-yi sandalī andākhta būdand. va ᶜaqrabak-i saᶜat baᶜd az fout dar rū-yi har daqīqa būda, hamun tour munda ast, ki dīgar tā bi hāl kūk nakarda and. Pardahā yi ashkāl bisyār khūb dāsht ki az hamun zamān munda ast.	This is the special palace of *Frederick the Great*. We saw the very room in which he died. The chair in which he expired, his writingtable, a time-piece, and other effects of Frederick, were all there. They had covered the chair with something as a mark of respect. And the hands of the time-piece have remained since his death in the very same position to a minute, never having been set since then. There were many beautiful paintings, left from that time.
کفتند وقتی که ناپلیون اوّل	Guftand vakhtī ki *Nāpulyūn*	They told me that when the

این شهر را فتح کرده ماهوتِ روی میز فردریک را پاره کرده است همان طور پاره را نگاهداشته اند	*Avval* īn shahrrā fath karda, māhūt-i rū yi mīz-i Fradarīk-rā pāra karda ast; hamun tour pārarā nigāh dāshta and.	first Napoleon took possession of this town, he tore the cloth on the table of Frederick, and that it has ever since been preserved in that state.
اطاقهای خوب داشت از آثار قدیم زیاد بود بعد پائین آمدیم جلو عمارت مهتابی بلندی است در روی تپه باغچهای بسیار خوب و حوضهای کوچک دارد از بلندی مجسمهای خوب قرار داده اند که از دهن آنها آب بحوض میریزد چشم انداز این مهتابی و بلندی در عالم نظیر ندارد وآن فوّارهٔ	Utāqhā-yi khūb dāsht. Az āsār-i qadīm zīād būd. Baʿd pāīn āmadīm. Jilou-i ʿimārat mahtābī-i bulandī-st. Dar rū-yi tapa bāghchahā-yi bisyār khūb va houzhā-yi kūchik dārad. Az bulandī mujassamahā-yi khūb qarār dāda and, ki az dahan-i unhā āb bi houz mīrīzad. Chashm-andāz-i īn mahtābī va bulandī dar ʿālam nazīr nadārad, va un favvāra-yi bu-	There were beautiful rooms, and many relics of antiquity. We then descended. In front of the palace there is a lofty terrace. In front of the eminence there are very beautiful gardens, with small basins of water. From the top they have arranged statues, from the months of which water flows into basins. The view from this terrace and this eminence has not its equal in the world. That lofty jet-

بزرگ محاذی این چشم انداز است	zurg muhāzī-yi īn chashm-andāz ast.	d'eau is opposite to this eminence.
خلاصه فوارها و باغها و خیابانهای خوب زیاد بود قدری گشتیم بعد سوارِ کالسکه شده راندیم در محلی آسیا خرابه دیده شد از عهد فردریک کبیر مانده است وتاریخی دارد معلوم شد وقتی که فردریک خواسته بود آنجارا بسازد هرچه کرده بود آسیارا از صاحبش بخرد که باغ ناقص نباشد راضی نشده بود	Khulāsa favvārahā va bāghhā va khīābānhā-yi khūb-i zīād būd. Qadrī gashtīm, ba^cd savār-i kālaska shuda, rāndīm. Dar mahallī *āsyā*-yi kharāba dīda shud, az ^cahd-i Fradarīk-i Kabīr mānda ast va tārīkhī dārad. Ma^clūm shud, vakhtī ki Fradarīk khāsta būd, ūn jārā bisāzad, har chi karda būd, āsyārā az sāhib-ash bikharad, ki bāgh nāqis na bāshad, rāzī na shuda būd.	In short, the fountains, the parks, and the beautiful avenues were numberless. After walking about for a while, we entered our carriage and drove to a place where we saw a ruined mill, which has remained from the time of Frederick the Great, and has a history. We gathered that when Frederick wished to build this place, he was unable, do what he would, to induce the proprietor of the mill to sell his property, so that the park might not remain incomplete. He would not consent; and
	Bi nishāna-yi ^cadālat īn ās-	

بنشانهٔ عدالت این آسیارا همانطور نگاهداشته اند	yārā hamuntour nigāh dāshta and.	the mill has been preserved in the same condition ever since as an example of justice.
بعد رفتیم بگرمخانه و نارنجستان از آجر وشیشه و غیره ساخته اند اما میانش نرفتیم همه گلها و درختهارا از حالابیرون آورده بودند جلو نارنجستان باغچه و حوض و مهتابی است مجسّمه های مرمر بسیار خوب و باغچهای خیلی قشنگ دارد از اینجا پلهٔ زیادی است	Baʿd raftīm bi garmkhāna va nāranjistān. Az ājur va shīsha va gheira sākhta and, ammā mīān-ash na raftīm; hama gulhā va dirakhthārā az hālā bīrūn āvurda būdand. Jilou-i nāranjistān bāghcha va houz va mahtābī-st. Mujassamahā-yi marmar-i bisyār khūb va bāghchahā-yi kheilī qashang dārad. Az īnjā palla-yi zīādī-	We next went to the hot-houses and orangeries (conservatories), which are constructed with brickwork, glass, and other appliances, but we did not enter them, the whole of the flowers and shrubs having been brought out of doors. In front of the conservatory there is a garden, a basin of water, and a terrace, with statues of marble, which have beautiful parterres of flowers, steps lead down from here, and flower beds are very nicely arranged on successive

levels. Here we walked about a little; and then, entering our carriage, we drove to the palace and summer residence of the wife of *Prince Charles*, a sister of the Queen of Prussia, (i. e. the wife of the *Emperor*), and mother of *Frederick Charles*. It has a pretty courtyard, with statues and ancient stone figures and sculptures, from *Egypt*, *Syria*, *Nineveh*, *Mosul*, etc., such as a leg, a head a shoulder, an arm (or hand), figures of animals and man large or small, imperfect or whole, collected therein of every kind, and fixed to the wall in an artistic manner. It was

---

st, ki martaba bi martaba bꞩgh ast, bisyꞩr khūb sꞩkhta and. Qadrı gashta, baᶜd savꞩr-i kꞩlaska shuda rꞩndım barꞩ-yi ᶜimꞩrat va yeilꞩq-i zan-i *Prins Shārl*, ki khꞩhar-i Malika-yi Prūs, yaᶜnı zan-i *Imparatūr*, va mꞩdar-i *Fradarīk Shārl* ast. Haiyꞩt-i bisyꞩr qashangı dꞩsht. Az ashkꞩl-i sangı va hajjꞩrı-yi qadım-i *Misr* va *Shām* va *Nīnavā* va *Mousil* va gheira, va mujassamahꞩ-yi mukhtalif, misl-i yak pꞩ, yak sar, kitf, dast, shakl-i heivꞩnꞩt va insꞩn, buzurg u kūchik va nꞩqis u tamꞩm-i hama nou'-ı jamᶜ namūda bi dıvꞩrhꞩ bi tarz-i qashangı nꞩsb karda and.

که مرتبه بمرتبه باغ است بسیار خوب ساخته اند قدری گشته بعد سوار کالسکه شده راندیم برای عمارت و ییلاق زن پرنس شارل که خواهر ملکهٔ پروس یعنی زن امپراطور ومادر فردریک شارل است حیاط بسیار قشنگی داشت از اشکال سنگی و حجاری قدیم مصر و شام و نینوا و موصل وغیره و مجسمهای مختلف مثل یکپا یکسر کتف دست شکل حیوانات و انسان بزرگ و کوچک و ناقص و تمام همه نوعی جمع نموده بدیوار ها بطرز قشنگی نصب کرده اند

معلوم بود که پرنس شارل و زنش علم و با سلیقه هستند خلاصه باغچهای خیلی خوب و فواره و چمن وغیره داشت	Maᶜlum bud, ki Prins Sharl va zan-ash ᶜalim va ba salıqa hastand. khulasa baghchaha-yi kheilı khub va favvara va chaman va gheira dasht.	evident that Prince Charles and his wife were persons of learning and taste. In short, most beautiful gardens, fountains, lawns, and the like, were there to be seen.
بالا رفته قدری در اطاق نشستیم زن پرنس شارل خیلی عذر خواهی و اظهار خجالت میکرد از اینکه دیر خبر شده است و میگفت تلگرافی کرده بودند که شما امروز نمیآیید کتابی آورد اسم خودرا در آنجا نوشتیم زن مسنّی است	Bala rafta qadrı dar utaq nishastım. *Zan-i Prins Shārl* kheilı ᶜuzrkhahı va izhar-i khajalat mıkard az ın, ki dır khabar shuda ast, va mıguft: "talagrafı karda budand, ki shuma imruz na mıayıd". Kitabı avurd, ism-i khudra dar unja navishtım. Zan-i musinnı-st.	We went upstairs and sat down a while in a room. The wife of Prince Charles offered many excuses, and expressed great regret that notice (of our visit) had been given to her late, saying: "They telegraphed to inform me that you would not come to-day". She brought out a book, in which we inscribed our name. She is an aged woman.
بعد برخاسته سوار کالسکه	Baᶜd barkhasta savar-i kalaska	On leaving this place, we

شدیم دم منزل زن فردریک شارل هم رفتیم خانه نبود دم در خیابان فردریک شارل دو مجسّمه مرال نر خوابیده بالای معجر بود بسیار خوب ساخته بودند راندیم از جاهای خوب گذشته رسیدیم بیک قصر کوچک بسیار خوش وضعی که مال امپراطور است باغچه های قشنگ و چشم انداز خوبی برودخانه عظیمی داشت	shudım. Dam-i manzil-i *Zan-i Fradarīk Shārl* ham raftım, khāna na būd. Dam-i dar-i khıābān-i Fradarık Shārl du mujassama-yi marāl-i nar-i khābıda bālā-yi maʿjar būd. Bisyār khūb sākhta būdand. Rāndım. Az jāhā-yi khūb guzashta, rasıdım bi yak qasr-i kūchik-i bisyār khushvazʿī, ki māl-i Imparātūr ast. Bāghchahā-yi qashang va chashmandāz-i khūbī bi rūd khāna-yi ʿazīmī dāsht.	drove to the residence of the wife of *Frederick Charles*. She was not at home. In front of the avenue leading to the gate of Frederick Charles, there were two statues of recumbent stags, on the top of the railings, most beautifully executed. We drove on, and passed some charming spots; among others a small pavilion most beautifully situated, which belongs to the Emperor. It has some pretty gardens, and a charming prospect over a large river.
بعد رفتیم بکالسکه بخار نشسته راندیم برای شهر در .	Baʿd raftīm bi kālaska-yi bukhār, nishasta rāndīm barāyi shahr.	We then returned to the city by train. On the route we

بین راه مردم بازی غریبی در آورده بودند چادر پوش قلندری درست کرده و دور چادر را کالسکه و اسب مقوّائی ساخته اطفال مردم سوار آن اسبها و کالسکه شده بودند چادر متّصل بسرعت چرخ میخورد کالسکه ها و اسبها و آدمهاهم دور میزدند خلاصه وارد منزل شدیم	Dar bein-i rāh mardum bāzī-yi gharībī dar āvurda būdand: Chādurpūsh-i qalandarī durust karda va dour-i chādur-rā kālaska va asp-i muqavvāī sākhta, atfāl-i mardum savār-i un asphā va kālaskahā shuda būdand va chādur muttasil bi surʿat charkh mīkhurd. Kālaskahā va asphā va ādamhā ham dour mīzadand. Khulāsa vārid-i manzil shudīm.	remarked a singular pastime which they had devised. The top part of a round tent had been pitched, and around the tent there were pasteboard carriages and horses, on which people's children rode, while the tent revolved with speed, causing the carriages, the horses, and their riders to go round also. Finally we reached home.
باغ وحشِ برلن	*Bāgh-i vahsh-i Barlin.*	*The Zoological Gardens of Berlin.*
روز ششم شهر ربیع الثانی	*Rūz-i shishum-i shahr-i Rabīʿassānī.*	*The 6th of the month Rabīʿassānī.*
بعد از نهار سفرای خارجه آمدند حضور ایلچی فرانسه	Baʿd az nahār sufarā-yi khārija āmadand huzūr. *Ilchī-yi Fa-*	After our breakfast the foreign representatives came to an

audience. The *French repre-*
sentative had not come, be-
cause, *M. Thiers* having re-
signed, he had no credentials.
We then went to another
chamber, and spoke to each
of the representatives, sepa-
rately, enquiring after their
health. Subsequently *Prince*
Bismarck came, and conver-
sed at some length. Next
Marshal Roon, the War Mi-
nister came; and then *Mar-*
shal Moltke, with whom we
conversed a little.

rānsa nayāmada būd; chun
Musyū Tyar istiʿfā karda,
ikhtyārnāma na dāshta ast.
Baʿd raftīm bi utāq-i dīgar.
Sufarārā yak yak aḥvāl-
pursi kardam. Baʿd *Prins Bīz-*
mārk āmad; kheilī bā ū suh-
bat shud. Baʿd *Mārshāl Rūn*,
vazīr-i jang, baʿd *Mārshāl*
Mulk āmada, qadrī suhbat
shud.

نیامده بود چون مسیو طیار
استعفا کرده اختیار نامه نداشته
است بعد رفتیم باطاق دیگر
سفرا را یک بیک احوال پرسی
کردم بعد پرنس بیزمارک آمد
خیلی با او صحبت شد بعد
مارشال رون وزیر جنگ بعد
مارشال ملک آمده قدری
صحبت شد

After this, changing our (state)
costume (for a private one),
we entered our carriage and
drove to the Zoological Gar-
dens. Today also (Whit-Mon-

Barkhāsta, taghyīr-i libās dāda,
savār-i kālaska shuda, raftīm
bi *bāgh-i vahsh*. Imrūz ham
rūz-i ʿīd-i Farangīān būd.
Jamīʿ-yi ahl-i shahr dar ha-

برخاسته تغییر لباس داده سوار
کالسکه شده رفتیم بباغ
وحش امروز هم روز عید
فرنکیان بود جمیع اهل شهر
در حرکت بودند جمعیت

زیاد کالسکه بسیار در راه و طرفین راه بودند موزیکان هم در باغ میزدند دریاچهای زیاد و اقسام مرغهای آبی در دریاچها بود	rakat būdand Jamʿīat-i zīād, kālaska-yi bisyār dar rāh va tarafein-i rāh būd. Mūzīkān ham dar bāgh mīzadand. Daryāchahā-yi zīād va aqsām-i murghhā-yi ābī dar daryāchahā būd.	day) was a festival of the Franks, and the whole population of the city were astir. There was an enormous crowd, and a great many carriages on the road and on both sides of the road. Bands were playing in the gardens. There were many ponds, and various species of aquatic fowl in the ponds.
بعد یکیک قفسهای بزرك خوب دیده شد که هر نوع حیوانی را در قفس علیحده کذاشته بودند انواع مرغهای شکاری از قراقوش و کوندر که مرغ شکاری معروف بزرکیست و از ینکی دنیا میآورند یکجفت از ان بود حیوان غریبی	Baʿd yak yak qafashā-yi buzurg-i khūb dīda shud, ki har nouʿ heivānīrā dar qafas-i ʿalāhidda guzāshta būdand. Anvāʿ-i *murghhā-yi shikārī*, az *qarāqūsh* va *kūndur*, ki murgh-i shikārī-yi maʿrūf-i buzurgī-st va az *Yangī Dunyā* mīāvarand, yak juft az un	Next we looked, one by one, at the beautiful large cages, in which the various kinds of beasts were kept apart. Different *birds of prey*, such as *eagles*, and a pair of *condors*, which are a well-known bird of prey brought from the *New-World* (America).

است رنگ سیاه تیره دارد بسیار مرغ مهیبی است اما چنگالش مثل قراقوش تیز نیست از جنس لاش خور است	būd. Heivān-i gharībī-st. Rang-i sīāh tīra dārad. Bisyār murgh-i muhībī-st, ammā changāl-ash misl-i qarāqūsh tīz nīst. Az jins-i *lāshkhur* ast.	It is a singular creature, of a dusky black colour, and of great ferocity; but its talons are not as sharp as those of the eagle, since it belongs to the class of *carrioneaters*.
دیکر اقسام درناهای افریق و هند و ینکی دنیا و غیره بود خیلی درشت تر و خوشکل تر از درناهای متعارفی ایران انواع طیوریکه در عالم بهم میرسد همه در آنجا موجود بود بنوشتن نمیآید آنچه اشکالی در کتابها دیده بودم در اینجا زنده دیدم	Dīgar aqsām-i *durnāhā-yi Afrīq* va *Hind* va *Yangī Dunyā* va gheira būd, kheilī durushttar va khushgiltar az durnāhā-yi mutaᶜārifī-yi Īrān. Anvāᶜ-i *tuyūrī*, ki dar ᶜālam bi ham mīrasad, hama dar unjā moujūd būd. Bi navishtan na mīāyad. Unchi ashkālī dar kitābhā dīda būdam, dar īnjā zinda dīdam.	There were various kinds of *cranes* from *Africa*, *India*, the *New-World*, and other parts; bigger and more beautiful than the common cranes of Persia. All the different species of birds produced in the whole world are there collected together, so that it is impossible to mention them all. What we had formerly seen portrayed in books, we here saw living.
بعد داخل دالان قفسهای	Baᶜd dākhil-i dālān-i qafashā-	We then entered the corridor

حیوانات درنده شدیم انواع
سباع که بتصور نمیآید بود
شیر یال دار افریق که جز
در کتاب ندیده بودم بسیار
عظیم الجثّه و مهیب یال
سیاه بسیار ضخیم ریخته
سرش بقدرِ سرِ فیل بلکه بزرکتر
چشمهای دریده خیلی مهیب
بدن خوشکل مثل مخمل
شیربان کوشت بلند کرد
بلند میشد کوشت بکیرد
سه چهار ذرع قدش بود

yi *heivānāt-i daranda* shudɪm. Anvaᶜ-i *sabāᶜ*, ki bi tasavvur na mɪɑyad, bud: *shīr-i yāldār-i* Afrɪq, ki juz dar kitɑb na dɪda bɑdam, bisyɑr ᶜazɪm al jussa va muhɪb, yɑl-i sɪɑh-i bisyɑr zakhɪm-i rɪkhta, sar-ash bi qadr-i sar-i fɪl, balki buzurgtar, chasmhɑ-yi darɪda, kheilɪ muhɪb, badan-i khushgil misl-i makhmal. Shɪrbɑn gɑsht buland kard. Buland mɪshud, gɑsht bigɪrad, sih chahɑr zarᶜ qadd-ash bɑd. Gɑshthɑrɑ rɑ-yi

of the *carnivorous quadrupeds*, — the beasts of prey. Here were wild beasts that cannot be imagined, *maned-lions* of Africa, — which I had not hitherto seen, save in books, — huge in bulk, terrible in appearance, with very thick black manes hanging down, their heads as large as those of elephants, or larger; with glaring eyes fearful to look on; with graceful bodies resembling velvet. The keeper held up a piece of flesh; the lion rose on his hind feet and seized the flesh. His stature was from three to four ells ($10^1/_2$ feet to 14 feet). The flesh was placed on

کوشتهارا روی عرابه کذاشته میکشیدند و میدادند	ʿarrāda guzāshta mīkashīdand va mīdādand.	a truck, and so conveyed from den to den and given to the beasts.
محلی که بدالان منظر دارد خانه خانه جای حیوانات است دری دارد از تخته ضخیم که با زنجیر بلند میکنند آن طرف در محلِ کردشِ حیواناتست در را که بلند میکنند حیوان بآن سمت میرود فوراً این در را انداخته اطاق را تمیز میکنند زمین اطاق را باتخته فرش کرده اند بسیار تمیز احدی نمیتواند نزدیك این حیوانات برود کوشت را هم از سوراخ پنجرها میدهند خلاصه مایل بودم	Mahallī, ki bi dālān manzar dārad, khāna khāna jāī heivānāt ast, darī dārad az takhta-yi zakhīm, ki bā zanjīr buland mīkunand. Untaraf-i dar mahall-i gardish-i heivānāt ast. Darrā ki buland mīkunand, heivān bi un samt mīravad; fouran īn darrā andākhta, utāqrā tamīz mīkunand. Zamīn-i utāqrā bā takhta farsh karda and bisyār tamīz. Ahadī na mītavānad nazdīk-i īn heivānāt biravad. Gūshtrā ham az sūrākhi panjarahā mīdihand.	The compartment which looks out on this corridor, and is subdivided to hold the different beasts, has a door of stout timber that can be raised by a chain. The other side of the door is where the animals walk about. When the door is raised, the beast goes to that other side; the door is then quickly lowered, and the den is swept ont. The compartment is very carefully floored with wood. No one is allowed to go near these creatures; and the flesh is given to them through the

مدتی تماشای این شیر را بکنم ولی از هجوم مردم تماشاچی ممکن نبود	Khulāsa māil būdam, muddat-ī tamāsha-yi īn shīrrā bikunam, valī az hujūm-i mardum-i tamāshāchī mumkin na būd.	bars of their cages. I was extremely tempted to stay and observe this lion a long while; but through the thronging of the crowds of spectators, this was impossible.
بعد چند ببر بسیار بزرك دیدم از ببرهای هند و افریق دو پلنك سیاه هم دیده شد از افریق که خیلی غریب و مهیب بودند شیرماده هم بود که چند بچه شیر همانجا زائیده و بچه هایش بزرك شده بودند	Ba^cd chand *babr*-i bisyār buzurg dīdam, az babrhā-yi *Hind* va *Afrīq*, du *palang-i sīāh* ham dīda shud az Afrīq, ki kheilī gharīb u muhīb būdand. Shīr-i māda ham būd, ki chand bacha-shīr hamunjā zāīda, va bachahā-yash buzurg shuda būdand.	I saw several enormous *tigers*, *African* and *Indian*; two *black leopards*, from Africa, very singular and terrific. There was a lioness whose cubs had been born aud bred on the premises.
پلنك زیاد یوز های مختلف کفتارهای عجیب الخلقه افریق که صداهای غریب میکردند	*Palang-i* zīād, *yūzhā*-yi mukhtalif, *kaftārhā*-yi ^cajīb al khilqa-yi Afrīq, ki sadāhā-yi gharīb mīkardand.	There were many *leopards*, various *chetahs*, strange-looking *hyaenas* from Africa that made curious noises

خلاصه قفسهای متعدد دیدیم که در هریك انواع حیوانات بود میمونهای مختلف و غیره دو فیل بود یکی بسیار بزرگ که از هند آورده بودند دیکری از افریقا فیل افریق بسیار تفاوت با فیل هند داشت کوشهایش خیلی بزرکتر و پهن تر بود	Khulāsa qafashā-yi muta^caddid dīdīm, ki dar har yak anvā^c-i heivānāt būd. Meimūnhā-yimukhtalif va gheira. Du *fīl* būd, yakī bisyār buzurg, ki az *Hind* āvurda būdand, dīgarī az *Afrīqā*. *Fīl-i Afrīq* bisyār tafāvut bā *fīl-i Hind* dāsht, gūshhāyash kheilī buzurgtar va pahntar būd.	In short, I saw numerous cages, in each of which were various animals many kinds of monkeys, and the like. There were two *elephants*; one very large, that had been brought from *India*; the other from *Africa*. The *African elephant* differs much from that of *India*, its ears being much broader and larger.
سه ظرّافه بود زبر هم بود که کور اسپ است بدنش خط خط و بسیار مقبول است بیزون بود که کاومیش وحشی افریق و ینکی دنیاست متعدد بودند بزرك و کوچك کاومیش تبت بود از اطرافش آنقدر پشم آویخته بود که	Sih *zarrāfa* būd. *Zabr* ham būd, ki *gūr-i-asp* ast. Badanash khatt khatt va bisyār maqbūl ast. *Bīzūn* būd, ki *gāv-i mīsh-i vahshī-yi Afrīq* va *Yangī Dunyā-st*; muta^caddid būdand buzurg u kūchik. *Gāv-i mīsh-i Tibbat* būd; az atrāf-ash unqadr	There were three *giraffes*, and a *zebra*, i. e., a *wild horse*, the body of which is in stripes, and very beautiful. Also many *bisons*, the *wild buffaloes* of *Africa* and the *New-World*; there were many, large and small; *buffaloes* (yaks?) of *Tibet*, from the sides of which so

که بزمین میکشید بسیار مهیب بود	pashm ᴀvikhta būd, ki bi zamīn mɪkashɪd; bisyar muhɪb būd.	much wool hung as to trail on the ground; they looked very ferocious.
لاما که حیوانی است مابین شتر و کاو و ارقالی و بز کوهی و غیره و بسیار تند میدوید توی باغچهای وسیع بود دورش معجر انواع ارقالی و بزِ کوهی و آهو بود از هند و افریق مثلاً ارقالی دیده شد بقدر اسپ باشاخهای بلند ضخیم تیز که هیچ شباهتی به ارقالیهای ایران نداشت انواع خوك و كراز حیوانات عجیب دیکر هم آنقدر در آنجا بود که بحساب نمی آید هر نوع	*Lāmā*, ki heivᴀnɪ-st mᴀbein-i *shutur*, va *gāv*, va *arqālī*, va *buz-i kūhī*, va gheira va bisyᴀr tund mɪdavɪd, tūyi bᴀghchahᴀ-yi vasɪ[c] būd, dour ash ma[c]jar. Anvᴀ[c]-i *arqālī* va *buz-i kūhī* va *āhū* būd az *Hind* va *Afrīq*, masalan arqᴀlɪ dɪda shud bi qadr-i asp, bᴀ shᴀkhhᴀ-yi buland-i zakhɪm-i tɪz, ki hɪch shabᴀhatɪ bi arqᴀlɪhᴀ-yi Irᴀn na dᴀsht. Anvᴀ[c]-i *khūg* u *gurāz*, heivānāt-i [c]ajɪb-i dɪgar ham unqadr dar un jᴀ būd, ki bi hisᴀb na mɪᴀyad. Har nou[c]-i	*Llamas*, an animal between the *camel*, *ox*, *argali*, *ibex*, and other species, and which runs very fast, were kept in spacious gardens enclosed with railings. There were *argalis*, *ibexes*, and *antelopes*, from *India* and *Africa*; for instance, there was one argali as big as a horse, with long, straight, sharp horns, having no resemblance to the argali of Persia. Also various kinds of *swine* and *wild boars*; curious animals, too, of other species, and in such varieties, were collected in that place

حیوانی که در هر اقلیمی بوده در آنجا جمع نموده اند در کمال نظافت و پاکیزگی خوراك هریك را میدهند	heivānī, ki dar har iqlīmī būda, dar un jā jam^c namūda and, dar kamāl-i nazāfat u pākīzagī khurāk-i har yakrā mīdihand.	as cannot be computed. All sorts of animals, wherever they may naturally exist, have been there brought together, and are there fed with all care and cleanliness.
انواع طوطیها و طاوسها و قراقاولهای طلائی استرالیا که بسیار قشنك بود انواع مرغهای خوش رنك در قفسی بسیار بزرك مشغول پرواز و بازی بودند	Anvā^c-i *tūtīhā* va *tāūs-hā* va *qarāqāūlhā-yi tilāī-yi Ustrālīā*, ki bisyār qashang būd, anvā^c-i *murghhā-yi* khush-rang dar qafas-ī bisyār buzurg mashghūl-i parvāz u bāzī būdand.	Various *parrots*, *peacocks*, *golden pheasants* of *Australia*, that are very pretty, were there; also many kinds of *birds* with magnificent plumage were flying about and disporting in large cages.
خلاصه اسم رئیس این باغ وحش که مرد فاضل عالمی است حکیم بودینوس است	Khulāsa ism-i raīs-i īn *bāgh-i vahsh*, ki mard-i fāzil-i ^cāli-mi-st, *Hakīm Būdīnus* ast.	The name of the director of these *Zoological Gardens* is *Doctor Bodinus*, a learned and distinguished man.

دیدنِ کارخانهٔ کروپ	*Dīdan-i kārkhāna-yi Krūp.*	*A visit to Krupp's works.*
یکساعت بغروب مانده رسیدیم بکار خانه کروپ مسیو کروب خودش سر راه آهن آمده بود شخص پیر بلندقدّ لاغری است تمام این کارخانه هارا خودش ساخته است توپ کل دول را از اینجا میدهد انواع توپها از توپ بزرك قلعه و توپ کشتی و توپ جنك صحرائی همه اینجا ساخته میشود	Yak sāᶜat bi ghurūb munda-rasīdīm bi *kārkhāna-yi Krūp.* *Musyū Krūp* khud-ash sar-i rāh-i āhan āmada būd. Shakhs-i pīr-i bulandqadd-i lāghirī-st. Tamām-i īn kār-khānahā-rā khudash sākhta ast. *Tūp-i* kull-i duvalrā az īnjā mīdihad. ᶜAnvāᶜ-i tūphā az *tūp-i buzurg-i qalᶜa* va *tūp-i kashtī* va *tūp-i jang-i sahrāī* hama īnjā sākhta mī-shavad.	At an hour to sunset we arrived at the *works of M. Krupp*, who came himself to the railway (to meet us). He is a tall, thin old man. He has himself, in a certain space of time, created the whole of these works and from this place he supplies cannon for all governments. Guns of every description, such as large *cannon for forts, cannon for ships*, and *cannon for field use in campaigns*, are all manufactured here.
دستگاه و کارخانهای بخار مثل یک شهر عظیمی است	*Dastgāh* va *kārkhānahā-yi bukhār* misl-i yak shahr-i	His *plant* and steam works resemble a mighty city. He

پانزده هزار عمله دارد که بجهت همه خانه و نشیمن ساخته و مزد و خرج میدهد بعد از وضع مخارج سالی ششصد هزار تومان نقد مداخل خود اوست	azīmī-st. Punzdah hazār ʿamala dārad, ki bi jihat-i hama khāna va nishīman sākhta va muzd u kharj mī-dihad. Baʿd az vazʿ-i *ma-khārij-i salī* shish-sad hazār tūmān naghd *madākhil-i* khud-i ūst.	employs 15,000 workmen, for the whole of whom he has erected houses and lodgings, paying them salaries and wages. After deducting his *expenditure*, his own yearly income amounts to 600,000 tūmāns.
خلاصه به کارخانهٔ چکش بخار رفتیم چکشهای غریبی است مثل کوه با زور بخار بانگارهٔ توپ میخورد بهر ترکیب که بخواهند آنرا درست میکنند وقتیکه چکش به توپ میخورد زمین کارخانه صدا میکرد و میلرزید چیز غریبی است	Khulāsa bi *kārkhāna-yi cha-kush-i bukhār* raftīm. Cha-kushhā-yi gharībī-st, misl-i kūh. Bā *zūr-i bukhār* bi an-gāra-yi tūp mīkhurad. Bi har tarkīb, ki bikhāhand, unrā durust mīkunand. Vakhtī ki chakush bi tūp mīkhurd, za-mīn-i kārkhāna sadā mīkard va mīlarzīd. Chīzī gharībī-st.	We went to the *shop of the steam hammers*. They are wonderful hammers, like mountains; and worked by *steam*, are used for forging cannons. They make these of any pattern they desire. When the hammer strikes the gun, the floor of the workshop groans and trembles. It was a marvellous thing.

همهٔ کارخانه را کشته بعضی توپهای بزرك و کوچکرا انداختند بعد رفتیم بخانه	Hama-yi kărkhānară gashta, ba^czĭ tūphā-yi buzurg va kū-chikră andākhtand, ba^cd raftĭm	We went all over the works, and they turned out some large and some small cannon.
که معین کرده بودند آنجا شام خوردیم شام خوبی دادند درختی در نارنجستان خانه	bi khāna, ki mu^ceyyan karda būdand. Unjă shām khurdĭm. Shăm-i khūbĭ dădand. Di-	We then went to a house which he had prepared, and there we dined. He gave us an excellent dinner. In the
دیده شد که برك آن دو ذرع و نیم طول و نیم ذرع عرض داشت	rakhtĭ dar nāranjistān-i khāna dĭda shud, ki barg-i un du zar^c u nĭm tūl va nĭm zar^c ^carz dăsht.	conservatory of this house we saw a tree, the leaves of which were two ells (seven feet) long, and half an ell (twenty-one inches) wide.
چکش بخار باوجود فاصله زیاد بااین اطاق زمین آنجارا مثل هنگام زلزله بحرکت میاورد	Chakush-i bukhār bă vujūd-i fāsila-yi zĭăd bi ĭn utăq, zamĭn-i ănjără misl-i hangām-i zalzala bi harakat mĭăvurd.	The steam-hammers, in spite of their great distance from this room, made the earth shake here as though there had been an earthquake.
یک توپ تهپر شش پوند بسیار اعلی مسیو کروپ با	Yak *tūp-i tahpur-i shishpound-i* bisyăr a^clā *Musyū Krūp* bă	*M. Krupp* made us a present of a most magnificent *breech-*

تمام اسباب بما پیشکش کرد	tamām-i asbāb bi mā pīsh-kash kard.	*loading six-pounder cannon*, with all its appliances.
بیان رودخانهٔ رن	*Beyān-i rūdkhāna-yi Ran.*	*Description of the Rhine.*
بشهر کوبلنس رسیدیم کالسکه ایستاده حاکم آنجا و غیره بحضور آمدند از قلعه آنجا توپ انداختند شهر بزرگیست	Bi shahr-i *Kūblans* rasīdīm. Kalaska īstāda hākim-i unjā va gheira bi huzūr āmadand. az qalʿa-yi unjā tūp andākhtand. Shahr-i buzurgī-st.	We next reached *Coblentz.* The train stopped; the Governor of the place, with others, came to an audience. The guns of the fortress fired a salute. It is a large place.
از پل رودخانهٔ رن کذشتیم اینجا رود رن کم عرض میشود و طرفین آن کوه است کنار رودخانه همه ده و قصبه و زراعت انکور و درخت کیلاس وغیره بود کیلاسها هم رسیده و پربار بود هرتاك را بیك چوب قطور بسته اند تمام	Az pul-i rūdkhāna-yi *Ran* guzashtīm. Injā rūd-i *Ran* kam ʿarz mīshavad, va tarafein-i un kūh ast. Kanār-i rūdkhāna hama dih va qasaba va zarāʿat-i angūr va dirakht-i gīlās va gheira būd. Gīlāshā ham rasīda va purbār būd. Har tākrā bi yak chūb qutūr	We crossed the *Rhine* river by a bridge, the river being narrow, with hills on either side. The bank of the river is all villages, towns, vineyards cherry-trees, and the like. The cherries were ripe and the trees laden with fruit. Each vine was bound to a

کوه و زمین تاکستان است شراب مشهور رن از همین انگورها عمل میآید	basta and. Tamām-i kūh va zamīn tākistān ast. *Sharāb-i* mashhūr-i *Ran* az hamīn angūrhā ʿamal mīāyad.	stout stake. The whole hill-side and the plain is one continuous vineyard, the famous *Rhein-wein* being produced from these very vines.
طرفین رودخانه راه آهن و متّصل کالسکه بخار در حرکت است راه کالسکه عراده و پیادهرو هم است خیلی پاکیزه و تمیز تمام زمین گلستان است و همه کوهها و صحراها انگور و درخت میوه و باغچهای گلکاری و خیابان و باندك مسافت شهر و قصبه است آدم حیرت میکند و از تماشا سیر نمیشود	Tarafein-i rūdkhāna rāh-i āhan va muttasil kālaska-yi bukhār dar harakat ast. Rāh-i kālaska-yi ʿarrāda va pīādarou ham ast, kheilī pākīza va tamīz. Tamām-i zamīn gulistān ast, va hama kūhhā va sahrāhā angūr va dirakht-i mīva va bāghchahā-yi gulkārī va khīābān, va bi andak masāfat shahr va qasaba ast. Adam heirat mīkunad va az tamāshā sīr na mīshavad.	On either side of the river there is a railway, and trains run continually. There are also roads for carriages, waggons, and pedestrians, well made and kept. The whole region is a garden. All the mountains and plains are grape-vines, fruit-trees, flower-gardens, and avenues; with towns and cities at frequent intervals. One wonders, and is never tired with admiring.
تکتك قصرهای خوب و	Taktak qasrhā-yi khūb va	Every now and then a beauti-

کوشکهای بزرك و کوچك از روی سلیقه با کمال قشنکی در کنار رودخانه و بالای کوهها که مشرف برودخانه است ساخته اند مثل بهشت

بعضی آثار قلعه خرابهای قدیم در کوهها و کنار رودخانه دیده شد تردد کالسکه های بخار و عمارات و سبزها و

کلهای طبیعی و مصنوعی آدم را واله میکرد تا چند فرسنك راه شبیه بود باول ورود خاك

کیلان و رودخانهٔ سفید رود

kūshkhā-yi buzurg u kūchik az rū-yi salīqa bā kamāl-i qashangī dar kanār-i rūdkhāna va bālā-yi kūhhā, ki mushrif bi rūdkhāna ast, sākhta and, misl-i bihisht. Baʿzī āsār-i qalʿa, kharābahā-yi qadīm dar kūhhā va kanār-i rūdkhāna dīda shud. Taraddud-i kālaskahā-yi bukhār va ʿimārāt va sabzahā va gulhā-yi tabīʿī va masnūʿī ādamrā vālih mīkard; tā chand farsang rāh shabīh būd bi avval-i vurūd-i khāk-i Gīlān va rūdkhāna-yi Safīd-rūd.

ful solitary pavilion, with large and small summer-houses, in the best taste and of the most graceful forms, are seen erected on the hills overlooking the stream, like a paradise. We also noticed some ruins of old castles on the mountains and on the river bank. Tho passing of the trains, the buildings, the verdure and flowers, both natural or artificial, put one beside one's self. For several leagues our road was (through a country) similar to that seen on first arriving in the land of Gīlān and by the river Safīd-rūd.

بعضی اوقات راه کالسکهٔ ما از روی پشت بامِ خانها و کوچهای دهات میگذشت خلاصه بتعریف نمی آید	Baʿzī ouqāt rāh-i kālaska-yi mā az rū-yi pusht-i bām-i khānahā va kūchahā-yi dihāt mīguzasht. khulāsa bi taʿrīf na mīāyad.	Sometimes our trains passed over the tops of the roofs of houses in streets of villages. In short, it was indescribable.
سرحد آلمان و بلجیک	*Sarhadd-i Almān u Baljīk.*	*The frontier of Germany and Belgium.*
قدری که رفتیم برود خانه کوچکی رسیدیم پل کوچکی هم داشت سر حدّ بلجیک و آلمان گویا همین رود خانه است اما خداوند عالم قادر طوایف و ممالک را چگونه از هم سوا کرده که عقل حیران است در آنِ واحد یکباره آدم زبان مذهب وضع خاک آب کوه زمین تغییر کرد که هیچ	Qadrī ki raftīm bi rūdkhāna-yi kūchikī rasīdīm. Pul-i kūchikī ham dāsht. *Sarhadd-i Baljīk* va *Almān* gūyā hamīn rūdkhāna ast. Ammā khudāvand-i ʿĀlam-i Qādir tavāif u mamālikrā chigūna az ham sivā karda, ki ʿaql heirān ast! Dar ān-i vāhid yakbāra ādam, zabān, mazhab, vazʿ, khāk, āb, kūh, zamīn taghyīr kard, ki hīch shabāhatī bi	We went on, and shortly reached a small stream with a little bridge over it, which appears to form the *frontier* between *Germany* and *Belgium.* But what a difference has the All-Wise and Almighty Creator placed between the two nations and the two countries! Man's mind is lost in amazement thereat. In one moment a total change came

شباهتی به آلمان نداشت کوهها قدری بلند تر و پر جنگل هوا سردتر زبان همه فرانسه مردمانش فقیرتر وضع و لباس قشون و مخلوق بالمره تغییر کرد و جمیع اهل بلجیك زبان فرانسه حرف میزنند زبانی هم خودشان علیحده دارند مذهبشان اغلب کاتولیك است

Almān na dāsht. kūhhā qadrī bulandtar va pur jangal, havā sardtar, zabān hama farānsa, mardumān-ash faqīrtar, vaz[c] u libās-i qushūn va makhlūq bil-marra taghyīr kard; va jamī[c]-i ahl-i Baljīk zabān-i farānsa harf mīzanand. Zabānī ham khud-i-shān [c]alāhidda dārand. Mazhab-i-shān aghlab kātūlīk ast.

over the people, the language, the religion, the appearance of the land and water, mountains, and plains; — all were different, nothing here resembling what is in Germany. The hills are somewhat higher and more wooded, the air is colder, all speak French, the people are somewhat poorer, the style and costume of soldier and civilian utterly different. The whole population of Belgium speak French, though they have a special dialect of their own; they are chiefly of the Catholic religion.

در وضع آلمان	*Dar vaz^c-i Almān.*	*Remarks about Germany.*
در آلمان زنها خیلی مشغول کار و زحمت هستند بخصوص در امر زراعت و باغبانی خیلی بیشتر از مردمانشان کار میکنند	Dar Almān zanhā kheilī mashghūl-i kār u zahmat hastand; bi khusūs dar amr-i zarā^cat va bāghbāni kheilī bīshtar az mardumān-i shān kār mī-kunand.	In Germany the women are very hard-working; especially at agriculture and in gardening they do much more than their husbands.
گوش اسپهای کالسکه و غیره را در آلمان با ماهوت قرمز وغیره میپوشانند که از مگس محفوظ باشد	Gūsh-i asphā-yi kālaska va gheirarā dar Almān bā māhūt-i qirmiz va gheira mī-pūshānand, ki az magas mahfūz bāshad.	The ears of the carriage-horses, and others, are covered over with red and other coloured cloths, as a protection against the flies.
در برلن و سایر شهرها اطفال کوچك کولهبار سربازی بدوش بسته توی کوچها میدوند و شیپور میزنند که از طفولیت	Dar *Barlin* va sāir-i shahrhā atfāl-i kūchik kūlabār-i sarbāzī bi dūsh basta tūyi kūchahā mīdavand va sheipūr mīzanand, ki az tufūliyat	In *Berlin*, and in other towns, the little boys fasten soldiers' knapsacks on to their backs, run about the streets, and play on fifes. So that they thus, from infancy

آنهارا عادت بلشکری میدهند	unhārā ᶜādat bi lashgarī mī-dihand.	upwards, learn to be soldiers.
سنك فرش کوچهارا بسیار خوب میکنند سنکهارا مربع کوچك بریده کار میکذارند خیلی خوب بهم وصل میکنند	*Sangfarsh-i kūchahārā* bisyār khūb mīkunand. Sanghārā murabbaᶜ, kūchik burīda, kār mīguzārand, kheilī khūb bi ham vasl mīkunand.	They *pave their streets* with stone most artistically. They use stones cut into small squares, and join them together very closely.
آجرهای فرنکستان مثل آجرهای ایران مربّع و بزرك نیست بلکه ترکیب آجر تراش طهران است	*Ajurhā-yi Firangistān* misl-i ājurhā-yi Irān murabbaᶜ va buzurg nīst; balki tarkīb-i ājur-i tarāsh-i *Tahrān* ast.	*The bricks of Firangistān* are not like those of Persia, large and square, but are of the shape of the cut bricks of *Tehrān*.
در وضع بلچیك	*Dar vazᶜ-i Baljīk.*	*Remarks about Belgium.*
مملکت بلچیك بسیار آزاد و رتق و فتق امورات با مجلس پارلمنت است که وکلا آنجا	Mamlikat-i Baljīk bisyār āzād, va ratq u fatq-i umūrāt bā *majlis-i Pārlamant* ast, ki vukalā unjā jamᶜ shuda hukm	The kingdom of Belgium is very free, the ordering of all matters being in the hands of the Parliament, where the

جمع شده حکم میکنند مجلس پارلمنت عمارتی عالی و در شهر است حال هم باز بود وکلا جمع بودند	mīkunand. Majlis-i Pārlamant ʿimārat-i ʿālī va dar shahr ast. Hāl ham bāz būd. Vukalā jamʿ būdand.	Deputies meet together and make laws. The Parliament House is a sumptuous edifice, and is in the city. It was in active session (when we arrived), the members being assembled.
روزنامه نویسانِ این ولایت بسیار آزاد هستند هرچه بنویسند از هیچکس باك ندارند	*Ruznāmanavīsān*-i īn vilāyat bisyār āzād hastand. Har chi binavīsand, az hīch kas bāk na dārand.	The editors of the news-papers in this country are extremely free. Whatever they may write, they are in fear of no one.
جمعیّت بروکسل قریب یکصد و هفتاد و دو هزار نفر است جمعیت کل ده کرور کسری است مالیات قریب سی و هفت	Jamʿīat-i Brūksal qarīb-i yaksad u haftād u du hazār nafar ast. Jamʿīat-i kull dah kurūr-kasrī-st; mālīāt qarīb-i sī u haft kurūr; qushūn dar	The population of Brussels is of about a hundred and seventy two thousand souls; that of all Belgium, ten crores and a fraction (five millions). Its income is about thirty-seven crores, its army

کرور قشون در وقت جنك صد هزار نفر	vakht-i jang sad hazār nafar.	in time of war, one hundred thousand.
سابقًا تمام این مملکت تابع هولاند بوده است چهل و دو سال قبل از این دولتین انکلیس و فرانسه و غیره جمع شده از آن دولت موضوع کرده به لیوپولد اوّل که داعی پادشاه انکلیس بوده داده اورا پادشاه کردند	Sābiqan tamām-i īn mamlikat tābi'-i Hūlānd būda ast. Chihil u du sāl qabl az īn, doulatein-i Inglīs va Farānsa va gheira jam^c shuda, az un doulat mouzū^c karda, bi *Līūpūld*-i *Avval*, ki dā^cī-yi pādishāh-i Inglīs būda, dāda, ūrā pādishāh kardand.	Formerly, the whole of this country was subject to Holland, but forty-two years ago, the kingdoms of England and France, with others, combined and separated it from that State, giving it to *Leopold I*, the maternal uncle of the Sovereign of England, and making him King.
سفر از بلژیک بانکلیس	*Safar az Baljīk bi Inglīs.*	*Journey from Belgium to England.*
صبح زود باکسالتِ بیخوابیِ شب برخاسته بتعجیل رخت پوشیدم بسیار سرد بود اهلِ	Subh-i zūd bā kasālat-i bī-khābī-yi shab barkhāsta bi ta^cjīl rakht pūshīdam. Bisyār sard būd. ahl-i shahr ham	In the morning we arose earlier than usual, thoroughly worn out with a sleepless night, and hastily dressed.

شهر هم هنوز خواب بودند یکفوج با موزیکان آمده پای عمارت صف کشیدند سواره هم بود پادشاه آمدند بکالسکه نشته از کوچها و خیابانها گذشته رسیدیم بکار همان کالسکه های پریروزی حاضر بود فوج سرباز با موزیکان وغیره بودند با پادشاه وداع کرده بکالسکه نشسته راندیم	hanūz khāb būdand. Yak fouj bā mūzīkān āmada, pāyi ʿimārat saff kashīdand; savāra ham būd. Pādishāh āmadand. bi kālaska nishasta, az kūchahā va khīābānhā guzashta, rasīdīm bi gār. Hamān kālaskahā-yi parīrūzī hāzir būd. Fouj-i sarbāz bā mūzīkān va gheira būdand. bā pādishāh vidāʿ karda bi kālaska nishasta rāndīm.	It was very cold. The inhabitants of the city were still asleep. A battalion of infantry, with their band, arrived and were drawn up in front of the palace. There were also some cavalry. The King came. We took our seats in a carriage, drove through streets and avenues, and arrived at the railway station. The same train was there in readiness which we had used two days previously. A battalion of infantry, with band, was drawn up; others were also there. We said adieu to the King, took our seat and left.
از مملکت فلاندر عبور شد	Az mamlikat-i Flāndar ʿubūr	We traversed the Flemish pro-

همه جا جلکه آبادی سبزه چمن باغ و گل است اینجا بزبان فلمنکی که هولاند باشد حرف میزنند خلاصه رسیدیم به بندر اوستاند تجارتگاه معتبری است کشتیهای زیاد بود شهر آبادی است از بروکسل تا اینجا سه ساعت کمتر راه بود کالسکه بخار امروز خیلی تند میرفت	shud. Hama jā julga, ābādī, sabza, chaman, bāgh u gul ast. Injā bi zabān-i Flamangī, ki Hulānd bāshad, harf mīzanand. khulāsa rasīdīm bi bandar-i *Ustānd.* tijāratgāh-i muʿtabarī-st. kashtīhā-yi zīād bud, shahr-i ābādī-st. Az *Brūksal* tā injā si sāʿat kamtar rāh bud. kālaska-yi bukhār imrūz kheilī tund mīraft.	vinces, where all was a flat plain, populous, green, grassy, full of gardens and flowers. In these parts the people speak Flemish; i. e., Dutch. We at length arrived at the sea-port town of *Ostend* — an important commercial town, where we found many ships. It is a flourishing place. We performed the distance from *Brussels* in less than three hours, as the train travelled at great speed today.
مأمورین بلژیك مرخّص شده حاکم و کار گذاران اوستان به حضور آمده نطق زیادی کردند بعد پیاده شده از اسکله داخل کشتی اعلیحضرت	Maʿmūrīn-i Baljīk murakhkhas shuda, hākim va kārguzārān-i Ustān bi huzūr āmada nutq-i zīādī kardand. Baʿd pīāda shuda az askala dākhil-i kashtī-yi *aʿlāhazrat-i pādi-*	The Belgian officials took their leave, and the Governor, with the functionaries of Ostend had an audience. They delivered very long speeches. We then alighted and passed from the

پادشاه انکلیس شدیم که موسوم به ویژیلانت است لارنسون صاحب وانکلیسهائی که همراه ما بودند معرفی و راهنمائی میکردند	*shāh-i Inglīs* shudīm, ki mousūm bi *"Vigilant"* ast. *Lāransūn sāhib* va Inglīsīhāī-ki hamrāh-i mā būdand, muᶜarrafī va rāhnamāyī mī-kardand.	wharf on board the ship of *Her Most Exalted Majesty the Sovereign of England*, which was named the *"Vigilant"*. *Mr Rawlinson* and the Englishmen who accompanied-us led the way and performed the presentations.
امیرال معتبر کشتی های انکلیس که موسوم بماک‌کلنتوك است و بسیاحت جزایر قطب شمالی چنندین دفعه رفته و مرد معروفی است استقبال آمده در کشتی بود صاحجنصبان دیکر بحری هم زیاد بودند	*Amīrāl*-i muᶜtabar-i kashtīhā-yi Inglīs, ki mousūm bi *"M' Clintock"* ast, bi sīāhat-i jazāyir-i qutb-i shamālī chandīn dafᶜa rafta va mard-i maᶜrūfī-st. Istiqbāl āmada dar kashtī būd. Sāhibmansa-bān-i dīgar-i bahrī ham zīād būdand.	The distinguished *Admiral* of the English ships who is named *M'Clintock*, has several times gone on Voyages to the islands of the North Pole, and enjoys a great reputation. He had come to meet us and was in the ship. There were also a great number of naval officers besides.
رفتیم باطاق مخصوص خودمان نشستیم کشتی بسیار تندرو	Raftīm bi utāq-i makhsūs-i khud-i-mān, nishastīm. Kash-	We went to the cabin specially designated for our use, and

خوبی است صدر اعظم با
عملهجات و بعضی دیگر در
کشتی ما وشاهزادگان و
سایرین در دو کشتی دیگر که
مثل همین کشتی بود بودند
خیلی منتظر شدیم تا بارها را
آوردند و همراهان جابجا
شدند من بواسطهٔ کسالت
باطاق پائین رفته قدری
استراحت کرده بعد آمدم بالا
روی میز ما میوهای خوب
بود هلوی بسیار اعلی انگور
سفید و سیاهِ بسیار معطّرِ
خوب میوهٔ موز که چیز
بسیار خوبی است خربزه
کوچک هم بود بسیار شیرین
این میوهارا کلاّ در گرمخانه

ti-yi bisyār tundrou-i khūbī-st. *Sadr aʿzam* bā ʿamalajāt va baʿzī dīgar dar kashtī-yi mā va shāhzādagān va sāirīn dar du kashtī-yi dīgar, ki misl-i hamīn kashtī būd, būdand. Kheilī muntazir shudīm tā bārhārā āvurdand va hamrāhān jā-bi-jā shudand. Man bi vāsita-yi kasālat bi utāq-i pāīn rafta, qadrī istirāhat karda, baʿd āmadam bālā Rūyi mīz-i mā mīvahā-yi khūb būd: hulū-yi bisyār aʿlā, angūr-i safīd u sīāh-i bisyār muʿattar-i khūb, mīva-yi mouz, ki chīz-i bisyār khūbī-st. Kharbuza-yi kūchik ham būd, bisyār shīrīn. In mīvahārā kullan dar garm-

there seated ourselves. The ship is very handsome and of great speed. *The Grand-Vizīr*, with our personal attendants, and a few others, were in our ship, the princes, and the remainder, were in two other vessels similar to her. We waited a considerable time for the baggage to be brought, and our travelling companions to take their places. On account of my drowsiness, I myself went below and took a little repose; after which I went up again. On the table I found some fine fruit, — excellent peaches, white and black grapes of exquisite aroma, some banana fruits, —

عمل میآورند و قیمتِ آنها بسیار کران است مثلًا یکخوشهٔ انکور را بدو هزار دینار میدهند وقس علی هذا	khāna ᶜamal mɪᴀvarand va qɪmat-i unhᴀ bisyᴀr girᴀn ast, masalan: yak khūsha-yi angūr rᴀ bi du hazᴀr dɪnᴀr mɪdahand, va qiss ᶜalᴀ hᴀzā.	which are very nice. There was also a small melon, — very sweet. These fruits are all raised in hothouses, and the price of them is very high. For instance, they sell a single bunch of grapes for two thousand (Persian mites (about twenty pence English); from whence the rest may be inferred.
خلاصه راندیم نهاری خوردیم همراهان را نهار خوبی داده بودند	khulᴀsa rāndɪm, nahᴀrɪ khurdɪm. hamrᴀhᴀnrā nahᴀr-i khūbɪ dᴀda būdand.	Well, we sailed on, and we had our luncheon. They gave our suite au excellent meal.
از بندر اوستاند الی دوور که اوّل خاك انکلیس است پنجساعت راه است و این دریای مانش به طوفان و .	Az bandar-i *Ustānd* ilᴀ *Dūvar*, ki avval i khᴀk-i Inglɪs ast, panj sᴀᶜat rᴀh ast va ɪn *Daryā-yi Mānsh* bi tūfᴀn va mouj-i zɪād maᶜrūf ast, ammā, al	From the port of *Ostend* to *Dover*, — the first place on the coast of England, — it takes five hours to cross; and the sea of the *British Çhan-*

موج زیاد معروف است امّا
الحمد للّه تعالی دریا بسیار آرام
مثلِ کفِ دست بود احوال
احدی برهم نخورد مثلِ سیاحتِ
روی رودخانه بود از عقبِ
سرِ ما سه کشتی بردیف
میآمد دو کشتی بزرگِ جنگیِ
زره پوش هم یکی دست راست
ما دیگری دست چپ برای
احترام میآمدند گاهی توپ
میانداختند قدری که رفتیم
کشتی دیگری آمد که دو برج
و در هر برجی دو توپ
داشت برجرا بهر طرف که
میخواستند میگرداندند این

hamdu l'Illāhi. taᶜālā, daryā bisyār ārām misl-i kaf-i dast būd. Ahvāl-i ahadī bar ham na khurd, misl-i siāhat-i rū-yi rūdkhāna būd. Az ᶜaqab-i sar-i mā si kashtī bi radīf mīāmad. Du kashtī-yi buzurg-i jangī-yi zarapūsh, ham yakī dast-i rāst-i mā, dīgarī dast-i chap barāyi ihtirām mīāmadand, gāhī tūp mīandākhtand. qadrī ki raftīm, kashtī-yi dīgarī āmad, ki du burj va dar har burjī du tūp dāsht. Burj-rā bi har taraf ki mīkhāstand mīgardāndand. In

nel is much noted for its storms and roughness. But, thanks be to God Most High, — the sea was very calm like the palm of one's hand, so that no one was incommoded. It was like a trip on a river. Behind us followed three ship, while two large ironclad ships of war accompanied us, to show us honour, the one to our right, the other to our left. Occasionnally they fired guns. When we had advanced a certain distance, there appeared another ship, with two turrets, and each turret with two guns; which turrets they

کشتی هم آهن پوش است کفتند زورِ پنج هزار اسپ دارد دیوارهٔ کشتی هم چندان از دریا بلند تر نبود میکفتند کلولهٔ توپهای این کشتی کشتیهای دیکر را خورد میکند دو سه تیر از توپهای آن انداختند بسیار صدا میکرد	kashtī ham āhanpūsh ast. Guftand zūr-i panj hazār asp dārad. Dīvāra-yi kashtī ham chandān az daryā bulandtar na-būd. Mīguftand gulūla-yi tūphā-yi īn kashtī kashtīhā-yi dīgar rā khurd mīkunad. Du si tīr az tūp-hā-yi ān andākhtand, bisyār sadā mīkard.	can turn round in any direction they choose. This ship also is covered with iron, and, as they said, has a steam power of five thousand horses. The ship's sides were not high out of the water. They informed me that the projectiles from her guns would smash to pieces the other ships. They fired two or three rounds from her guns, which made much noise.
کشتیهای تجارتی و غیره بسیار آمد و رفت میکردند تا نزدیك شدیم بسواحل انکلیس کوه های کنار دریا پیدا شد کشتی جنکی زیادی باستقبال آمد همه توپ انداختند روی	Kashtīhā-yi tijāratī va gheira bisyār āmad u raft mīkardand, tā nazdīk shudīm bi savāhil-i Inglīs. Kūhhā-yi kanār-i daryā peidā shud. Kashtī-yi jangī-yi ziādī bi	Many merchant ships came and went, as well as others. At length, as we neared the English coasts, the hills on the sea-shore became visible, and a large number of men-

دریا از کشتی وقایق و کشتیهای بخار بزرک که بزرکان و نجبای انکلیس در آنها نشته بتماشا آمده بودند پر بود کوههای سواحل چندان بلند نیست و سنکش سفید رنک مثل معدنِ کچ است	istiqbāl āmad. Hama tūp andākhtand. Rū-yi daryā az kashtī va qāyiq va kashtīhā-yi bukhār-i buzurg, ki buzurgān va nujabā-yi Inglīs dar unhā nishasta bi tamāshā āmada būdand, pur būd. Kūhhā-yi savāhil chandān buland nīst va sang-ash safīdrang misl-i ma'dan-i gach ast.	of-war hove in sight, coming to meet us. They all fired guns. The surface of the sea was covered with ships, and boats, and large steamers, in which the magnates and nobles of the English had seated themselves, and were come forth to witness the spectacle. The hills on the coast are not very high: their stones are white, like quarries of lime.
خلاصه کشتی رسید به بندر دوور سکوی سنکی طولانی ساخته اند تا کشتی در بندر از موج و طوفان محفوظ باشد خیلی توی دریا آمده است بالای آن زن و مرد و خانمها و	Khulāsa kashtī rasīd bi bandar-i *Dūvar*. Sakkū-yi sangī-yi tūlānī sākhta and, tā kashtī dar bandar az mouj u tūfān mahfūz bāshad, kheilī tū-yi daryā āmada ast. Bālā-yi ān zan u mard va khānumhā va	Our ship now reached the port of *Dover*, where they have constructed a long stone pier, so that the ships in the harbour may be safe from storms and the waves. It projects a great distance into the sea.

نجبا و افواج و سوارِ بسیار
بودند اینجا ایستادیم پسرهای اعلیحضرت پادشاه انکلستان با وزیر دول خارجه لورد کرانویل و اعیان و اشراف لندن همه
آمده بودند پسر وسطی پادشاه دوك ادمبورك و پسر سیمی پرنس ارتور در کشتی ایستادیم پسرهای پادشاه وزیر
خارجه ایشیك آقاسی باشی پادشاه که مردی معتبر و هم پیشخدمت باشی است توی
کشتی آمدند رفتیم توی اطاق نشسته صحبت کردیم تا

nujabā va afvāj va savār-i bisyār būdand. Injā īstādīm. Pisarhā-yi aʿlāhazrat-i *pādishāh-i Inglistān* bā vazīr-i duval-i khārija *Lord Granville* va aʿyān va ashrāf-i *Landan* hama āmada būdand. Pisar-i vasatī-yi pādishāh *Duke Edinburgh* va pisar-i siyumī *Prince Arthur.* Dar kashtī īstādīm. pisarhā-yi pādishāh, vazīr-i khārija, ishik āghāsī bāshī-yi pādishāh, ki mardī muʿtabar va ham pīshkhidmat bāshī-st, tū-yi kashtī āmadand. Raftīm tū-yi utāq, nishasta suhbat

Upon it were women and men, ladies and nobles, infantry and cavalry, in great numbers. Here we stopped. The sons of her Majesty the *Queen of England*, with the Secretary for Foreign Affairs, *Lord Granville*, and the notables and authorities of *London*, had all arrived, — the second son of the Sovereign, the *Duke of Edinburgh*, — and the third son, *Prince Arthur.* We stood up in the ship; the Sovereign's sons, the Foreign Secretary, and the Chief Usher of the Sovereign, — a man of consideration and official in waiting, came. We went

بارهارا از کشتی بردند بیرون پسر دومی ملکه جوان بسیار خوشروی با بنیهٔ است چشمهای زاغ و قدری ریش دارد قدّش چندان بلند نیست سنّش باید بیست و هفت هشت سال باشد پسر سیّمی که از او کوچکتر است قدری رویش باریکتر و جثّهاش کمتر است ایشیك آقاسی باشی اسمش لورد سیدنی مرد پیری قوی بنیهٔ است	kardɪm, tᴀ bᴀrhᴀrᴀ az kashtɪ burdand bɪrᴜn. Pisar-i duyumɪ-yi malika javᴀn-i bisyᴀr khushrᴜ-yi bᴀ-bunyaɪ-st, chashmhᴀ-yi zᴀgh va qadrɪ rɪsh dᴀrad. qadd-ash chandᴀn buland nɪst. Sinn-ash bᴀyad bɪst u haft, hasht sᴀl bᴀshad. Pisar-i siyumɪ, ki az ᴜ kᴜchik-tar ast, qadrɪ rᴜ-y-ash bᴀrɪk-tar va jussa-y-ash kamtar ast. Ishɪk ᴀghᴀsɪ bāshɪ, ism-ash *Lord Sidney*, mard-i pɪrɪ, qavɪbunyaɪ-st.	into the cabin, sat down, and conversed until the baggage was carried out of the ship. The Queen's second son is a youth with a very pleasing countenance, and stout. He has crow's eyes (bluish grey) and a small beard, in stature he is not tall; his age must be twenty-seven or twenty-eight. The third son is shorter than he, and his complexion is darker, his body slighter. The Chief Usher (Lord Chamberlain) is named *Lord Sydney*. He is a robust old man.
خلاصه برخاسته از اسکله بالا رفتیم ازدحام و جمعیت غریبی بود سوار کالسکه بخار شدیم من و پسرهای پادشاه و صد	Khulāsa barkhᴀsta az askala bᴀlᴀ raftɪm. Izdihᴀm va jamʿɪat-i gharɪbɪ bᴜd. Savᴀr-i kᴀlaska-yi bukhᴀr shudɪm.	At length we rose and went up on the jetty, where there was a wonderful assembly. We took our seat in a railway

اعظم و وزیر خارجهٔ انگلیس و
پیشخدمت باشی در یک
کالسکه نشستیم بسیار کالسکه
های خوب بود هیچ جا چنین
واگونها دیده نشده بود آهسته
چند قدمی رفتیم بعمارتیکه
غذا حاضر کرده بودند پیاده
شدیم من رفتم به اطاق
کوچکی حکیم الممالک که
چندی بود اینجا بود دیده
شد بعد گفتند حاکم شهر
دوور نطقی حاضر کرده است
باید بخواند رفتم بتالاری
بالای پلهٔ بلندی ایستاده هٔ

Man u pisarhā-yi Pādishāh va sadr aʿzam va vazīr-i khārija-yi Inglīs va pīshkhid-mat bāshī dar yak kālaska nishastīm. Bisyār kālaskahā-yi khūbī būd, hīch chunīn vāgunhā dīda na-shuda būd. Āhista chand qadamī raftīm bi ʿimāratī-ki ghazā hāzir karda būdand. Pīāda shudīm. Man raftam bi utāq-i kūchikī Hakīm al-Mamālik, ki chandī būd injā būd, dīda shud baʿd guftand *hākim*-i shahr-i *Dūvar* nutqī hāzir karda ast, bāyad bikhānad. Raftīm bi tālārī bālā-yi pilla-yi bulandī

carriage, — I, the Sovereign's sons, the Grand Vazīr, the Foreign Secretary, and the Principal Official in Waiting, being together in one compartment. They were exceeding beautiful carriages; none such had hitherto been seen. We gently went forward a few feet; and, at a building where they had prepared food, we alighted. I went into a small room. The Hakīm al Mamālik, who had been here some time, was admitted. They then told me the *Governor* of the town of *Dover* had prepared a speech which he must recite. I went into a

شاهزادها و اعیان انکلیس شاهزادها و سایر نوکرهای ما بودند حاکم نطقی را مفصّلا خواند بسیار تعریف و تمجید از ما بود ما هم جواب دادیم لارنسون بانکلیسی بیان کرد مردم دست میزدند بعد برکشته رفتیم سرِ نهار همراهان همه بودند غذای کرمِ پخته و میوه و غیره آوردند خوردیم بعد برخاسته باز با همان اشخاص در کالسکه بخار نشته راندیم همه جا از بغل

istāda. Hama shāhzādahā va a^cyān-i Inglīs, shāhzādahā va sāir-i noukarhā-yi mā būdand. Hākim nutqī-rā mufassalan khānd; bisyār ta^crīf u tamjīd az mā būd. Mā ham javāb dādīm. *Lāransūn* bi inglīsī beiān kard; mardum dast mīzadand. Ba^cd bargashta raftīm sar-i nahār. Hamrāhān hama būdand. Ghazā-yi garm-i pukhta va mīva va gheira āvurdand, khurdīm. Ba^cd barkhāsta bāz bā hamān ashkhās dar kālaska-yi bukhār nishasta rāndīm. Hama jā

hall and stood at the top of a high flight of steps, the whole of the English princes and notables, our princes and others, with our servants, being present, and the Governor (Mayor) recited his speech at great length, in which there was much praise and laudation of us. We replied, and *Rawlinson* explained in English. The people clapped (their) hands. Returning from thence, we went to breakfast, accompanied by all the princes. They served hot cooked food, fruit, and other things, of which we partook. Then arising, we returned to our train, and

took our seat in a railway-carriage with the same personage. We started. Everywhere we passed over the bosoms of mountains and across valleys, traversing numerous tunnels, of which two were about a quarter of a league in length, very dark and suffocating.	az baghal-i kūh va darra mī-raftīm. az tūnalhā-yi muta^{c}ad-did guzashtīm, ki du tā-yi az ānhā bi qadr-i rub^{c}-i far-sang va bisyār tārīk va khafa būd.	كوه و درّه ميرفتيم از تونلهاى متعدّد كذشتيم كه دوتاى از آنها بقدر ربع فرسنك و بسيار تاريك و خفه بود
The country in England has no resemblance to that in other territories. It has much forest, large trees, population without interval, and enormous cultivation. The wealth of the English is famous throughout the world, there is no need to describe it (here).	Zamīn-i Inglīs hīch shabāhatī bi sāir-i zamīnhā nadārad. Jangal-i zīād dārad: Di-rakhthā-yi qavī, ābādī-yi muttasil, zarā^{c}at-i zīād. Ta-mavvul-i Inglīshā ma^{c}rūf-i dunyā-st zarūr bi navishtan nīst.	زمين انكليس هيچ شباهتى بساير زمينها ندارد جنكل زياد دارد درختهاى قوى آبادى متّصل زراعت زياد تمول انكليسها معروف دنياست ضرور بنوشتن نيست

از نزدیک قصبه و آبادی شیسلهورست کذشتیم که مقر ناپلیون سوم بوده هم آنجا فوت شده است قبرش هم آنجا ست کالسکهٔ بخار بطوری تند میرفت که امکان نداشت کسی جائی را ببیند از بس تند میرفت از عرّادها آتش درآمد یک کالسکه سوخت کم مانده بود که همه بسوزد کالسکه ها را نکاه داشته آمدند پائین خاموش کردند درست شد دو باره براه افتادیم تا رسیدیم باول شهر لندن	Az nazdīk-i qasaba va ābādī-yi *Chiselhurst* guzashtīm, ki maqarr-i Nāpulyūn-i Siyum būda. Ham ānjā fout shuda ast. Qabr-ash ham ānjā-st. Kālaska-yi bukhār bi tourī tund mīraft, ki imkān na-dāsht kasī jāī-rā bibīnad. Az bas tund mīraft, az ʿarrāda-hā ātash dar āmad. Yak kālaska sūkht. Kam munda būd ki hama bisūzad. Kālaskahā-rā nigāh dāshta āmadand pāīn, khāmūsh kardand, du-rust shud. Du bāra bi rāh uftādīm tā rasīdīm bi avval-i shahr-i *Landan*.	We passed by the town and outlying districts of *Chiselhurst*, the abode of Napoleon III, and where he died. His tomb is also there. The train travelled at so furious a rate that it was impossible for one to distinguish any place. From the rapidity of our motion, fire came out of the wheels, and one carriage caught fire. It wanted but little for all to be burnt. They stopped the train, got down, and extinguished the fire. All was right, and again we went on until we reached the beginning of the city of *London*.
دیکر آبادی و جمعیت و	dīgar ābādī va jamʿīat va	Again it is impossible to des-

بزرگی شهر و کثرت راه آهن که علی الاتّصال کالسکه از هر طرف عبور و مرور میکند و از دود کارخانها وغیره نمی توان شرح داد ما از روی پشت بام ها میراندیم	buzurgī-yi shahr va kasrat rāh-i āhan, ki ʿala 'l ittiṣāl kālaska az har ṭaraf ʿubūr u murūr mīkunad va az dūd-i kārkhānahā va gheira namītavān sharh dād. mā az rū-yi pusht-i bāmhā mīrāndīm.	cribe the prosperity, the populousness, the extent of the city, the numbers of lines of railway over which incessantly the trains come and go in every direction, the smoke of the manufactories, and the like. We travelled over the exteriors of the roofs of the houses. | Thus we reached the station and stopped.
خلاصه رسیدیم بکار ایستادیم تماشاچی و جمعیّتی زیاده از حدّ نظام انکلیس سواره زره پوش خاصّه نوّاب ولیعهد	Khulāsa rasīdīm bi gār, īstādīm. tamāshāchī va jamʿīatī zīāda az hadd, niẓām-i Inglīs, savāra-yi zarapūsh-i khāṣṣa, navvāb-i *Valīʿahd-i Inglīs* maʿrūf bi "*Prince*	There was an assemblage of spectators, and a crowd, beyond all limits; there were the armour-wearing English household cavalry; there was the Nawwāb the *Heir-Apparent of* England, known as

انکلیس معروف بـه پـرنس دوکال همهٔ وزرا و اعیان واشراف حـاضر بـودنـد پیاده شده من و ولیعهد و صـدر اعظم و لردمورلی مـهـمـانـدار بکالسکه روبازی نشسته راندیم	*de Galles*", hama-yi *vuzarā* va a^cyān va ashrāf hāzir būdand. Pīāda shuda man va Vali^cahd va Sadr a^czam va Lord Morley, mihmāndār bi kālaska-yi rūbāzī nishasta rāndīm.	the *Prince of Wales*; and the whole of the *Ministry*, of the notables, and of the nobles, were present. We alighted. I, the Heir-Apparent, the Grand-Vazīr, and *Lord Morley*, — the Lord-in-Waiting upon us, took our seats in an open carriage, and drove off.
طـرفین راه و بامها و بالاخـانها مملوّ از زن و مـرد وبـچه بود بسیار اظهار خوشحالی میکردند هورا میکشیدند دستمال تکان میدادند دست میـزدنـد خلاصه معرکهٔ غریبی بود من متّصل بـا سر و دست تعارف	Tarafein-i rāh va bāmhā va bālākhānahā mamlū az zan u mard u bacha būd. Bisyār izhār-i khushhālī mīkardand, hūrā mīkashīdand, dastmāl takān mīdādand, dast mīzadand. Khulāsa ma^crika-yi gharībī būd. Man muttasil bā sar va dast ta^cāruf mīkar-	Both sides of the road, the roofs, the upper stories of the houses, were fall of women, men, and children, who exhibited much joy and pleasure by shouting hurrahs, by waving handkerchiefs, by clapping hands. It was a surprising turmoil. I saluted incessantly with head and hands.

میکردم جمعیت تماشاچی انتها
نداشت جمعیت این شهر را
متجاوز از هشت کرور نفس
میکفتند زنهای بسیار خوشکل
دارد نجابت و بزرکی و وقار
و تمکین از روی زن و مرد
میریزد معلومست که ملّت
بزرکی است و مخصوصًا
خداوند عالم قدرت و توانائی
و عقل و هوش و تربیّت
بانها داده است این است
که مملکتی مثل هندوستانرا
مسخّر کرده و در ینکی دنیا
و سایر جاهای عالم هم
متصرّفات معتبره دارند

dam. Jamʿīat-i tamāshāchī intihā na-dāsht. Jamʿīat-i īn shahr-rā mutajāviz az hasht kurūr nafas mīguftand. Zanhā-yi bisyār khushgil dārad. Najābat va buzurgī va vaqār va tamkīn az rū-yi zan u mard mīrīzad; maʿlūm ast ki millat-i buzurgī-st va makhsūsan Khudāvand-i ʿālam qudrat va tavānāī va ʿaql va hūsh va tarbīyat bi ānhā dāda ast. Īn ast, ki mamlikatī misl-i *Hindūstān*-rā musakhkhar karda va dar *Yangī Dunyā* va sāir-i jāhā-yi ʿalam ham mutasarrifāt-i muʿtabara dārand.

The crowd of spectators was never-ending. The population of the city is said to be over eight crores (four millions) of souls. It has most lovely women. The nobleness, the greatness, the gravity and sedateness of the women and men shine out from their countenance. One sees and comprehends that they are a great people, and that the Lord of the Universe has bestowed upon them power and might, sense and wisdom, and enlightenment. Thus it is that they have conquered a country like *India*, and hold important possessions in *America* and elsewhere.

رفتن بقصرِ ویندزور

روز بیست و چهارم ربیع الثانی باید برویم به قصرِ ویندزور که مقرّ اعلیحضرتِ ویکتوریا پادشاه انکلیس است با کالسکهٔ بخار یکساعت مسافت است خلاصه رخت پوشیده باصدر اعظم ولارد مورلی سوار کالسکه شده رفتیم جمعیتِ زیاده از حدّ سرِ راه و طرفین راه ایستاده بودند آنقدر کالسکه بود که حساب نداشت از خیابان هایدپارك و شهر کذشته رسیدیم بکار سوارِ کالسکهٔ

Raftan bi qasr-i Windsor.

Rūz-i bīst u chahārum-i Rabīʿ as sānī. Bāyad biravīm bi *qasr-i Windsor*, ki maqarr-i *Aʿlāhazrat-i Victoria*, Pādishāh-i Inglīs ast. Bā kālaska-yi bukhār yak sāʿat masāfat ast. Khulāsa rakht pūshīda bā *Sadr Aʿzam* va *Lord Morley* savār-i kālaska shuda raftīm. Jamʿīat-i zīāda az hadd sar-i rāh va tarafein-i rāh īstāda būdand. Anqadr kālaska būd, ki hisāb nadāsht. Az khīābān-i *Hydepark* va shahr guzashta rasīdīm bi gār. Savār-i kālaska-yi bu-

Visit to Windsor Castle.

24th Rabīʿ as sānī. — We have to go to *Windsor Castle*, the residence of *Her Majesty Victoria*, Sovereign of England, which is one hour's journey by rail. So we dressed, and then taking our seat in the carriage with the *Grand-Vazīr* and *Lord Morley*, started. Crowds beyond limit were standing at the ends and on both sides of our road. There were that number of carriages that no one could count them. Passing along the drive in *Hyde Park*, and through the town, we reached the station, and took

بخار شدیم کالسکه های بسیار اعلی و طرفینِ کالسکه یکپارچه از بلور بود از جاهای آباد و صحرا و چمن گذشتیم تا قصر ویندزور از دور پیدا شد مثل قلعه چهار برجی بنظر میآید نزدیك رسیده پیاده شده سوارِ کالسکهٔ اسپی شدیم جمیع ملتزمین ما هم بودند پای پلّهٔ قصر پیاده شدیم اعلیحضرت پادشاه تا پای پلّه استقبال کردند پائین آمده دست ایشانرا گرفته بازو داده رفتیم بالا از اطاقها و دالانهای قشنك که پردهای

khār shudīm. Kālaskahā-yi bisyār aʿlā va tarafein-i kālaska yak pārcha az bulūr būd. Az jāhā-yi ābād va sahrā va chaman guzashtīm, tā *Qasr-i Windsor* az dūr peidā shud. Misl-i qalʿa-yi chahār burjī bi nazar mīāyad. Nazdīk rasīda, pīāda shuda, savār-i kālaska-yi aspī shudīm. Jamīʿ-i multazimīn-i mā ham būdand. Pā-yi pilla-yi qasr pīāda shudīm. Aʿlāhazrat-i Pādishāh tā pā-yi pilla istiqbāl kardand. Pāīn āmada dast-i īshānrā giriftā, bāzū dāda, raftīm bālā. Az utāqhā va dālānhā-yi qashang, ki

our seat in the train. The carriages were most sumptuous; each side being a single sheet of plate glass. We traversed well cultivated places, fields, and green meadows; and at length *Windsor Castle* rose to view at a distance, appearing like a fortress with four turrets. Arriving near thereto, we alighted and got into a carriage. All our suite were of the party. At the foot of the steps of the Castle we alighted. Her Majesty the Sovereign advanced to meet us at the foot of the staircase. We got down, took her hand, gave our arm, went up stairs,

اشکالِ خوب داشت گذشته داخل اطاقِ مخصوص شده روی صندلی نشستیم	pardahā-yi ashkāl-i khūb dāsht, guzashta, dākhil-i utāq-i makhsūs shuda, rū-yi sandalī nishastīm.	passed through pretty rooms and corridors hung with beautiful portraits, and entering a private apartment, took our seat.
پادشاه اولاد و متعلقان و خدّام خودشان‌را معرّفی کردند ما هم شاهزادها و صدر اعظم و غیره را معرّفی کردیم لارد شامیرلاند که وزیر دربار پادشاهی است نشان ژارتیر مکلّل بالماس را که بزانوبند معروف است و از نشانهای بسیار معتبر انگلیس است برای ما آورد پادشاه برخاسته بدست خودشان نشان را بما	Pādishāh oulād va mutaᶜalliqān va khuddām-i khud-i shān-rā muᶜarrafī kardand. Mā ham shāhzādahā va Sadr Aᶜzam va gheira-rā muᶜarrafī kardīm. *Lord Shāmīrlānd*, ki vazīr-i darbār-i pādishāhī-st, *nishān-i* "*jarretière*" i mukallal bi almās-rā, ki bi zānūband maᶜrūf ast, va az nishānhā-yi bisyār muᶜtabar-i Inglīs ast, barāyi mā āvurd. Pādishāh barkhāsta bi dast-i khud-i shān nishān-rā bi mā zadand	The Sovereign presented her children, relations, and officers. We, too, on our part, presented our princes, the Grand-Vazīr, and the others. The *Lord Chamberlain*, who is the Minister of the Court of the Sovereign, brought for us the *Insignia of the Order of the Garter* set in diamonds; i. e., the knee-tie, which is one of the most esteemed English Orders. The Sovereign rose, and with her own hand decorated us with the Order

زدند و حمایلش را انداختند جوراب بند بلندرا هم دادند	va hamāyil-ash-rā andākhtand; jurābband-i buland-rā ham dādand.	and cast the ribbon upon us, presenting us at the same time with a long stocking-tie.
خلاصه نشان‌را باحترامِ تمام گرفته نشستیم منهم نشان و حمایل آفتاب مکلّل به الماس را با نشان تصویر خود بپادشاه انگلیس دادم ایشان هم با کمال احترام قبول کرده بخود زدند	Khulāsa nishānrā bi ihtirām-i tamām girifta nishastīm. Man ham nishān u hamāyil-i *āftāb*, mukallal bi almās rā, bā nishān-i tasvīr-i khud bi Pādishāh-i Inglīs dādam. Ishān ham bā kamāl-i ihtirām qabūl karda bi khud zadand.	I received the Order with the utmost respect, and sat down. I too presented to the English Sovereign the Order of the *Sun*, set in diamonds, and also the Order of my own Portrait, which she received with all honour and put them on herself.
بعد برخاسته سرِ میز رفتیم سه دخترِ پادشاه و یك پسرِ کوچکی که هنوز از پیشِ ایشان جائی نمیرود و اسمش لیوپولد است نشسته بودند این پسر امروز الی کار باستقبال آمده	Baʿd barkhāsta sar-i mīz raftīm. Si dukhtar-i Pādishāh va yak pisar-i kūchikī, ki hanūz az pīsh-i īshān jāī na-mīravad va ism-ash *Leopold* ast, nishasta būdand. In pisar imrūz ilā gār bi istiqbāl āmada būd.	We then rose and went to table. Three daughters of the Sovereign and one young son, who does not yet go anywhere away from her, and whose name is *Leopold*, were already seated. This son to-day had come to the sta-

بود بسیار جوانِ خوشکلی است لباس اکوسی پوشیده بود وضع لباس اکوسی این است که زانوها الی ران مکشوف است	Bisyār javān-i khushgilī-st. Libās-i *Akūsī* pūshīda būd. Vaz^c-i libās-i *Akūsī* īn ast, ki zānūhā ilā rān makshūf ast.	tion to meet me. He is a very good looking young man. He wore the *Scotch* costume. The peculiarity of the *Scotch* costume is this: the knees are left visible up to the thighs.
یك دختر شانزده سالهٔ پادشاه هم همیشه در خانهٔ ایشان است هنوز شوهر ندارد دو دخترِ دیگرِ شان شوهر دارند شاهزادهگان و صدر اعظم و لارد گرانویل و غیره بودند نهارِ خوبی خورده شد میوهای خوب سرِ نهار بود	Yak dukhtar-i shānzdah sāla-yi pādishāh ham hamīsha dar khāna-yi īshān ast, hanūz shouhar na-dārad. Du dukhtar-i dīgar-i shān shouhar dārand. Shāhzādagān va *Sadr A^czam* va *Lord Granville* va gheira būdand. Nahār-i khūbī khurda shud; mīvahā-yi khūb sar-i nahār būd.	One of the Sovereign's daughters, sixteen years of age, is always at home with her, and has not a husband as yet. Her other two daughters have husbands. The princes, the *Grand-Vazīr*, *Lord Granville*, and others, were present. A beautiful breakfast was eaten. There were some fine fruits at the breakfast.
بعد پادشاه دست مارا گرفته	Ba^cd Pādishāh dast-i mārā girifta, bi utāq-i rāhatgāh	The Sovereign again took my hand and led me to a pri-

باطاق راحتکاه برده خودشان رفتند	burda, khud-i shān raftand.	vate apartment, she herself going away.
		The English Fire-Brigade.
امروز قبل از دیدن وزراء و غیره تلمبه چیان انکلیس آمده در باغ جلو عمارت مشق کردند نردبانها کذاشته بخیال اینکه عمارت مرتبه بالا آتش کرفته است بچابکی و جلدی تمام از نردبان بالا رفته مردم سوخته و نیم سوخته و سالم بعضی را بدوش کشیده پائین آوردند بعضی دیکررا طناب بکمرشان بسته بزمین	Imrūz, qabl az dīdan-i vuzarāʿ va gheira, *tulumbachīān-i Inglīs* āmada dar bāgh, jilou-i ʿimārat mashq kardand. Nardubānhā guzāshta bi kheiyāl-i īn, ki ʿimārat martaba-yi bālā ātash girifta ast, bi chābukī va jaldī-yi tamām az nardubān bālā rafta, mardum-i sūkhta va nīmsūkhta va sālim, baʿzīrā bi dūsh kashīda, pāīn āvurdand, baʿzī-yi dīgarrā, tanāb bi kamar-i-	To-day, before seeing the Ministers and others, the *English Fire-Brigade* came, and in the garden in front of our palace went through their exercise. They planted ladders, with the supposition that the upper floor of the palace was on fire; they mounted these ladders with perfect celerity and agility, and brought down people who were burnt, half-burnt, or unharmed, some taken up on their shoulders, and others

فرود آورنند	shān basta, bi zamīn furūd āvurdand.	let down by ropes made fast round their waists.
برای استخلاص مردم اختراع خوبی کرده اند امّا تعجّب در این است که از یکطرف این نوع اختراعات و اهتمامات برای استخلاص انسان از مرك میکنند از طرف دیکر در قورخانهای ولویچ انکلیس و کروپ آلمان اختراعات تازه از توپ و تفنك و کلوله و غیره برای زود تر و بیشتر کشتن جنس انسان میکنند و هر کس اختراعش بهتر و	Barāyi *istikhlās-i mardum* ikhtirāʿ-i khūbī karda and, ammā taʿajjub dar īn ast, ki az yak taraf īn nouʿ-i ikhtirāʿāt va ihtimāmāt barāyi *istikhlās-i insān az marg* mīkunand, az taraf-i dīgar dar qūrkhānahā-yi *Vūlvīch-i Inglīs* va *Krūp-i Almān*, ikhtirāʿāt-i tāza az tūp va tufang va gulūla va gheira barāyi *zūdtar u bīshtar kushtan-i jins-i insān* mīkunand; va har kas ikhtirāʿ-ash bihtar va zūdtar talaf mīkunad,	They have invented a beautiful means of *saving men.* But, the wonder is in this, that on the one hand, they take such trouble and originate such appliances for the salvation of man from death, when, on the other hand, in the armouries, arsenals, and workshops of *Woolwich* in *England*, and of *Krupp* in *Germany*, they contrive fresh engines, such as cannons, muskets, projectiles, and similar things, for the *quicker and more multitudinous slaughter of the human race.* He whose invention destroys

زودتر انسان‌را تلف میکند افتخارها مینماید و نشانها میگیرد	iftikhārhā mīnamāyad va nishānhā mīgīrad.	man more surely and expeditionsly prides himself thereon, and obtains decorations of honour.
از کتابِ روزنامهٔ سفر همایونی بمازندران	*Az kitāb-i rūznāma-yi safar-i humāyūnī bi Māzandarān.*	*From the diary of the royal journey to Māzandarān.*
جمعهٔ هفتم رمضان از پول بکجور باید رفت از اردو بفاصلهٔ قلیلی بقریهٔ پول رسیدیم امامزادهٔ ایست در پول موسوم بامامزاده علی بالای کوه مشرف بقریه درخت جنکلی زیاد بود میکفتند امامزاده نظر کرده است هرکس از شاخهای آنها	Jumᶜa-yi haftum-i Ramazān az *Pūl* bi *Kujūr* bāyad raft. Az urdū bi fāsila-yi qalīlī bi qarīa-yi Pūl rasīdīm. *Imāmzādaī*-st dar Pūl, mousūm bi *Imāmzāda yi ᶜAlī.* Bālā-yi kūh, mushrif bi qarīa dirakht-i jangalī-yi zīād būd. Mīguftand Imāmzāda nazar karda ast, har kas az shākhhā-yi	On Friday the 7th of the month of Ramazan we must ride from *Pūl* to *Kujūr*. From the camp, after a short distance, we reached the village of Pūl. There is an "*Imāmzāda*" 1) in Pūl, named "*Imāmzāda-yi Alī*". At the summit of the mountain, near the village, were many forest-trees. They said that the Imāmzāda had

1) "Imamzada" means a persian Saint, or his tomb.

قطع کند یقینا خواهد مرد از آن جهت است که اهل ولایت این اشجار را قطع نمیکنند	unhā qat^c kunad, yaqīnan khāhad murd. Az un jihat ast, ki ahl-i vilāyat īn ashjārrā qat^c na mīkunand.	ordained, that whosoever cut off a branch of these trees, would surely die. For this reason the people in these parts do not fell these trees.
از گردنه لاشك گذشته صحرای لاشك پیدا شد از عجایب اینکه چند سال قبل که اینجا آمده بودیم صحرای لاشك خشك بود دو سال است دریاچهٔ در وسط جلگهٔ لاشك پیدا شده وآب زیادی جمع شده دور دریاچه نزدیك یك فرسخ است اطراف آن نی زیاد روئیده انواع مرغابی دارد	Az gardana-yi *Lāshk* sahrā-yi *Lāshk* peidā shud. Az ^cajāib īn, ki chand sāl qabl, ki īnjā āmada būdīm, sahrā-yi *Lāshk* khushk būd. Du sāl ast, daryāchaī dar vasat-i julga-yi *Lāshk* peidā shuda va āb-i zīādī jam^c shuda. Dour-i daryācha nazdīk-i yak farsakh ast. Atrāf-i un nei-yi zīād rūīda, va anvā^c-i murghābī dārad, va āb bi	After crossing the pass of *Lāshk* the plain of Lāshk was seen. It is a wonder that, when we came here some years ago, the plain of Lāshk was dry. Two years ago a lake formed itself in the middle of the valley of Lāshk and a great quantity of water collected there. The circumference of the lake is of almost one farsakh. All round the lake many reeds and rushes have sprung up, and all kinds of water-fowl are there. The

و آب بجزئی نسیمی متموّج میشود	juzʿɪ-yi nasɪmɪ mutamavvaj mɪshavad.	water becomes wavy at the slightest blowing of the zephyr.
حقیقةً خیلی عجیب است هر کس چیزی میگوید بعضی میگویند سیل آمد و اینجا دریاچه شد	Haqɪqatan kheilɪ ʿajɪb ast. Har kas chɪzɪ mɪgᴜyad: Baʿzɪ mɪgᴜyand seil ᴀmad va ɪnjᴀ daryᴀcha shud.	Truly it is very wonderful. Every one says something: Some say that a flood came and that the lake was (thus) formed.
بعضی میگویند برف زیاد آمد و آب شد و این دریاچه تشکیل یافت بهر تقدیر حالا دریاچه خیلی بزرگی است و عجب تر اینکه همین زمینها که آب گرفته دریاچه شده است چندین سال بود که مابین اهالی کجور در مالکیّت	Baʿzɪ mɪgᴜyand barf-i zɪᴀd ᴀmad va ᴀb shud, va ɪn daryᴀcha tashkɪl yaft. Bi har taqdɪr hᴀlᴀ daryᴀcha-i kheilɪ buzurgɪ-st, va ʿajɪbtar ɪn, ki hamɪn zamɪnahᴀ, ki ᴀb girifta daryᴀcha shuda ast, chandɪn sᴀl bᴜd ki mᴀbein-i ahᴀlɪ-yi Kujᴜr dar mᴀlikɪyat-	Others say that a great quantity of snow fell and turned to water and so the lake found its origin. In any case it is now a very big lake. It is especially wonderful, that just about the possession of this same piece of ground, which the water has covered and turned into a lake, the inhabitants of Kujᴜr quarrelled several years ago and appea-

آن منازعه بود که عرض بدیوانخانهٔ عدلیّه کرده بودند حالا که این اراضی را آب گرفته دریاچه شده است قطع نزاع گردیده	i un munāzaʿa būd, ki ʿarz bi dīvānkhāna-yi ʿadlīya karda būdand. Hālā, ki īn arāzīrā āb girifta, daryācha shuda ast, qatʿ-i nizāʿ gardīda.	led to the High Court of Judgment. Now that the water has taken possession of this ground and has turned it into a lake, the law-suit has come to an end.

APPENDIX.

Some of the titles most used in speaking.

1. *How to address the Shāh.*

اعلیحضرت همایونی	aᶜlāhazrat-i humāyūni.	Your most gracious Majesty.
قبلهٔ عالم	qibla-yi ᶜālam.	Pole of the World.
بلی قربان شوم	bálī, qurbān shavam!	Yes, may I be your sacrifice! [1]

2. *The Sons of the Shāh.*

حضرت والا	hazrat-i vālā.	Your Royal Highness.

3. *Other Royal Princes.*

نواب والا	navvāb-i vālā.	Your Highness.
سرکار والا	sarkār-i vālā.	

4. *Princesses.*

نواب عالیّه	navvāb-i ᶜālīa.	Royal Highness.

1) Used only by the Shah's subjects.

شاهزاده خانم	shāzda (for *shāhzāda*) khānum.	Princess.
امیرزاده خانم	amīrzāda khānum.	

5. *The Grandvizier.*

حضرت اجلّ	hazrat-i ajall.	Your Highness.
آقای صدر اعظم	aghā-yi Sadr a^czam.	Prince Minister.

6. *All Viziers (State-Ministers) and Mullahs (Divine Ministers).*

جناب عالی	janāb-i ^cālī.	Your Excellency.

7. *Seyids (descendants of the Prophet Muhammed)* [1]).

آقا	Aghā.

8. *Governors (unless they have a higher personal title, as that of Prince).*

خان حاکم	khān-i hākim.
آقای بیگلربیگی	āghā-yi baglarbagī.

1) The Seyids are easily recognized by their green belts and green or dark blue turbans.

9. *All ladies and gentlemen whatever rank they may hold.*

سرکار	sarkār.	Madam, Sir.

10. *Women.*

خانم	khānum.	addressing a lady.
باجی	bājī.	addressing an inferior.

Measures of Length.

انگشت	angusht.	a finger's breadth.
وجب	vajab.	a span.
ذراع	zirā^c.	a cubit.
ذرع	zar^c.	a yard.
میدان اسپ	meidān-i asp.	the length of a horse's gallop.
فرسخ فرسنگ	farsakh or farsang.	a parasang (about 6,2 kilometres or $3\frac{3}{4}$ English miles).

Weights.

جو گندم	jou or gandum.	a barley-corn or a wheat-corn (0,048 g).

نخود	4 gandum = 1 nukhud.	a small chick pea (0,192 g. or $\frac{1}{144}$ of an ounce).
مثقال	24 nukhud = 1 miskāl.	(4,6 g. or nearly $\frac{1}{6}$ ounce).
سیر	16 miskāl = 1 sīr.	(73,6 g.).
چارك	10 sīr = 1 chārak.	a quarter of a man.
من	4 chārak = 1 man.	(2,44 kg. or $7\frac{1}{4}$ lbs.).
خروار	100 man = 1 kharvār.	(donkey load, 244,40 kg. or 725 lbs.).

Money.

قران یک هزار	qarān or yak hazār.	a kran (silver coin) or 1000 dinars (an obsolete infinitesimal coin) has
شاهی	shāhī.	20 shāhī. (copper).
تومان	tūmān.	10 krans make one *tumān* (at present worth about 4 sh.)
پول سفید	pūl-i safīd.	silver coin (white money).
پول سیاه	pūl-i sīāh.	copper coin (black money).
صد دینار	sannār (for sad dīnār, see p. 6).	(a hundred dinars) a two shahī copper coin.

دو هزاری	du hazārī.	(2000 dinars) a two kran piece.

Gold coins are very rare. A tumān is generally paid in 5 two krān pieces.

The following terms are used, like the English "guinea" for values not represented by amy actual coins.

عباسی	ʿabbāsī.	4 shahis.
پناهاباد	panāhābād.	10 "
چهار عباسی	chahār abbāsī.	depreciated krans worth only 16 shahis instead of 20.
ریال	rīāl.	1 kran 5 shahis.

Banknotes and foreign money.

اسکناس	askinās.	banknote.
برات	barāt.	cheque.
لیره	līra.	£
امپریال	impariāl.	Russian imperial.
منات	manāt.	Rouble.

ENGLISH-PERSIAN VOCABULARY.

A.

abandon	ترک کردن	tark kardan
abreviated	مختصر	mukhtasar
abreviation	اختصار	ikhtisār
abdication	استعفا	isti'fā
abdomen	شکم	shikam
abhorrence	نفرت	nifrat
ability	قابلیت	qābilīat
abject	خوار, زلیل	khār, zalīl
abjectness	خواری, زلالت	khārī, zalālat
able	زرنگ	zarang
ablution	وضو	vuzū
abode	منزل, مکان	manzil, makān
— (plur.)	منازل, اماکن	manāzil, amākin
abolish	موقوف کردن	mouqūf kardan
about, around	دور, گرد	dour, gird
— nearly	تقریباً	taqrīban
— concerning	در خصوص	dar khusūs
above	بالا	bālā
above mentioned	مذکور	mazkūr
	مزبور	mazbūr

abridged	مختصر	mukhtasar
abroad	خارج	khārij
abscess	دنبل	dumbal
abscence	غیبت	gheibat
absent	غایب	ghāib
absolute	مطلق	mutlaq
abstinence	پرهیز	parhīz
absurd	بی خود	bī-khud
to abuse (bad language)	فحش دادن	fuhsh dādan
— ill usage	بد رفتاری	bad raftārī
acacia	اقاقیا	aqāqiā
academy	دار الفنون	dār ul funūn
accept	قبول کردن	qabūl kardan
accident	اتفاق	ittifāq
accidentally	اتفاقاً	ittifāqan
accompany	همراه رفتن	hamrāh raftan
according to	موافق	muvāfiq-i
accordingly	بنابر این	binā bar īn
accountant	محاسب	muhāsib
accountbook	دفتر	daftar
accounts	حساب	hisāb
accredited (dipl.)	مقیم	muqīm
accuracy	دقت	diqqat
accurate	دقیق	daqīq
accusation	ادّعا	iddiʿā
accustom (oneself)	عادت کرفتن	ʿādat giriftan
accustomed	آموخته	āmūkhta
ache	درد	dard

acid	ترش	tursh
acquaintance	آشنای	āshnāī
acquire	حاصل کردن	hāsil kardan
acquit	رها کردن	rihā kardan
acrobat	بازیگر	bāzī gar
act	کار, فعل plur: افعال	kār, fiʿl plur: afʿāl
— (of a play)	پرده	parda
to act	کردن (کن)	kardan (kun)
— (in a play)	بازی در آوردن	bāzī dar āvurdan
actor	مقلّد	muqallid
adapt	منسوب کردن	mansūb kardan
add (figures)	جمع زدن	jamʿ zadan
addition	اضافه	izāfa
— (in arithmetic)	جمع	jamʿ
address (of a letter)	عنوان	ʿinvān
adieu	وداع	vidāʿ
adjective	اسم صفت	ism-i sifat
adjutant	آجودان	ājūdān
administration	اداره	idāra
admiral	امیر البحر	amīr ul bahr
	دریا بیگی	daryā bagī
admire	حظّ کردن	hazz kardan
admission	دخول	dukhūl
adopt	تبنی کردن	tabannī k.
adore	پرستیدن	parastīdan
adult	بالغ	bāligh
adulterated	مخلوط	makhlūt
adultery	زنا	zinā

advance (to)	پیش رفتن	pīsh raftan
advancement	ترقی	taraqqī
advantage	فایده	fāida
plur:	فواید	favāyid
advantageous	مفید	mufīd
adventure	واقعه	vāqiʿa
	plur: وقایع	vaqāiʿ
advertise	اعلان کردن	iʿlān kardan
advice	نصیحت	nasīhat
	plur: نصایح	nasāyih
advocate	وکیل	vakīl
affair	کار	kār
afflicted	پریشان	parīshān
afraid	ترسان	tarsān
afresh	از سرِ نو	az sar-i nou
after	بعد از	baʿd az
afternoon	عصر	ʿasr
afterwards	بعد از آن	baʿd az ān
again	باز ,دیگر	bāz, dīgar
against	بر ضدّ	bar zidd-i
age	عمر	ʿumr
agent	گماشته	gumāshta
agio	صرف	sarf
agreement	قرار	qarār
agriculture	زراعت	zarāʿat
ague	تپِ لرز	tap-i larz
aigrette	جیقه	jīqa
aim (to)	قراول گرفتن	qarāvul giriftan
air	هوا	havā

alas!	افسار	afsūs
alchemy	کیمیا	kīmiā
alcohol	الکحول	alkuhūl
alcove	شاه نشین	shāh nishīn
alight (to)	پاین امدن	pāīn āmadan
alike	برابر	barābar
alive	زنده	zinda
all	همه	hama
alliance	معاهده	muʿāhida
allow (to)	اذن دادن	izn dādan
almanac	تقویم	taqvīm
almighty	قادر	qādir
almond	بادام	bādām
almost	قریب	qarīb
alms	خیرات	kheirāt
alone	تنها	tanhā
aloud	بلند	buland
alphabet	ا ب	alif bē
also	هم	ham
alteration	تغییر	taghyīr
although	اکرچه	agarchi
altogether	بالکلّ	bilkull
always	همیشه	hamīsha
amazed	حران	heirān
ambassador	سفیر , ایلچی	safīr, īlchī
	plur: سفرا	sufarā
amber (straw attractor)	که ربا	kah-rubā
amble	یرغه	yurgha
among	میان	mīān

amorous	عاشق	ʿāshiq
amulet	تعویذ	taʿviz
amusement	تفرج	tafarruj
ancestors	اجداد	ajdād
anchor	لنگر	langar
ancient	قدیم	qadīm
and	و	u, va
anecdote	نقل	naql
angel	فرشته	firishta
anger	تغیّر	tagheiyur
angle	کنج	kunj
animal	حیوان	heivān
	plur: حیوانات	heivānāt
annalist	واقعه نگار	vāqiʿa nigār
annul (to)	باطل کردن	bātil kardan
another	دیگر , غیر	dīgar, gheir
answer	جواب	javāb
ant	مورچه	mūrcha
— (white ant)	موریانه	mūrīāna
antediluvion	قبل از طوفان	qabl az tūfān
antiquities	انتیقه	antīqa
anxious	دلتنگ	diltang
any	هیچ	hīch
apart	جدا	judā
aperient	مسهل	mushil
apologize	عذر خواستن (خواه)	ʿuzr khāstan (khāh)
apoplexy	سکته	sakta
apothecary	دواساز	davāsāz
apparent	ظاهر	zāhir
appetite	اشتها	ishtihā

apple	سیب	sīb
appointment	ماموریت	maʿmūrīat
appreciate	غنیمت شمردن (شمار)	ghanīmat shumurdan (shumār)
apprentice	شاگرد	shāgird
approve	پسندیدن (پسند)	pasandīdan (pasand)
apricot	زرد آلو قیسی	zard ālū qeisī
apron	پیش‌بند	pīshband
apt	مناسب	munāsib
Arabia	عربستان	ʿarabistān
Arab	عرب	ʿarab
arabian	عربی	ʿarabī
arabic	عربی	ʿarabī
arch	طاق محراب	tāq mihrāb
archives	دفتر	daftar
argument	دلیل	dalīl
	plur: دلایل	dalāyil
arid	خشک	khushk
aristocracy	نجبا	nujabā
arithmetic	حساب	hisāb
arm	بازو	bāzū
arms	اسلحه	aslaha
army	قشون	qushūn
around	دور	dour
arrange	ترتیب دادن	tartīb dādan
arrest (to)	حبس کردن	habs kardan
arrive	رسیدن (رس)	rasīdan (ras)
arrival	ورود	vurūd
arriving	وارد	vārid

arrogance	غرور	ghurūr
arrogant	مغرور	maghrūr
arrow	تیر	tīr
arsenal	قورخانه	qūrkhāna
art	فن	fann
	plur: فنون	funūn
artificial	ساختگی	sākhtagī
artillery	توپخانه	tūpkhāna
artillery man	توپچی	tūpchī
artist	استاد	ustād
ash	زبانِ گنجشك	zabān-i gunjishk
ashamed (to be)	خجالت کشیدن	khajālat kashīdan
ashes	خاکستر	khākistar
ask (to)	پرسیدن (پرس)	pursīdan (purs)
asleep	خوابیده	khābīda
asparagus	مارچوبه	mārchūba
ass	خر	khar
assassin	قاتل	qātil
assassination	قتل	qatl
assault	حمله	hamla
assembly	مجلس	majlis
	plur: مجالس	majālis
assist	کمك کردن	kumak kardan
assistant	معاون	muʿāvin
associate	شریك	sharīk
	plur: شرکا	shurakā
astray	گمراه	gumrāh
astrologer	منجم	munajjim
astrology / astronomy	علم نجوم	ʿilm-i nujūm

asylum	بست	bast
athlete	پهلوان	pahlavān
atom	ذره	zarra
atrocity	ظلم	zulm
attack (to)	حمله بردن	hamla burdan
attempt	قصد	qasd
attentive	متوجه	mutavajjih
auction	هراج	harrāj
aunt (paternal)	عمه	ʿamma
— (maternal)	خاله	khāla
authentic	صحيح	sahīh
author	مصنف	musannif
autograph	دست خط	dast khatt
autumn	پاييز	pāīz
avalanche	بهمن	bahman
avarice	بخل	bukhl
avaricious	بخيل	bakhīl
avenue	خيابان	khīābān
average (on an)	روی هم رفته	rū-yi ham rafta
avoid	حذر کردن	hazar kardan
awake	بيدار	bīdār
away	دور	dūr
awful	مهيب	muhīb
awning	سايه بان	sāyabān
axe	تبر	tabar
axiom	قاعده	qāida
	plur: قواعد	qavāʿid
axis	ميل	mīl

B.

baby	بچه	bacha
back	پشت	pusht

backgammon	نرد	nard
backwards	پش	pas
bad	بد	bad
badness	بدی	badī
bag	کیسه	kīsa
baggage	اسباب	asbāb
bake (to)	پختن (پز)	pukhtan (paz)
baker	نان‌وای	nānvāī
balance (large)	قاپون	qāpūn
(small)	ترازو	tarāzū
balcony	مهتابی	mahtābī
ball	کره	kurra
— (dance)	مهمانیِ بال	mihmānī-yi bāl
bamboo	نیِ هندی	nei-i hindī
band (music)	موزیکان	mūzīkān
banishment	اخراجِ بلد	ikhrāj-i balad
bank (of river)	کنار	kanār
— (money)	بانك	bānk
banker	صراف	sarrāf
banknote	اسکناس	askinās
bankrupt	مفلس	muflis
bankruptcy	افلاس	iflās
banner	علم	ʿalam
banquet	مهمانی	mihmānī
baptism	تعمید	taʿmīd
barbarian / barbarous	وحشی	vahshī
barber	دلاك	dallāk
bare	لخت	lukht

barefoot	پا برهنه	pā barahna
bareheaded	کله برهنه	kala barahna
barley	جو	jou
barn	انبار	ambār
barracks	سرباز خانه	sarbāz khāna
barrel	پیپ	pīp
— (of a gun)	لوله	lūla
barren	خشك	khushk
barricade	سنگر	sangar
base	پست	past
basil	ریحان	reihān
basin	طست لگن	tasht, lagan
basket	سبد	sabad
bastard	حرامزاده	harāmzāda
bastinado	چوب و فلکه	chūb u falaka
bastinado (to)	چوب زدن	chūb zadan
bastinadoed (to be)	چوب خوردن	chūb khurdan
bath	حمام	hammām
battle	جنگ	jang
bayonet	نیزه	neiza
bazaar	بازار	bāzār
be (to)	بودن (باش)	būdan (bāsh)
bead	مهره	muhra
beak	نك	nuk
beam (wood)	تیر	tīr
bean	لوبیا	lūbīā
bear	خرس	khirs
beard	ریش	rīsh
beast	بهیمه	bahīma
	plur: بهایم	bahāyim
beat (to)	زدن (زن)	zadan (zan)

beautiful	قشنگ	qashang
beauty	حسن	husn
beaver	سگِ آبی	sag-i ābī
because	زیرا که	zīrā ki
become (to)	شدن (شو)	shudan (shou)
becoming	شایسته	shāyasta
bed	رختِ خواب	rakht-i khāb
bedstead	تختِ خواب	takht-i khāb
bedroom	خوابگاه	khābgāh
bee	زنبور	zambūr
beef	گوشتِ گاو	gūsht-i gāv
beer	آبِ جو	āb-i jou
beetle	سن	sin
beetroot	چقندر	chuqundur
— (red)	لبو	labū
before	قبل	qabl
beg (to)	استدعا کردن	istidʿā kardan
— (alms)	گدای کردن	gadāī kardan
beggar	گدا	gadā
begin	گرفتن (گیر)	giriftan (gīr)
beginner	مبتدی	mubtadī
behind	عقب	ʿaqab
believe	باور کردن	bāvar kardan
bell	زنگ	zang
belly	شکم	shikam
below	زیر	zīr
belt	کمر بند	kamar band

bench	سکو	sakū
bend (trans)	پیچاندن	pīchāndan
— (intrans)	پچیدن (پیچ)	pīchīdan (pīch)
bend (subst)	پیچ و خم	pīch u kham
besides	علاوه از	ᶜalāva az
besiege	محاصره کردن	muhāsira kardan
best	بهترین	bihtarīn
bet (to)	شرط بستن	shart bastan
better	بهتر	bihtar
between	میان	mīān
beyond	آن طرف	ān taraf
bible	توریت و انجیل	tourāt va anjīl
bier	تابوت	tābūt
big	بزرگ , کلفت	buzurg, kuluft
bigotry	تعصب	taᶜassub
bill	حساب	hisāb
— (of exch.)	برات	barāt
bind (to)	بستن (بند)	bastan (band)
bird	مرغ	murgh
birth	تولد	tavallud
biscuit	نان خشك	nun-i khuchk
bit	پاره	pāra
bite (to)	گزیدن	gazīdan
bitter	تلخ	talkh
black	سیاه	sīāh
blackguard	حرامزاده	harāmzāda
blacksmith	آهنگر	āhangar
blade (sword, knife)	تیغه	tīgha
blame	تقصیر , عیب	taqsīr, ᶜeib
	plur: عیوب	ᶜūyūb

blanket	پتو	patū
— (of a horse)	جل	jul
blasphemy	کفر	kufr
bleed (to)	خون گرفتن رگ زدن	khūn giriftan, rag zadan
blessed	مبارك	mubārak
blind	کور	kūr
block (to)	مسدود ساختن	masdūd sākhtan
blood	خون	khūn
bloodthirsty	خونخوار	khūnkhār
blossom (to)	شگفتن	shiguftan
blottingpaper	کاغذِ آب‌کش	kāghaz-i ābkash
blow (to)	وزیدن (وز)	vazīdan (vaz)
— (with the breath)	پف کردن	puf kardan
blue	آبی	ābī
blunt	کند	kund
board	تخته	takhta
boast (to)	لاف زدن	lāf zadan
boat (rowing)	کرجی	karajī
body	تن ، بدن	tan, badan
— dead	مرده	murda
boil (to)	جوشانیدن	jūshānīdan
bold	دلیر	dilīr
bolster	بالش	bālish
bolt	چفت	chift
bomb	خمپاره	khumpāra
bone	استخوان	ustukhān
book	کتاب	kitāb
	plur: کتب	kutub

bookbinder	صحاف	sahhāf
bookbinding (the)	جلد	jild
boot	چکمه	chakma
border	حاشیه	hāshīa
born	زاده	zāda
borrow	امانت گرفتن	amānat giriftan
— (money)	قرض کردن	qarz kardan
botany	علم نباتاتی	ʿilm-i nabātātī
both	هر دو	har du
bottle	شیشه	shīsha
bottom	ته	tah
bough	شاخ	shākh
bouquet	گلدسته	guldasta
bow	کمان	kamān
to bow	تعارف کردن	taʿāruf kardan
bowl	کاسه	kāsa
box (big)	صندوق	sandūq
— (small)	جعبه	jaʿba
— (on the ear)	سالی	sīlī
box (to)	مشت زدن	musht zadan
boxtree	شمشاد	shamshād
boy	پسر	pisar
bracelet	دست بند	dastband
braces	بندِ شلوار	band-i shalvār
brackish	شور	shūr
brain	مغز	maghz
brand	داغ	dāgh
brandy	کونیاك	kūnyāk
brass	برنج	birinj
bravo!	به به	bah! bah!

bread — نان — nān, nun
breadth — پهنای — pahnāī
break (to) — شکستن (شکن) — shikastan (shikan)
breakfast — نهار — nahār
breast — سینه — sīna
— (female) — پستان — pistān
breath — نفس — nafas
to breathe — نفس کشیدن — nafas kashīdan
breeches — شلوار — shalvār
breechloader — ته پر — tah pur
breeze — نسیم — nasīm
brick (unburnt) — خشت — khisht
— (burnt) — آجر — ājur
bride — عروس — ʿarūs
bridegroom — داماد — dāmād
bridge — پل جسر — pul, jisr
bridle — جلو — jilou
brigand — رهزن — rahzan
bright — روشن — roushan
bring — آوردن (آر) — āvurdan (ār)
broad — پهن — pahn
broker — دلال سمسار — dallāl, simsār
bronze — چودن — chūdan
brooch — سنجاق — sanjāq
broom — جاروب — jārūb
broth — آبگوشت — ābgūsht
brother — برادر — barādar
brown — قهوهٔ — qahvaī
brush — پاك کن — pāk kun

buckle	سگک	sagak
bud	غنچه	ghuncha
buffalo	گاوِ میش	gāv-i mīsh
bug	ساس	sās
— (poisonous)	گنه مله	gana, malla
build	بنا کردن	banā kardan
builder	بنّا	bannā
building	عمارت	ʿimārat
bulb	پیاز	pīāz
bullet	گلوله	gulūla
bunch	خوشه	khūsha
burden	بار	bār
burial	دفن	dafn
burn (trans)	سوزاندن	sūzāndan
— (intrans)	سوختن (سوز)	sūkhtan (sūz)
burst	ترکیدن (ترك)	tarakīdan (tarak)
bush	بوته	buta
business	کار	kār
busy	مشغول	mashghūl
but	لیکن	likan
butcher	قصّاب	qassāb
butler	پیش خدمت	pīsh-khidmat
butter	کره	kara
— (clarified)	روغن	roughan
butterfly	شاه پرك	shāh parak
button	دکمه	dukma
buy	خریدن (خر)	kharīdan (khar)
buyer	مشتری	mushtarī

C.

cabbage	کلم	kalam
cage	قفس	qafas
cake	نانِ شیرینی	nān-i shīrīnī
calamity	بلا	balā
calf	گوساله	gūsāla
calico	چیت ,قلمکار	chīt, qalamkār
call	صدا کردن	sadā kardan
called	مسمیٰ	musammā
camel	شتر	shutur
camomile	بابونه	bābūna
camp	اردو	urdū
camphor	کافور	kāfūr
canal	نهر ,جوب	nahr, jūb
candle	شمع	sham^c
candlestick	شمعدان	sham^cdān
canc	نی	nei
cannon	توپ	tūp
canter	چارنعل	chārnaˀl
canvas	کرباس	karbās
cap	کلاه	kulāh
capable	قابل	qābil
capacity	قابلیت	qābilīaᶜt
cape	سر	sar
caper	کبر	kabar
capital	پای تخت	pāyi takht
caprice	تلونِ مزاج	talavvun-i mizāj
captain	سلطان	sultān
captive	اسیر	asīr
caravan	قافله , کاروان	qāfila, kāravān

caravanserai	کاروانسرا	kārvānsarā
carcass	لاش	lāsh
card (play)	گنجفه	ganjafa
— (visiting)	گارت	gārt
care	فکر	fikr
careful	خبردار	khabardār
careless	بی خبر	bī khabar
carnation	میخک	mīkhak
carpenter	نجار	najjār
carpet (general)	فرش	farsh
— (knotted)	قالی	qālī
— (woven)	گلیم	gilīm
— (felt)	نمد	namad
carriage	کالسکه	kālaska
carrier	حمال	hammāl
carrot	هویج	havīj
carry	بردن (بر)	burdan (bar)
cartridge	فشنگ	fishang
to carve	تراشیدن (تراش)	tarāshīdan (tarāsh)
carving	نقش	naqsh
cascade	آبشار	ābshār
cash	پول نقد	pūl-i naghd
to cast (in a mould)	ریختن (ریز)	rīkhtan (rīz)
castle	قصر قلعه ارك	qasr, qalʿa, ark
castor oil	روغن چراغ	roughan chirāgh
to castrate	آخته کردن	ākhta kardan
cat	گربه	gurba
— (long haired Persian cat)	براق	burrāq
catalogue	فهرست	fihrist

to catch	گرفتن (گیر)	giriftan (gīr)
cauldron	دیگ	dīg
cauterize	داغ کردن	dāgh kardan
cavalry	سواره	savāra
cavern	غار	ghār
caviar	تخمِ ماهی	tukhm-i māhī
to cease	تمام شدن	tamām shudan
ceiling	سقف	saqf
celebrated	مشهور معروف	mashhūr, maʿrūf
celery	کلفس	kalafs
cellar	زیر زمین	zīr zamīn
centre	مرکز	markaz
ceremony	رسم	rasm
— plur.	رسوم	rusūm
certain	یقین	yaqīn
certificate	تصدیق	tasdīq
— (of a servant)	کاغذِ رضامندی	kāghaz-i rizāmandī
chain	زنجیر	zanjīr
chair	صندلی	sandalī
chalk	گلِ سفید	gil-i safīd
chamberlain	پیشخدمت حضور	pīshkhidmat-i huzūr
chancery	دفتر	daftar
chandelier	چهل چراغ	chihil chirāgh
chandler	بقال	baqqāl
to change	عوض کردن	ʿavaz kardan
chapter	باب	bāb
character	خصلت	khaslat
charcoal	زغال	zughāl

chargé d'affaires	شارژدفر کفیل امور	chārjdafar, kafīl-i umūr
charity	کرم	karam
charm	طلسم	talism
chastity	عصمت	ʿasmat
cheap	ارزان	arzān
cheapness	ارزانی	arzānī
cheating	تقلب	taghallub
cheese	پنیر	panīr
chemist	عطار دواساز	ʿattār, davāsāz
cheque	برات	barāt
cherry (sweet)	گیلاس	gīlās
— (sour)	آلوبالو	ālubālū
chess	شطرنج	shatranj
chest (human)	سینه	sīna
chestnut	شاه بلوط	shāh balūt
chicken	جوجه	jūja
chief	رئیس خان	raʿīs, khān
child	بچه	bacha
childhood	بچه‌گی	bachagī
chimney	دودکش	dūdkash
chin	زنخ	zanakh
China	چین	Chīn
China, Chinese	چینی	chīnī
chintz	قلمکار	qalamkār
choke	خفه شدن	khafa shudan
cholera	وبا	vabā
choose	اختیار کردن	ikhtīār kardan
Christ	حضرتِ عیسی	Hazrat-i ʿĪsā
Christian	عیسوی	ʿĪsavī

chronicle	تاریخ تواریخ	tārīkh plur: tavārīkh
church	کلیسیا	kalīsyā
cinnamon	دار چینی	dār-chīnī
circle	دایره	dāira
circumcision	ختنه	khatna
cistern	آب انبار	āb-ambār
citadel	قلعه	qalʿa
city	شهر	shahr
civility	ادب	adab
claim	طلب	talab
—	ادعا	iddiʿā
claimant	مدعی	muddaʿī
class	قسم ,طبقه	qism, tabaqa
claw	چنگال	changāl
clay	گل	gil
clean	پاک	pāk
clear	صاف	sāf
to cleave	شکافتن شکاف	shikāftan (shikāf)
clergyman	کشیش	kashīsh
clever	با هوش	bā hūsh
climate (water and air)	اب و هوا	āb u havā
to cling	چسپیدن چسپ	chaspīdan (chasp)
cloak	عبا	ʿabā
clock	ساعت مجلسی	sāʿat-i majlisī
to close	بستن بند	bastan (band)
cloth	ماهوت	māhūt
to clothe	پوشیدن پوش	pūshīdan (pūsh)
— (causal)	پوشاندن پوشان	pūshāndan (pūshān)
clothes	رخت	rakht
	لباس	libās

cloud	ابر	abr
clove	میخک	mīkhak
clover	شبدر	shabdar
coachhouse	کالسکه خانه	kālaskakhāna
coachman	کالسکه‌چی	kālaskachī
coal	زغالِ سنگ	zughāl-i sang
coarse	درشت	durusht
coast	کنار	kanār
—	ساحل	sāhil
— (plur.)	سواحل	savāhil
coat (persian)	سرداری	sardārī
cobweb	تارِ عنکبوت	tār-i ʿankabūt
cock	خروس	khurūs
coffee	قهوه	qahva
coffin	تابوت	tābūt
coin	سکه	sikka
to coin	ضرب کردن	zarb kardan
cold (adj.)	سرد	sard
to catch cold	سرما خوردن	sarmā khurdan
collar	یقه	yakha
to collect	جمع کردن	jamʿ kardan
collyrium	سرمه	surma
colonel	سرهنگ	sarhang
colour	رنگ	rang
colt	کره	kurra
column	ستون	sutūn
comb	شانه	shāna
to comb	شانه زدن	shāna zadan
to come	آمدن (آ)	āmadan (ā)

comet	ستاره‌دنباله دار	sitara-yi dumbala-dar
comic	مضحک	muzhik
command	حکم فرمان	hukm, farman
to command	فرمودن فرما	farmudan (farma)
commentary	تفسیر	tafsir
commerce	تجارت	tijarat
companion	رفیق	rafiq
to compare	مقابله کردن	muqabila kardan
comparatively	بالنسبه	bi'n nisba
compass	قبله نما	qibla nama
compensation	مکافات	makafat
complaint	شکایت	shikayat
complete	تمام	tamam
compliments	سلام	salam
composed	مرکب	murakkab
to conceal	پنهان کردن	panhan kardan
concerning	در خصوص	dar khusus
concession	امتیاز	imtiaz
conciliation	مصالحه	musalaha
condition	حال	hal
	plur: احوال	ahval
— (stipul)	شرط	shart
	plur: شروط	shurut
to condole	تعزیه کردن	ta'zia kardan
conduct	رفتار	raftar
confectioner	شیرینی‌ساز	shirinisaz
confederacy	معاهده	mu'ahida
to confess	اقرار کردن	iqrar kardan
confidence	اعتقاد	i'tiqad
confidentially	محرمانه	mahramana

to confirm	تصدیق کردن	tasdīq kardan
to confiscate	ضبط کردن	zabt kardan
conformably	موافق	mavāfiq
confusion	شلوق	shulūq
to congratulate	تبریك کردن	tabrīk kardan
conjurer	ساحر	sāhir
to conquer	فتح کردن	fath kardan
to consent	راضی بودن	rāzī būdan
consolation	تسلی	tasallī
consul	قونسل	qūnsul
consulate	قونسلگری	qūnsulgarī
contagion	سرایت	sarāyat
contagious	مسری	musrī
content	راضی	rāzī
to contradict	ردّ کردن	radd kardan
contrary	ضدّ عکس	zidd, ʿaks
contrivance	تدبیر	tadbīr
convalescence	شفا	shafā
convent	دیر	deir
conversation	صحبت	suhbat
cook	آشپز	āshpaz
to cook	پختن پز	pukhtan (paz)
cool	خنك	khunuk
copper	مس	mis
coppersmith	مسگر	misgar
copy	سواد	savād
cork	چوبِ پنبه	chūb-i pamba
corkscrew	پیچ	pīch

corn	غله	ghalla
corner	کنج	kunj
corporal	وکیل	vakīl
corpulent	چاق	chāq
to correct	تصحیح کردن	tas-hīh kardan
correspondence	مکاتبه	mukātiba
corridor	دالان	dālān
corrupt	خراب	kharāb
cost	قیمت	qīmat
cotton	پنبه	pamba
cough	سلفه	sulfa
to count	شمردن شمار	shumurdan (shumār)
counterfeit	ساختگی	sākhtagi
country	ولایت	vilāyat
countryseat	ییلاق	yeilāq
couplet (verse)	بیت	beit
courage	دلیری	dilīrī
courier	چاپار	chāpār
court	دربار	darbār
courtesan	جنده	jinda
cover	پوشش	pūshish
to cover	پوشاندن پوشان	pūshāndan (pūshān)
cow	گاو	gāv
coward	ترسو	tarsū
crab	خرچنگ	kharchang
crack	ترک	tarak
cradle	گهواره	gahvāra
cravat	گردن‌بند	gardanband
cream	خامه	khāma

to create	آفریدن آفرین	āfarīdan (āfarīn)
creator	خالق	khāliq
creature	مخلوق	makhlūq
credentials	اختیار نامه	ikhtīār nāma
creditor	طلب کار	talab-kār
crime	تقصیر	taqsīr
cripple	چلاغ	chulāgh
crooked	خم کج	kham, kaj
crop	حاصل	hāsil
to cross	عبور کردن	ʿubūr kardan
crow	کلاغ	kalāgh
crowd	جمعیت	jamʿīat
crown	تاج	tāj
to crucify	به صلیب زدن	bi salīb zadan
cruel	ظالم	zālim
cruelty	ظلم	zulm
to crush	خورد کردن	khurd kardan
to cry	داد زدن	dād zadan
crystal	بلور	bulūr
cucumber	خیار	khīār
cultivated	آباد	ābād
cultivation	زراعت	zarāʿat
cup	فنجان	finjān
cupboard	دولابچه	dūlābcha
cupola	گنبد	gumbad
curb	دهنه	dahana
curds and whey	ماست	māst
cure	علاج	ʿilāj
curiosity	کنج کاوی	kunj kāvī
curl	زلف	zulf

currants	سبزه	sabza
currier	دباغ	dabbāgh
currycomb	قشو	qashou
curse	لعنت	laʿnat
curtain	پرده	parda
cushion	بالش	bālish
custom	رسم	rasm
custom-house	گمرك خانه	gumruk-khāna
to cut	بریدن (بر)	burrīdan (burr)
cypress	سرو	sarv

D.

dagger	خنجر	khanjar
dam	سدّ	sadd
damage	خرابی	kharābī
"	ضرر	zarar
Damascus	شام	Shām
damasked (steel)	جوهر دار	jouhar-dār
to dance	رقصیدن (رقص)	rakhsīdan (rakhs)
danger	خطر	khatar
dangerous	خطرناك	khatarnāk
daring	جرأت	jurʿat
dark	تاریك	tārīk
darkness	تاریکی	tārīkī
date (fruit)	خرما	khurmā
— (time)	تاریخ	tārīkh
daughter	دختر	dukhtar
day	روز	rūz
dead	مرده	murda

deaf	کر	kar
dealing	معامله	muʿāmala
dear (beloved)	عزیز	ʿazīz
— (expensive)	گران	girān
death	مرگ	marg
debt	قرض	qarz
debtor	بدهکار	bidih kār
decanter	تنگ	tung
to decay	پوسیدن (پوس)	pūsīdan (pūs)
deceit	تقلّب	taqallub
to decorate	زینت دادن	zīnat dādan
decoration (order)	نشان	nishān
to deduct	کم کردن	kam kardan
deep	گود	goud
defeat	شکست	shikast
to defend	حمایت کردن	himāyat kardan
defendant	مدّعیٰ الیه	muddaʿā ileihi
degree	درجه	daraja
delicious	لذیذ	lazīz
delight	لذت	lazzat
to deliver	تسلیم کردن	taslīm kardan
deluge	طوفان	tūfān
demon	دیو	dīv
demon of the desert	غولِ بیابانی	ghūl-i bīābūnī
denial	انکار	inkār
dentist	دندان ساز	dandān-sāz
to depose (office)	معزول کردن	maʿzūl kardan
deposit	امانت	amānat
deputy	نایب	nāyib

derision	ریش خند	rīsh-khand
to descend	پایین آمدن	pāīn āmadan
to describe	تعریف کردن	ta'rīf kardan
description	بیان	beyān
desert	بیابان	bīābūn
deserving	سزاوار	sazāvār
desire	آرزو	ārzū
to despair	مأيوس شدن	māyūs shudan
to despise	بهیچ نشمردن	bi hīch na shumurdan
destiny	بخت	bakht
to destroy	خراب کردن	kharāb kardan
detail	تفصیل	tafsīl
devil	شیطان	sheitān
dew	شبنم	shabnam
dialogue	گفتگو	guftugū
diamond	الماس	almās
diarrhoea	اسهال	is'hāl
diary	روزنامه	rūznāma
— (of a journey)	سفر نامه	safar-nāma
dictionary	لغت	lughat
to die	مردن (میر)	murdan (mīr)
difference	فرق تفاوت	farq, tafāvut
different	جورِ دیگر	jūr-i dīgar
difficult	مشکل	mushkil
to dig	کندن (کن)	kandan (kan)
to digest	تحلیل کردن	tahlīl kardan
dignity	شان	shān
diligent	کارکن	kār-kun

to dine	شام خوردن	shām khurdan
dining-room	سفره خانه	sufra-khāna
dinner	شام	shām
direction	سمت	samt
directly	الآن	al ān
director	رئیس	ra'īs
dirt	کثافت	kasāfat
dirty	چرك , کثیف	chirk, kasīf
to discharge	جواب دادن	javāb dādan
discipline	انتظام	intizām
discontented	ناخوشنود	nā-khushnūd
to discover	پیدا کردن	peidā kardan
to disgrace	رسوا کردن	rusvā kardan
dish	دیس	dīs
— (food)	خوراك	khurāk
disinterested	بی غرض	bī-gharaz
to dismiss	مرخص کردن	murakhkhas kardan
disobedient	سرکش	sarkash
dispersed	متفرق	mutafarriq
displeased	کج خلق	kaj-khulq
dispute	دعوا	da'vā
to dissolve	حل کردن	hall kardan
distance	مسافت	masāfat
distant	دور	dūr
to distribute	تقسیم کردن	taqsīm kardan
district	بلوك	bulūk
ditch	خندق	khandaq
ditto	ایضاً	eizan
to dive	غوطه خوردن	ghūta khurdan
to divide	قسمت کردن	qismat kardan

divine	آلهی	ilāhī
divorce	طلاق	talāq
to do	کردن (کن)	kardan (kun)
doctor	حکیم	hakīm
dog	سگ	sag
— (sporting)	طوله	tūla
— (greyhound)	تازی	tāzī
doll	عروسك	ʿarūsak
dome	گنبد	gumbad
domestic	خانگی	khānagī
domicile	منزل	manzil
door	در	dar
— (to shut the door)	در را پیش کردن	dar-rā pīsh kardan
— (to bolt the door)	در را چفت کردن	dar-rā chift kardan
— (to open the door)	در را وا کردن	dar-rā vā kardan
dot	نقطه	nuqta
double	دو لا	du lā
doubt	شك	shak
dough	خمیر	khamīr
dove	قمری	qumrī
down	پایین	pāīn
dragoman	مترجم	mutarjim
draper	بزاز	bazzāz
draft	برات	barāt
	حواله	havāla
draughtsboard	تختهٔ نرد	takhta-yi nard
to draw	کشیدن (کش)	kashīdan (kash)
drawer (furniture)	جعبه	jaʿba
drawers	زیر جامه	zīr-jāma
dreadful	مهیب	muhīb

to dream	خواب دیدن	khāb dīdan
dress	لباس	libās
to dress	رخت پوشیدن	rakht pūshīdan
to drill	مشق کردن	mashq kardan
to drink	خوردن (خور)	khurdan (khur)
to drip	چکیدن (چك)	chakīdan (chak)
to drive	راندن (ران)	rāndan (rān)
— (in a carriage)	سوار کالسکه رفتن	savār-i kālaska raftan
drop (of liquor)	قطره	qatra
	چکه	chaka
drowned	غرق	gharq
druggist	عطار	ʿattār
drum	طبل	tabl
»	بالابان	bālābān
drunk	مست	mast
dry	چشك	khushk
duck	اوردك	urdak
dumb	لال	lāl
dun (horse)	سمند	samand
dung	پهین	pahīn
dungeon	دستاق خانه	dustākh-khāna
durability	دوام	davām
during	ما دام	mā dām
dust	گرد و خاك	gard u khāk
to dust	گرد گرفتن	gard giriftan
duster	دست مال	dastmāl
duty	تکلیف	taklīf
to dye	رنگ زدن	rang zadan
dynasty	سلسله	silsila

E.

each	هر یکی	har yakī
eagle	قره قوش	qara-qūsh
ear	گوش	gūsh
— (of corn)	خوشه	khūsha
early	زود	zūd
earring	گوشواره	gūshvāra
earth	زمین خاک	zamīn, khāk
earthenware	کوزهٔ	kūzaī
earthquake	زلزله	zalzala
ease	راحت	rāhat
easy	آسان	āsān
east	مشرق	mashriq
The East	مشرق زمین	mashriq-zamīn
to eat	خوردن (خور)	khurdan (khur)
ebony	آبنوس	ābnūs
edifice	عمارت	ʿimārat
to educate	تربیت کردن	tarbīat kardan
education	تربیت	tarbīat
effect	اثر	asar
egg	تخم	tukhm
— (fried)	تخمِ نیم رو	tukhm-i nīm-rū
— soft boiled	تخمِ نیم بند	tukhm-i nīm band
egotism	خود پرستی	khud-parasti
either-or	یا یا	yā_yā
elastic	جهنده	jahanda
elbow	مرفق	mirfaq
— (plur:)	مرافق	marāfiq

to elect	گزیدن (گزین)	guzīdan (guzīn)
elegant (in clothes)	خوش لباس	khush-libās
element	عنصر	ʿunsur
— (plur)	عناصر	ʿanāsir
elephant	فیل	fīl
elm	نارون	nārvan
eloquence	فصاحت	fasāhat
eloquent	فصیح	fasīh
embassy	سفارت کبری	safārat-i kubrā
to embezzle	خیانت کردن	khīānat kardan
to embrace	بغل گرفتن	baghal giriftan
embroidery	گلدوزی	guldūzī
emerald	زمرد	zumurrud
emery	سنباده	sumbāda
emetic	مستفرغ	mustafrigh
emperor	امپراطور	imparātūr
empress	امپراتریس	imparātrīs
employed	مشغول	mashghūl
empty	خالی	khālī
enamel	مینا	mīnā
enclosed (in a letter)	لفاً	laffan
end	آخر	ākhir
to end	تمام شدن	tamām shudan
enemy	دشمن	dushman
energy	شوق	shouq
engagement	وعده	vaʿda
engine	ماشین	māshīn
engineer	مهندس	muhandis
English	انگلیس	inglīs
enough	بس	bas
»	کافی	kāfī

to enter	داخل شدن	dākhil shudan
envelope	پاکت	pākat
envious	حسود	hasūd
envirous	اطراف	atrāf
envy	حسد	hasad
equal	برابر	barābar
error	غلط	ghalat
to escape	رستن (ره)	rastan (rah)
especially	خصوصاً	khusūsan
etc	و غیره	va gheira
eternity (without beginning)	ازل	azal
— (without end)	ابد	abad
eunuch	خواجه آغا	khāja, āghā
Europe	فرنگستان	Farangistān
European	فرنگی	Farangī
evening	شام	shām
every	هر	har
ewer	آفتابه	āftāba
exact	درست	durust
to exaggerate	مبالغه کردن	mubālagha kardan
examination	امتحان	imtihān
example	مثل	masal
excellency	جناب عالی	janāb-i ʿālī
except	بغیر	bi gheir
exception	استثنا	istisnā
exchange (money)	صرف	sarf
to exchange	عوض کردن	ʿavaz kardan
excrement	گه	guh

excuse	عذر	ʿuzr
executioner	میر غضب	mīr ghazab
exercise	مشق	mashg
existence	وجود	vujūd
existent	موجود	moujūd
to expect	منتظر بودن	muntazir būdan
to expel	بیرون کردن	bīrūn kardan
to expend	خرج کردن	kharj kardan
experienee	تجربه	tajruba
expert	اهلِ خبره	ahl-i khibra
to explain	بیان کردن	beiān kardan
to export	بخارج بردن	bi khārij burdan
extra ordinary	فوق العاده	fouq al ʿāda
eye	چشم	chashm
eyebrow	ابرو	abrū
eyeglass	عینك	ʿeinak

F.

face	صورت	sūrat
facing	رو برو	rū bi rū
fact	حقیقت	haqīqat
factory	کارخانه	kārkhāna
to fade	پژمردن (پژمیر)	pajmurdan (pajmīr)
to faint	بی هوش شدن	bī hūsh shudan
fairy	پری	parī
faith	وفا	vafā
faithful	وفادار	vafādār
faithless	بی وفا	bī vafā
falcon	قوش	qūsh
to fall	افتادن (افت)	uftādan (uft)

false	دروغی	durūghī
fame	نام و ننگ	nām u nang
family	عیال و اطفال	ʿayāl u atfāl
famous	مشهور	mash-hūr
fan	باد بزن	bād-bizan
fanatic(al)	متعصب	mutaʿassib
fancy	خیال	kheyāl
far	دور	dūr
farewell	وداع	vidāʿ
farrier	نعل بند	naʿl band
fast (well fixed)	محکم	muhkam
to fast	روزه گرفتن	rūza giriftan
fat (subst.)	پی	pī
— (adj.)	چاق	chāq
father	پدر والد	padar, vālid
fault	عیب تقصیر	ʿeib, taqsīr
favour	التفات	iltifāt
favourite	عزیز	ʿazīz
fayence	کاشی	kāshī
fear	ترس و باك	tars u bāk
to fear	ترسیدن (ترس)	tarsīdan (tars)
feast	مهمانی	mihmānī
feastday	عید	ʿīd (vulg. ʿeid)
feather	پر	par
fee	انعام	inʿām
to feed	پروردن (پرور)	parvardan (parvar)
feeling	حس	hiss
felt	نمد	namad
female	ماده	māda
fertile	حاسل ده	hāsil-dih

fetters	پا بند	pā-band
fever (intermittent)	نوبه	nouba
— (trembling)	تپ لرز	tap-i larz
few	کم	kam
field	صحرا	sahrā
— (in compositions)	زار	zār
fig	انجیر	anjīr
to fight	دعوی کردن	da'vā kardan
figure	شکل	shakl
to fill	پر کردن	pur kardan
to filter	صاف کردن	sāf kardan
filth	کثافت	kasāfat
filthy	کثیف	kasīf
finance	مالیات	malīāt
to find	پیدا کردن	peidā kardan
fine	نازک	nāzuk
a fine	جریمانه	jarīmāna
to fine	جریمانه کردن	jarīmāna kardan
finger	انگشت	angusht
to finish	تمام کردن	tamām kardan
fire	آتش	ātash
— (to light the fire)	آتش روشن کردن	ātash roushan kardan
— (to put out the fire)	آتش خاموش کردن	ātash khāmūsh kardan
firewood	هیزم	hīzum
fireworks	آتش بازی	ātashbāzī
first	اول	avval

fish	ماهی	māhī
fist	مشت	musht
fitting	باندازه	bi andāza
to fix	نصب کردن	nasb kardan
flag	بیرق	beiraq
— vulg:	بیدق	beidaq
flame	شعله	shuʿla
flattery	تملّق	tamalluq
flea	کهك	kahk
to flee	فرار کردن	farār kardan
flesh	گوشت	gūsht
flint	سنگِ چقماق	sang-i chaqmāq
flock	گله رمه	gala, rama
flood	سیل	seil
flour	آرد	ārd
flowing	جاری	jārī
flower	گل	gul
flute	نی	nei
fly	مگس	magas
to fly	پریدن (پر)	parīdan (par)
foal	کره	kurra
foam	کف	kaf
fog	مه	mih
to fold	تا کردن	tā kardan
the following	ذیل	zeil
food	خوراك	khurāk
fool	خر	khar (ass.)
foot	پا	pā
for	برای	barāyi

to forbid	منع کردن	man^c kardan
forehead	پیشانی	pīshānī
foreign	غریب	gharīb
Foreign Affairs	امورِ خارجه	umūr-i khārija
forest	جنگل	jangal
forgery	ساختگی	sākhtagī
to forget	فراموش کردن	farāmūsh kardan
to forgive	عفو کردن, بخشیدن (بخش)	afv kardan, bakhshīdan (bakhsh)
fork	چنگال	changāl
form	صورت	sūrat
former (previous)	سابق	sābiq
fort	قلعه	qala^c
fortunate	خوش بخت	khush-bakht
— (unfortunate)	بد بخت	bad-bakht)
fortune	بخت	bakht
fountain	فوّاره	favvāra
fowl	مرغ	murgh
fox	روباه	rūbāh
frame	قاب چهار چوبه	qāb, chahār-chūba
free	آزاد	āzād
freedom	آزادی	āzādī
freemason	فرامسون	farāmasūn
freeze	یخ بستن	yakh bastan
French	فرانسوی	farānsavī
fresh	تازه	tāza
Friday	جمعه	jum^ca
friend	دوست	dūst
friendly	دوستانه	dūstāna

friendship	دوستی	dūstī
to frighten	ترسانیدن (ترسان)	tarsānīdan (tarsān)
frock	فستان	fistān
frog	قرباغه	qurbāgha
from	از	az
frontier	سرحدّ	sar-hadd
frost	سرما	sarmā
fruit	میوه	mīva
to fry	بریان کردن	birīān kardan
full	پر	pur
fun	تفرج	tafarruj
funny	مضحك	muzhik
fur	پوستین	pūstīn
furlough	مرخصی	murakhasī
furnace	تنور	tanūr
furniture	مبل و اسباب	mubl u asbāb
future	آینده	āyanda

G.

gall	زهره	zahra
gallnut	مازو	māzū
to gallop	دویدن (دو)	davīdan (dou)
— (causal)	دواندن (دوان)	davāndan (davān)
— (a horse)	تاختن (تاز)	tākhtan (tāz)
gambling	قمار بازی	qumār-bāzī
game	بازی	bāzī
gaol	حبس	habs
garden	باغ	bāgh
gardener	باغبان	bāghbān vulg: bāghbūn
garlic	سیر	sīr

garnet	لعل	la'l
garter	جراب بند	jurāb band
gate	دروازه	darvāza
gate-keeper	دربان	darbān
gazelle	آهو	āhū
gelding	اخته	ākhta
general (army)	سرتیپ	sartīp
general (adjective)	عمومی	'umūmī
generation	پشت	pusht
gentle	ملایم	mulāyim
gentleman	نجیب	najīb
genuine	صحیح	sahīh
geography	جغرافیا	jughrāfīā
geometry	هندسه	handasa
ghost	روح	rūh
— (Holy Ghost)	روح القدس	Rūh al quds
gift	پیشکش	pīshkash
gilt	مطلا	mutallā
ginger	زنجبیل	zanjabīl
girl	دختر	dukhtar
to give	دادن (ده)	dādan (dih)
glass	شیشه	shīsha
— (wine glass)	گلاس	gilās
— (tea glass)	استقام	istaqām
— (looking glass)	آینه	āina
glory	جلال	jalāl
glue	سریشم	sirīshum
to go	رفتن (رو)	raftan (rou)
goat	بز	buz

God	خدا	Khudā
,	الله	Allāh
gold	طلا	tilā
,	زر	zar
goldsmith	زرگر	zargar
good	خوب	khūb
good-bye	خدا حافظ	khudā hāfiz
goods	مال	māl
goose	قاز	qāz
gospel	انجیل	anjīl
gourd	کدو	kadū
gout	نقرس	niqris
government	حکومت	hukūmat
governor	حاکم	hākim
gradually	کم کم	kam-kam
grain	دانه	dāna
grammar	صرف و نحو	sarf u nahv
grandfather	جدّ	jadd
grandmother	جدّه	jadda
grandvizier	صدر اعظم	Sadr aʿzam
grape	انگور	angūr
grass	علف	ʿalaf
grateful	حق شناس	haqq shanās
gratis	مفت	muft
grave (tomb)	قبر گور	qabr, gūr
gravel	ریگ	rīg
gray	خاکستری	khākistarī
— (horse)	قزل	qizil
grease	چربی	charbī

greasy	چرب	charb
great	بزرگ	buzurg
green	سبز	sabz
greens	سبزی	sabzī
greyhound	سگ تازی	sag-i tāzī
grief	غم	gham
to grind	سابیدن (ساب)	sābīdan (sāb)
grocer	بقال	baqqāl
groom	مهتر	mihtar
ground	زمین	zamīn
to grow (veget)	رستن (رو)	rustan rū
— (persons and animals)	بزرگ شدن	buzurg shudan
guarantee	ضمانت	zamānat
guard	کشیک	kashīk
guess	قیاس	qīās
guest	مهمان	mihmān
guide	بلد	balad
gulf (sea)	خلیج	khalīj
gun	تفنگ	tufang
— (double barrelled)	دو لوله	du lūla
— (breech loader)	تهپر	tahpur
— (muzzle loader)	دهن پر	dahan pur
gunner	توپچی	tūpchī
gut	روده	rūda
gutter	راه آب	rāh-i āb
gymnasium	زور خانه	zūr-khāna
gymnastics	ورزش	varzish
gypsum	گچ	gaj

gipsy	کولی	koulī

H.

habitation	مسکن	maskan
— (plur.)	مساکن	masākin
hail	تگرگ	tagarg
hair	مو	mū
half	نیم نصف	nīm, nisf
hall	ایوان	eivān
hammer	چکوش	chakush
hand	دست	dast
handful	مشت	musht
handkerchief	دست مال	dast māl
handle	دسته	dasta
to hang	آویزان کردن	āvīzān kardan
to happen	اتفاق افتادن	ittifāq uftādan
happy	خوش وقت	khush-vakht
harbour	لنگر گاه	langar-gāh
hard	سخت	sakht
harem	اندرون	andarūn
harm	ضرر	zarar
harness	یراق	yarāq
harvest	درو حاصل	dirou, hāsil
haste	عجله	ʿajala
hasty	دست پاچه	dast-pācha
hat	کلاه	kulāh
hatred	کین	kīn
haughtiness	غرور	ghurūr
haughty	مغرور	maghrūr
hawk	قوش	qūsh

hay	یونجه	yūnja
head	سر	sar
headache	دردِ سر	dard-i sar
health	صحت	sihhat
„	احوال	ahvāl
„	سلامتی	salāmatī
to hear	شنیدن (شنو)	shanīdan (shanou)
heart	دل	dil
heat	گرمی	garmī
heathen	کافر	kāfir
heaven	بهشت	bihisht
heavy	سنگین	sangīn
hedgehog	خار پشت	khār-pusht
heel	پاشنه	pāshna
height	بلندی	bulandī
heir	وارث	vāris
hell	دوزخ	dūzakh
„	جهنم	jahannam
helmet	خود	khūd
help	کمك	kumak
hen	مرغ	murgh
here	اینجا	īnjā
hero	بهادر	bahādur
hideous	زشت	zisht
high	بلند	buland
Highness	حضرت والا	hazrat-i vālā
hill	تپه	tapa
to hinder	منع کردن	manʿ kardan
hire	کرایه	kirāya
history	تاریخ	tārīkh

to hit	زدن (زن)	zadan (zan)
hog	خوك	khūk
to hold	نگاه داشتن	nigāh dāshtan
hole	سوراخ	sūrākh
holiday	روزِ تعطيل	rūz-i taᶜṭīl
hollow	خالى	khālī
holtsters	قبل	qubul
holy	مقدس	muqaddas
honest	درست کار	durust-kār
honey	عسل	ᶜasal
honour	آبرو	ābrū
to honour	احترام کردن	iḥtirām kardan
hoof	سم	sum
hook	قلاب	qullāb
hoopoe	هدهد	hudhud
	شانه سر	shāna-sar
hope	اميد	umīd
hopeful	اميدوار	umīdvār
hopeless	نااميد	nā-umīd
horizon	عفق	ᶜufuq
horn	شاخ	shākh
horse	اسپ	asp
— (pack-horse)	يابو	yābū
horse-shoe	نعل	naᶜl
horseman	سوار	savār
hospitable	مهمان دوست	mihmān-dūst
hospital	مريض خانه	marīz-khāna
hot	داغ	dāgh
hotel	مهمان خانه	mihmān-khāna
hour	ساعت	sāᶜat

house	خانه	khāna
household	خانوار	khānavār
human	انسانی	insānī
humble	مظلوم	mazlūm
hunger	گرسنگی	gurusnagī
hungry	گرسنه	gurusna
— (vulg.)	گشنه	gushna
hunt	شکار	shikār
hunter	شکارچی	shikārchī
hurry	عجله	ʿajala
to hurt	رنجانیدن (رنجان)	ranjānīdan (ranjān)
husband	شوهر	shouhar
hyacinth	سنبل	sumbul
hyaena	کفتار	kaftār
hypocrisy	ریا	rīā
hypothesis	فرض	farz

I.

ibex	بزِ کوهی	buz-i kūhī
ice	یخ	yakh
idea	خیال	kheyāl
idiom	اصطلاح	istilāh
idiot	بی شعور	bī shuʿūr
idle	بی کار	bī-kār
idol	بت	but
if	اگر	agar
ignorant	نادان	nā·dān
ill	نا خوش	nā·khush
illness	ناخوشی	nākhushī
illumination	چراغان	chirāghān
image	تمثیل	tamsīl

to imagine	تصور کردن	tasavvur kardan.
imitation (plur)	تقلید (تقالید)	taqlīd (taqālīd)
immediately	الآن	al ān
imperfect	ناقص	nāqis
imperial	شاهنشاهی	shāhinshāhī
to import (goods)	داخل کردن	dākhil kardan
importance	اهمیت	ahammīat
important	مهم	muhimm
impossible	غیر ممکن	gheir mumkin
improbable	دور	dūr
impure	نا پاك	nā-pāk
incense	بخور	bukhūr
inclination	میل	meil
income	مداخل	madākhil
to increase	افزودن (افزا)	afzūdan (afzā)
indeed	البته	albatta
independent	خود مختار	khud mukhtār
index	فهرست	fihrist
India	هند	Hind
"	هندوستان	Hindūstān
indigo	نیل	nīl
infancy	بچگی	bachagī
infant	بچه طفل	bacha, tifl
infantry	پیاده	piāda
infection	سرایت	sirāyat
influence	نفوذ	nufūz
influenza	زکامِ فرنگی	zukkām-i farangī
information	اطلاع	ittilā[c]
ingratitude	نمک بحرامی	namak bi harāmī
inhabitant	ساکن	sākin

inhabitant (plur.)	سکنه	sakana
inheritance	میراث	mīrās
inheritor	وارث	vāris
ink	مرکب	murakkab
inlaidwork	خاتم کار	khātim-kār
inn	مهمان خانه	mihmān-khāna
innocent	بی گناه	bī-gunāh
insect	جانور	jānvar
— (vulg.)		jūnavar
inside	اندرون	andarūn
to insist	اصرار کردن	isrār kardan
insolent	بی ادب	bī adab
instead	عوض	ʿavaz
instruction	تعلیم	taʿlīm
instrument	آلت	ālat
insult	فحش	fuhsh
to insult	فحش دادن	fuhsh dādan
insurance	بیمه	bīma
intellect	عقل	ʿaql
intention	مقصود	maqsūd
interesting	دل چسپ	dil-chasp
interference	مداخله	mudākhila
internal	داخلی	dākhilī
interpreter	مترجم	mutarjim
interval	فاصله	fāsila
intoxicated	مست	mast
intoxicating	مسکر	muskir
intrenchment	سنگر	sangar
to introduce (to one another)	معرفی کردن	muʿarrafī kardan
to intrust	سپردن (سپار)	supurdan (sipār)
inundation	سیل	seil

invention	ایجاد	ījād
»	اختراع	ikhtirāʿ
inventory	سیاهه	sīāha
to invite	دعوت کردن	daʿvat kardan
iron	آهن	āhan
irregular (troops)	غیر نظامی	gheir-nizāmī
irrigation	آبیاری	ābyārī
island	جزیره	jazīra
itch	خارش	khārish
ivory	عاج	āj
— (of the walrus)	شیر ماهی	shīr-māhī
ivy	لبلب	lablab

J.

jackall	شغال	shaghāl
jade	یشم	yashm
jam	مربا	murabbā
jealousy	رشك	rashk
Jesus	حضرت عیسی	Hazrat-i ʿIsā
Jew	یهودی	Yahūdī
jockey	چابك سوار	chābuk-savār
to join	پیوستن (پیوند)	peivastan (peivand)
joint	بند	band
journal	روز نامه	rūz-nāma
journey	سفر	safar
joy	خوشی	khushī
Judas-tree	ارغوان	arghavān
judge (coranic law)	حاکمِ شرع	hākim-i sharʿ
» (civil law)	حاکم عرف	hākim-i ʿurf
judgment	حکم	hukm

jug	کوزه kūza
to jump	جستن (جه) jastan (jah)
just	عادل ʿādil
justice	عدل انصاف ʿadl, insāf

K.

to keep	نگاه داشتن nigāh dāshtan
keeper	مستحفظ mustahfiz
keepsake	یادگار yādgār
kettle	کتری katrī
key	کلید kalīd
— (of a carriage)	آچار āchār
to kick	لگد زدن lagad zadan
— (vulg.)	laghat zadan
to kill	کشتن (کش) kushtan (kush)
kind (species)	قسم qism
— (plur.)	اقسام aqsām
kind (friendly)	مهربان mihribān
king	پادشاه pādishāh
»	شاه shāh
»	ملك malik
kiss	بوسه būsa
— (vulg.)	ماچ māch
kitchen	آشپز خانه āshpaz khāna
knee	زانو zānū
to kneel	زانو نشستن zānū nishastan
knife	کارد kārd
— (penknife)	چاقو chāqū
to knit	بافتن (باف) bāftan (bāf)
to knock	کوبیدن (کوب) kūbīdan (kūb)

knot	گره	girih
to knot	گره زدن	girih zadan
to know	دانستن (دان)	dānistan (dān)
knowledge	دانش علم	dānish, ilm
known	معلوم	maʿlūm

L.

labour	کار	kār
labourers	عمله فعله	ʿamala, faʿala
lace	توری	tūrī
ladder	نردبان	nardubān
lady	خانم	khānum
lake	دریاچه	daryācha
lamb	بره	barra
lame	لنك	lang
lamentation	ناله	nāla
lamp	چراغ	chirāgh
lance	نیزه	neiza
lancet	نیشتر	nīshtar
land	زمین	zamīn
lane	کوچه	kūcha
language	زبان	zabān
lantern	فانوس	fānūs
large	بزرگ	buzurg
lark	چکاوك	chakāvuk
last	آخر	ākhir
late	دیر	dīr
latitude	عرض	ʿarz
to laugh	خندیدن (خند)	khandīdan (khand)
laughable	مضحك	muzhik
laughter	خنده	khanda

laundress	رخت‌شور	rakhtshūr
law	قانون	qānūn
coranic law	شرع	sharʿ
common law	عرف	ʿurf
lawcourt	دیوان خانه	divān-khāna
lawsuit	مرافعه	murāfaʿa
lawn	چمن	chaman
laxative	مسهل	musʿhil
to lay	گذاشتن (گذار)	guzāshtan (guzār)
lazy	تنبل	tambal
lead	سرب	surb
leaf	برگ ورق	barg, varaq
lean	لاغر	lāghir
to lean	تکیه دادن	takīa dādan
to learn	یاد گرفتن	yād giriftan
learned	عالم	ʿālim
learning	علم	ʿilm
leather	چرم تیماج	charm, tīmāj
leave	اذن	izn
to leave	ترک کردن	tark kardan
leech	زالو	zālū
left	چپ	chap
leg	پا	pā
legation	سفارت	safārat
legible	خوانا	khānā
leisure	فرصت	fursat
lemon	لیمو	līmū
lemonade	شربت لیمو	sharbat-i līmū
to lend	امانت دادن	amānat dādan
length	طول	tūl

lentils	عدس	ʿadas
leopard	پلنك	palang
less	كمتر	kamtar
lesson	درس	dars
letter (epistle)	كاغذ	kāghaz
— (alphab.)	حرف	harf
lettuce	كاهو	kāhū
lexicon	لغت	lughat
liar	دروغ گو	durūgh-gū
liberality	سخاوت	sakhāvat
liberty	آزادی	āzādī
library	كتب خانه	kutub-khāna
to lick	ليسيدن (ليس)	līsīdan (līs)
lid	سر پوش	sar-pūsh
lie	دروغ	durūgh
to lie (mentir)	دروغ گفتن	durūgh guftan
to lie (coucher)	خوابيدن (خواب)	khābīdan (khāb)
lieutenant	نايب	nāyib
life	زندگی	zindagī
lifetime	عمر	ʿumr
to lift	بلند كردن	buland kardan
light (subst.)	نور	nūr
— (adj.)	سبك	sabuk
to light	روشن كردن	roushan kardan
lightning	برق	barq
like	مثل	misl
to like	پسند كردن	pasand kardan
likeness	شباهت	shabāhat
lily	زنبق	zambaq
lime	آهك	āhak

limit	حدّ	hadd
line	خطّ	khatt
linen	کتان	kattān
lining	استر	astar
linseed	بزرك	bazrak
lion	شیر	shīr
lip	لب	lab
list	فهرست	fihrist
to listen	گوش دادن	gūsh dādan
lithography	چاپ	chāp
litter (travelling)	تخت روان	takht-i ravān
little	خورده	khurda
to live	زنده بودن	zinda būdan
liver	جگر	jigar
load	بار	bār
local	محلی	mahallī
lock	قفل	qufl
— (vulg.)		(qulf)
locust	ملخ	malakh
logic	منطق	mantiq
long	دراز	dirāz
to look	نگاه کردن	nigāh kardan
loose	شل	shul
to lose	گم کردن	gum kardan
loss	ضرر	zarar
lost	گم	gum
loud	بلند	buland
louse	شپش	shipish
love	عشق	ʿishq
to love	دوست داشتن	dūst dāshtan

to be in love	عاشق بودن	ʿāshiq būdan
lover	عاشق	ʿāshiq
low	پست	past
lucerne (hay)	یونجه	yūnja
luck	بخت	bakht
luggage	اسباب	asbāb
lunar	قمری	qamarī
lunatic	دیوانه	dīvāna
lunch	نهار	nahār
lung	شش	shush
luxury	عیش	ʿeish

M.

mace	گرز	gurz
»	چماق	chumāgh
mad	دیوانه	dīvāna
madness	دیوانگی	dīvānagī
magic	جادوگری	jādū-garī
magnet	آهن ربا	āhan-rubā
magpie	زاغ	zāgh
mail (armour)	زره	zira
maimed	چلاق	chulāgh
maize	ذرت	zurrat
majesty	اعلیحضرت	aʿlāhazrat
major	یاور	yāvar
to make	ساختن (ساز)	sākhtan (sāz)
male	نر	nar
man (kind)	آدم	ādam
»	انسان	insān
— (plur.)	ناس	nās
— (male)	مرد	mard

man (plur. men)	مردها	mardhā
— » people)	مردم	mardum
mane	یال	yāl
mange	خارش	khārish
manger	آخور	ākhur
manna	گز	gaz
— (biblical)	من	mann
manner	طور	tour
— (plur.)	اطوار	atvār)
manœuvres	جنگ هفت لشکر	jang-i haft lashgar
manuscript (adject)	خطی	khattī
many	بسیار خیلی	bisyār, kheilī
map	نقشه	naqsha
marble	مرمر	marmar
to march	کوچ کردن	kūch kardan
mare	مادیان	mādīan
mark	نشان علامت	nishān, ʻalāmat
to mark	علامت گذاشتن	ʻalāmat guzāshtan
market	بازار	bāzār
marriage	عروسی	ʻarūsī
marrow (bone)	مغز	maghz
marrow (vegetable)	کدوچه	kadūcha
to marry (a woman)	زن گرفتن	zan giriftan
» (a man)	شوهر کردن	shouhar kardan
martingale	سینه بند	sīna-band
martyr	شهید	shahīd
masculine	مذکر	muzakkar
mason	بنّا	bannā
massacre	قتل	qatl
mast (of a tent)	دیرك	dīrak

master	آقا	āghā
mat	حصیر	hasīr
match (lucifer)	کبریت	kibrīt
— (wax match)	شمعچه	sham'cha
mattress	دوشک	dūshak
mausoleum	مقبره	maqbara
meadow	چمن	chaman
meal	غذا	ghazā
meaning	معنی	ma'nī
measles	سرخک	surkhak
measure	اندازه	andāza
meat	گوشت	gūsht
to meddle	مداخله کردن	mudākhila kardan
mediation	واسطه	vāsita
medicine	دوا	davā
medlar	ازگیل	azgīl
to meet	ملاقات کردن	mulāqāt kardan
meeting	مجلس	majlis
melody	نوا آهنگ	navā, āhang
melon	گرمک	garmak
	خربوزه	kharbūza
— (water melon)	هندوانه	hindavāna
— (vulg.)		handūna
to melt	گداختن (گداز)	gudākhtan (gudāz)
memorandum	یاد داشت	yād-dāsht
memory	یاد	yād
"	خاطر	khātir
to mend	تعمیر کردن	ta'mīr kardan
mentioned	مذکور	mazkūr
merchant	تاجر	tājir
— (plur.)	تجار	tujjār

merciful	رحیم	rahīm
merciless	بی رحم	bī rahm
mercury	جیوه	jīva
message	پیغام	peighām
metal	فلز	filiz
metre (verse)	وزن	vazn
middle	میان وسط	miān, vasat
mighty	توانا	tavānā
mild	ملایم	mulāyim
military	نظامی	nizāmī
milk	شیر	shīr
milkpot	شیردان	shīrdān
mill	آسیا	āsyā
millet	ارزن	arzan
minarat	مناره	manāra
mind	خاطر	khātir
mine	معدن	ma'dan
minister	وزیر	vazīr
ministry	وزارت	vazārat
mint (for coinage)	ضراب خانه	zarrāb-khāna
» (plant)	نعنا	na'nā
minute (time)	دقیقه	daqīqa
minutely	با دقت	bā diqqat
miracle	معجزه	mu'jiza
mirage	آب یزید	āb-i Yazīd
mirror	آینه	āina
mischief	شیطانی	sheitānī
miser	بخیل	bakhīl
miserable	پریشان	parīshān
misfortune	بلا	balā

to miss (the aim)	خطا کردن	khatā kardan
missionary	کشیش مرسل	kashīsh, mursil
mist	مه	mih
mistake	غلط	ghalat
mistrustful	بدگمان	bad-gumān
to mix	امیختن (امیز)	āmīkhtan (āmīz)
»	قطی کردن	qātī kardan
mixed	مخلوط قاطی	makhlūt, qātī
moat	خندق	khandaq
mockery	ریش خند	rīsh-khand
modest	شرم سار	sharm-sār
moist	نم تر	nam, tar
moisture	رطوبت	rutūbat
moment	آن	ān
money	پول	pūl
money-changer	صراف	sarrāf
monkey	میمون	meimūn
monopoly	انحصار	inhisār
month	ماه	māh
— (arabic)	شهر	(shahr)
moon	ماه	māh
moonlight	مهتاب	mahtāb
morals	اخلاق	akhlāq
more	بیشتر	bīshtar
morning	صبح	subh
morter	هاونگ	hāvang
mosque	مسجد	masjid
mosquito	پسه	pasha
most	اکثر	aksar
moth	بید	bīd

mother	مادر	mādar
mother of pearl	صدف	sadaf
motion	حرکت	harakat
— (plur.)	حرکات	harakāt
to mount	سوار شدن	savār shudan
mountain	کوه	kūh
mourning	تعزیه دراى	ta'zīa-dārī
mouse	موش	mūsh
mouth	دهن	dahan
to move (trans.)	حرکت دادن	harakat dādan
— (intrans.)	حرکت کردن	harakat kardan
much	خیلی, بسیار	kheilī, bisyār
mud	گل	gil
mulberry	توت	tūt
mule	قاطر	qātir
mule-driver	قاطرچی	qātirchī
muleteer	چاروادار	chārvadār
murder	قتل	qatl
mushroom	قارچ	qārch
music	ساز	sāz
musician	مطرب	mutrib
musk	مشك	mishk
musket	تفنگ	tufang
musketeer	تفنگچی	tufangchī
muslin	ململ	malmal
mustachios	سبیل	sibīl
mustard	خردل	khardal
mute	لال	lāl
mutineer	یاغی	yāghī
mutiny	طغیان	tughyān

mutton	گوشت گوسفند	gūsht-i gūsfand
muzzle-loader	دهن پر	dahan-pur
mystic	صوفی	sūfī
mysticism	تصوف	tasavvuf

N.

nail (finger)	ناخن	nākhun
— (of iron or wood)	میخ	mīkh
naked	لخت	lukht
name	اسم	ism
— (plur.)	اسامی	asāmī
named	نام	nām
namely	یعنی	yaʿnī
napkin	دستمال	dast-māl
narcissus	نرگس	nargis
narrow	تنگ	tang
nasty	مکروه	makrūh
nation	ملّت	millat
natural	طبیعی	tabīʿī
nature	طبعیت	tabʿīat
near	نزدیک, قریب	nazdīk, qarīb
nearly	تقریباً	taqrīban
necessary	لازم	lāzim
neck	گردن	gardan
necktie	گردن بند	gardan-band
nectarine	شلیل	shalīl
to need	لازم داشتن	lāzim dāshtan
needle	سوزن	sūzan
negation	انکار	inkār
neglect	غفلت	ghaflat

negro	زنگی	zangī
vulg: negro man slave	کاکا سیاه	kākā sīāh
vulg: slave girl	دده سیاه	dada sīāh
to neigh	شیهه زدن	sheiha zadan
neighbour	همسایه	ham-sāya
neighbourhood	همسایگی	ham-sāyagī
neither-nor	نه نه	na-na
nephew (brother's son)	برادر زاده	barādar zada
— (sister's son)	همشیره زاده	hamshīra-zāda
nest	لونه	lūna
net	توره	tura
neutral	بی طرف	bī-taraf
neutrality	بی طرفی	bī-tarafī
new	نو ,تازه	nou, tāza
news	خبر	khabar
nice	مرغوب	marghūb
niche	طاقچه	tāqcha
niece (the same as nephew)		
night	شب	shab
nightingale	بلبل	bulbul
no	نه خیر	na-kheir
noble	شریف ,نجیب	sharīf, najīb
nobody	هیچ کس	hīch-kas
noise	صدا	sadā
nomads	ایلات	īlāt
nom de plume	تخلّص	takhallus
noon	ظهر	zuhr
north	شمال	shamāl
north-pole	قطبِ شمال	qutb-i shamāl
nose (obsol.)	دماغ (بینی)	damāgh (bīnī)

nosebag (of a horse)	توبره	tūbra
note (letter)	رقعه	ruqᶜa
nothing	هیچ نه	hīch-na
to nourish	پروردن (پرور)	parvardan (parvar)
novelty	تازگی	tāzagī
now	حالا	hālā
numbed	بی حس	bī hiss
number	عدد	ᶜadad
numerous	متعدّد	mutaᶜaddid
nun	راهبه	rāhiba
nurse	دایه	dāya (vulg. tāya)
nut (hazelnut)	فندق	funduq
— (walnut)	گردو	girdū
— (cocoanut)	نارگیل	nārgīl
nutmeg	جوز	jouz

O.

oak	بلوط	ballūt
oar	پارو	pārū
oath	قسم	qasam
»	سوگند	sougand
obedience	اطاعت	itāᶜat
obliged (grateful)	ممنون	mamnūn
obscene	فاحش	fāhish
to observe	ملاحظه کردن	mulāhaza kardan
obstacle	مانع	māniᶜ
obvious	پیدا, ظاهر	peidā, zāhir
occasion	موقع	mouqaᶜ
occasionally	گاه گاه	gāh-gāh
occident	مغرب	maghrib
occupation	مشغولیت	mashghūlīat

occupied	مشغول	mashghūl
to occur	واقع شدن	vāqiʿ shudan
ocean	بحرِ محیط	bahr-i muhīt
ode	غزل	ghazal
to offend	رنجانیدن (رنجان)	ranjānīdan (ranjān)
offer	تقدیم	taqdīm
office	مأموریت	maʿmūrīat
— (place of business)	دفتر	daftar
officer	صاحب منصب	sāhib mansab
official	رسمی	rasmī
officially	رسماً	rasman
often	خیلی	kheilī
oil	روغن	roughan
castor oil	روغن چراغ	roughan chirāgh
olive oil	روغنِ زیتون	roughan-i zeitūn
linseed oil	روغنِ بزرك	roughan-i bazrak
kerosine oil	نفت	naft
oily	روغنی	roughanī
old (persons or animals)	پیر	pīr
— (things)	کهنه	kuhna
olive	زیتون	zeitūn
onager (wild ass)	گورِ خر	gūr-i khar
once	يك دفعه	yak dafʿa
onion	پیاز	piāz
only	فقط	faqat
onyx	سنك سلیمانی	sang-i suleimānī
open	باز ,وا	bāz, vā

to open	وا کردن	vā kardan
operation	عمل کاری	ʿamalkārī
opinion	رئی	raī
opium	تریاك	taryāk
opposite	رو برو	rū bi rū
opposition	مخالفت	mukhālifat
to oppress	ظلم کردن	zulm kardan
oppression	ظلم	zulm
oppressor	ظالم	zālim
orange	پرتقال	purtuqāl
— (tangerine)	نارنگی	nārangī
— (bitter or.)	نارنج	nāranj
orangery	نارنجستان	nāranjistān
order	نظم	nazm
— (command)	حکم , فرمان	hukm, farmān
to order	فرمودن (فرما)	farmūdan (farmā)
ordinary	عادی	ʿādī
orient	مشرق زمین	mashriq-zamīn
oriental	مشرق زمینی	mashriq-zamīnī
origin	اصل	asl
original	اصلی	aslī
ornament	زینت	zīnat
ornamented	مزین	muzayyan
orphan	یتیم	yatīm
orthography	املا	imlā
ostrich	شتر مرغ	shutur-murgh (camel bird)
other	دیگر	dīgar
otter	سگِ آبی	sag-i ābī
ottoman	عثمانی	ʿusmānī

outpost	قراول	qarāvul
outside	بیرون	bīrūn
oval	تخمِ مرغی	tukhm-i murghī
oven	کوره	kūra
overseer	ناظر	nāzir
to overwhelm	غالب شدن	ghālib shudan
to owe	بده کار بودن	bidih-kār būdan
owl	جغد	jughd
owner	صاحب	sāhib
ox	گاو	gāv
oyster	صدف	sadaf

P.

pace	قدم	qadam
to pack	بستن (بند)	bastan (band)
pack-horse	یابو	yābū
packing-needle	جوال دوز	javāl-dūz
packsaddle	پالان	pālān
padlock	قفل	qufl
— (vulg.)		qulf
page	صفحه	safha
— (boy)	غلام بچه	ghulām bacha
pail	دلو, سطل	dalv, satl
pain	درد	dard
pains	زحمت	zahmat
paint	رنگ	rang
to paint	نقاشی کردن	naqqāshī kardan
painter	نقاش	naqqāsh
pair	جفت	juft
palace	عمارت	ʿimārat
pale	کمرنگ	kamrang

palm tree	نخل	nakhl
— (date-tree)	درختِ خرما	dirakht-i khurmā
pan	تاوه	tāva
panther	پلنگ	palang
paper	کاغذ	kāghaz
parade	سان	sān
parade-ground	میدان مشق	meidān-i mashq
paradise	بهشت , فردوس	bihisht, firdous
paragraph	فصل	fasl
— (plur.)	فصول	fusūl
parasang (4 miles)	فرسخ , فرسنگ	farsakh, farsang
parasol	آفتاب گیر	āftāb-gīr
parcel	بسته	basta
pardon	عفو	ʿafv
to beg pardon	عذر خواستن	ʿuzr khāstan
pardon!	ببخشید	bibakhshīd!
parents	والدین	vālidein
parliament (members of)	وکلای ملّت	vukalā-yi millat
parsee	گبر	gabr
parsley	جعفری	jaʿfarī
part	قسمت	qismat
partiality	طرفداری	taraf-dārī
particular	مخصوص	makhsūs
partner	شریك	sharīk
partnership	شراکت	sharākat
pass (mountain)	گردنه , کوتل	gardana, kūtal
to pass	گذشتن (گذر)	guzashtan (guzar)
passenger	مسافر	musāfir
passport	تذکره , باشپورت	tazkara, bāshpurt
past	گذشته	guzashta

pasture	چراگاه	charā-gāh
to pasture	چریدن (چر)	charīdan (char)
to patch	وصله کردن	vasla kardan
patience	صبر	sabr
patriot	وطن پرست	vatan-parast
pattern	نمونه	namūna
pavement	سنگ فرش	sang-farsh
pavillion	کلاهِ فرنگی	kulāh-i farangī
pawn	گرو	girou
to pay	پول دادن	pūl dādan
pea	نخود فرنگی	nukhud-i farangī
peace	صلح	sulh
peach	هلو	hullū
peacock	طاوس	tāūs
pear	گلابی	gulābī
pearl	مروارید	murvārīd
peasant	دهاتی ،رعیت	dahātī, raʿīat
pebble	ریگ	rīg
peddler	خورده فروش	khurda-furūsh
to peel	پوست کندن (کن)	pūst kandan (kan)
peg	میخ	mīkh
pelican	مرغ سقا	murgh-i saqqā
pen	قلم	qalam
pencil	مداد	midād
pendulum	لنگر	langar
peninsula	نیم جزیره	nīm-jazīra
pension	مستمری	mustamarrī
people	مردم	mardum
pepper	فلفل	filfil

peppermint	نعنا	na'nā
(5) percent	صد و (پنج)	sad u (panj)
perfect	کامل	kāmil
perfume	خوشبوی ,عطر	khushbūī, 'atr
perhaps	شاید	shāyad
to perish	هلاك شدن	halāk shudan
permission	اذن	izn
to permit	گذاشتن (گذار)	guzāshtan (guzār)
perquisite	مداخل	madākhil
Persia	ایران	Irān
Persian	ایرانی	Irānī
— (language)	فارسی	fārsī
person	شخص	shakhs
to perspire	عرق کردن	'araq kardan
petition	عرض	'arz
petitioner	عارض	'āriz
petroleum	نفت	naft
phaeton	درشکه	durushka
pheasant	قرهقاول	qaraqāvul
philosopher	حکیم آلهی	hakīm-i Illāhī
philosophy	حکمت ,فلسفه	hikmat, falsafa
photograph	عکس	'aks
photographer	عکّاس	'akkās
physician	طبیب ,حکیم	tabīb, hakīm
to pick	چیدن (چین)	chīdan (chīn)
pickles	ترشی	turshī
pick-pocket	جیب بر	jīb-burr
picture	تصویر	tasvīr
piebald	ابلق	ablaq
piece	تکه	tikka

to pierce	سفتن	suftan
pig	خوک , گراز	khūg, gurāz
pigeon	کبوتر , کفتر	kabūtar kaftar
pilgrim (to Mecca)	حاجی	hājī
— plur.	حجاج	hajāj
— (to other shrines)	زوّار	zavvār
pilgrimage	حج , زیارت	hajj, zīārat
pill	حب	habb
pillage	چپو	chapou
pillar	ستون	sutūn
pillow	بالش	bālish
pin	سنجاق	sanjāq
pine-tree	کاج	kāj
pink (flower)	میخک	mīkhak
pink (colour)	پشت گلی	pusht-i gulī
pious	دیانت دار	dīānat-dār
pipe (hubble-bubble)	قلیان	qalyān
— (turkish)	چپق	chupukh
— (tube)	لوله	lūla
pipe-clay	گل سفید	gil-i safid
pistachio	پسته	pista
pistol	طپانچه	tapāncha
pit	چاه	chāh
pity (sympathy)	رحم	rahm
it is a pity	افسوس است	afsūs ast
place	جا	jā
plague	طاعون	ta'ūn
plain	صحرا	sahrā
plaintiff	مدّعی	mudda'ī
to plait	بافتن (باف)	bāftan (bāf)

plane	رنده	randa
plane-tree	چنار	chinār
planet	سیاره	seyyāra
plant	سبزی	sabzī
plaster	گچ	gaj
— (medical)	مرهم	marham
plate	بشقاب	bushqāb
platform	سکو	sakkū
play	بازی	bāzī
to be pleased	پسندیدن (پسند)	pasandīdan (pasand)
if you please	التفات کرده	iltifāt karda
pleasure	عیش	ʿeish
plenipotentiary	وزیر مختار	vazīr mukhtār
plenty	فراوان	farāvān
plough	خیش	khīsh
to pluck	چیدن (چین)	chīdan (chīn)
plum	آلو	ālū
plunder	چپو	chapou
pocket	جیب	jīb
poem	شعر, نظم	shiʿr, nazm
poet	شاعر	shāʿir
poison	زهر	zahr
police	پلیس	pulīs
polite	باادب	bā adab
politeness	ادب	adab
politics	پلیتیک	pulītīk
pomegranate	انار	anār
pomp	حشمت	hashmat
pond	حوض	houz
pony	یابو	yābū

poor	فقیر	faqīr
poplar	تبریزی	tabrīzī
poppy	خشخاش	khashkhāsh
population	جمعیت	jamʿīat
porcupine	جوجه تیغه	jūja tīgha
porter	دربان	darbān
— (carrier)	حمال	hammāl
portmanteau	یخدان	yakhdān
portrait	شبیه , تمثال	shabīh, timsāl
to possess	داشتن (دار)	dāshtan (dār)
possible	ممکن	mumkin
post	چاپار	chapar
postage-stamp	تمبر	tambr (timbre)
post-office	پوست خانه	pūst-khāna
pot	کاسه	kāsa
— (earthenwar)	کوزه	kūza
potato	سیب زمینی	sīb-i zamīnī
potter	کوزه گر	kūza-gar
to pound	کوبیدن (کوب)	kūbīdan (kub)
to pour	ریختن (ریز)	rīkhtan (rīz)
poverty	فقر	faqr
powder	سفوف	sufūf
— (gun p.)	باروت	barūt
power	زور	zūr
praise	تعریف	taʿrīf
to pray	نماز خواندن	namāz khāndan
prayer	نماز	namāz
preacher	واعظ	vaʿiz
preaching	وعظ	vaʿz
precious	قیمتی	qīmatī

precipice	پرت گاه	part-gāh
preface	دیباچه	dībācha
to prefer	ترجیح دادن	tarjīh dādan
pregnant	آبستن	ābastan
to prepare	حاضر کردن	hāzir kardan
preparations	تدارك	tadāruk
presence	حضور	huzūr
present (adjective)	حاضر	hāzir
— (gift)	پیشکش	pīshkash
to preserve	نگاه داشتن	nigāh dāshtan
— (fruit)	مربا کردن	murabbā kardan
press (printer's)	مطبع	matbaᶜ
— (Minister of the Press)	وزیر انطباعات	vazīr-i intibāᶜāt
to press	فشاردن (فشار)	fishārdan (fishār)
pretext	بهانه	bahāna
pretty	قشنك	qashang
to prevent	مانع شدن	māniᶜ shudan
previous	سابق	sābiq
price	قیمت	qīmat
pride	غرور	ghurūr
priest (muhammedan)	ملا	mullā
— (christian)	کشیش	kashīsh
prince	شاهزاده	shāhzāda
— (vulg.)		shāzda
princess	شاهزاده خانم	shāzda khānum
to print	چاپ کردن	chāp kardan
prison	حبس	habs
	دستاق خانه	dustākh-khāna
prisoner	محبوس	mahbūs
— (of war)	اسیر	asīr

privilege	امتیاز	imtīāz
probably	احتمال میرود	ihtimāl mīravad
to procure	پیدا کردن	peidā kardan
produce	حاصل	hāsil
profession	پیشه	pīsha
professor	معلّم	mu'allim
progress	ترقی	taraqqī
promenade	گردش	gardish
to promise	وعده کردن	va'da kardan
pronunciation	تلفّظ	talaffuz
»	لهجه	lahja
proof	دلیل	dalīl
property	ملک	milk
prophet	پیغمبر	peighambar
prose	نثر	nasr
prostitute	جنده	jinda
to protect	حمایت کردن	himāyat kardan
protection	حمایت	himāyat
protocol	صورت مجلس	sūrat-i majlis
proud	مغرور	maghrūr
proverb	مثل	masal
provident	دور اندیش	dūr-andīsh
province	مملکت	mamlikat
»	ولایت	vilāyat
provisions	خوراك	khurāk
prudence	هوش	hūsh
prudent	هوشیار	hūshyār
psalm	زبور	zabūr
puberty	بلوغ	bulūgh

public	عام	ʿāmm
public-house	میخانه	mei-khāna
pudding	شیرینی	shīrīnī
to pull	کشیدن (کش)	kashīdan (kash)
pulpit	منبر	mambar
pulse	نبض	nabz
pumice-stone	سنگِ پا	sang-i pā
pump	طلمبه	tulumba
pumpkin	کدو	kadū
punctually	بوقت	bi vakht
to punish	تنبیه کردن	tambīh kardan
punishment	تنبیه	tambīh
pupil	شاگرد	shāgird
pure	پاك , خالص	pāk, khālis
purgative	مسهل	mus-hil
purgatory	اعراف	iʿrāf
purple	بنفشه رنگ	binafsha-rang
purpose	مقصود	maqsūd
purse	کیسه	kīsa
to pursue	تعقیب کردن	taʿqīb kardan
to push	تکان دادن	takān dādan
to put	گذاشتن (گذار)	guzāshtan (guzār)
— (nearly obsolete)	نهادن (نه)	nihādan (nih)
to put on (clothes)	پوشیدن (پوش)	pūshīdan (pūsh)
to put out (a light)	خاموش کردن	khāmūsh kardan

Q.

quail	بلدرچین	baldarchīn
quality	خصلت	khaslat
quantity	مقدار	miqdār
quarantine	کرنتین	karantīn

quarrel	دعوی	daʿvā
quarry	معدنِ سنگ	maʿdan-i sang
quarter	ربع , چهاریک	rubʿ, chahār-yak
quatrain	رباعی	rubāʿī
queen	ملکه	malika
queer	غریب	gharīb
question	سؤال	suʿāl
— (affair)	مسأله	masʿala
to question	پرسیدن (پرس)	pursīdan (purs.)
quick	زود	zūd
quicksilver	جیوه , سیماب	jīva, sīmāb
quiet	آرام	ārām
quietly	یاواش	yāvāsh
quilt	لحاف	lahāf
quince	به	bih
quinine	گنه گنه	gana-gana
quite	تماماً	tamāman

R.

rabbit (tame)	خرگوش خانگی	khargūsh-i khānagī
racing	اسپ دوانی	asp-davānī
radish	تربچه	turbcha
rafter	تیر	tīr
rag	کهنه	kuhna
railing	دست انداز	dast-andāz
railroad	راهِ آهن	rāh-i āhan
rain	باران , بارش	bārān, bārish
to rain	باریدن (بار)	bārīdan (bār)

ram	قوچ	qūch
ramparts	خاکریز	khākrīz
rank	منصب	mansab
rare	کم یاب	kam-yāb
rarely	ندرةً	nudratan
rat	موش سلطانیه	mūsh-i Sultānīa [1]
raw	خام	khām
razor	تیغِ دلاکی	tīgh-i dallākī
to reach	رسیدن (رس)	rasīdan (ras)
to read	خواندن (خوان)	khāndan (khān)
ready	حاضر	hāzir
real	صحیح	sahīh
really	حقیقةً	haqīqatan
to reap	درو کردن	dirou kardan
reason	عقل	ʿaql
— (cause)	سبب	sabab
rebel	یاغی	yāghī
rebellion	طغیان	tughyān
to receive	گرفتن (گیر)	giriftan (gīr)
reception	پذیرائی	pazīrāī
to reckon	حساب کردن	hisāb kardan
to recognize	شناختن (شناس)	shanākhtan (shanās)
recommendation	سفارش	safārish
— (letter of r.)	سفارشنامه	safārish-nāma
recompense	انعام	inʿām
recruit	جدید	jadīd
red	قرمز	qirmiz

1) *Mouse of Sultania*, so called because *Sultania* is the only place in which the rat is to be found in the highlands of Persia.

reed	نی	nei
reflet métallique tiles	کاشیِ طلائی	kāshī-yi tillāī
reform	اصلاح	islāh
refuge	پناه	panāh
— (asylum)	بست	bast
to refuse	قبول نکردن	qabūl nakardan
regiment	فوج	fouj
register	دفتر	daftar
regret	تاسف	ta'assuf
to regret	افسوس خوردن	afsūs khurdan
regular (troops)	نظامی	nizāmī
regularly	باقاعده	bā qā'ida
reign	سلطنت	saltanat
rein	دسته جلو	dasta-jilou
relation (kin)	قوم و خویش	qoum u khīsh
to release	وِل کردن	vil kardan
religion	مذهب, دین	mazhab, dīn
to remain	ماندن (مان)	māndan (mān)
remedy	چاره, علاج	chāra, 'ilāj
I remember	یادم است	yād-am ast
to remind	یاداوری کردن	yādāvarī kardan
to remove	بر داشتن (بر دار)	bar dāshtan (bar dār)
renewal	تجدید	tajdīd
rent (of a house)	اجاره	ijāra
repairs	تعمیر	ta'mīr
repeatedly	مکرر	mukarrar
repentance	پشیمانی	pashīmānī
repentant	پشیمان	pashīmān
repetition	تکرار	takrār

reproach	ملامت	malāmat
republican	جمهوری	jumhūrī
reputation	آبرو	ābrū
request	خواهش	khāhish
to request	خواستن (خواه)	khāstan (khāh)
research	تفحص	tafahhus
to resign	استعفا کردن	istiʿfā kardan
responsible	مسئول	masʾūl
responsibility	مسئولیت	masʾūlīat
rest (remainder)	باقی	bāqī
— (repose)	راحت	rāhat
result	نتیجه	natīja
resurrection	قیامت	qīāmat
return	مراجعت	murājaʿat
to return	بر گشتن	bar gashtan (bar gard)
revenge	انتقام	intiqām
review (military)	سان	sān
revolt	فساد	fisād
revolver	طپانچهٔ شش لوله	tapāncha-yi-shish-lūla
reward	انعام	inʿām
rheumatism	درد استخوان	dard-i-ustukhān
rhinoceros	کرگدن	kargadan
rhubarb	ریباس	rībās
rhyme	ردیف	radīf
rib	دنده	danda
ribbon	نوار	navār
rice (in the field)	شلتوك	shaltūk
— (cleared from the husk)	برنج	birinj

rice (plain boiled)	چلو	chilou
— (cooked with meat and spices)	پلو	pilou
rich	با دولت	bā doulat
riches	دولت	doulat
to ride	سوار شدن	savār shudan
rider	سوار	savār
ridiculous	مضحك	muzhik
rifle	تفنگ گلوله زن	tufang-i gulūla-zan
right	راست	rāst
ring	حلقه	halqa
— (finger r.)	انگشتر	angushtar
ringlet	زلف	zulf
ripe	رسیده	rasīda
to ripen	رسیدن (رس)	rasīdan (ras)
to rise	بر خواستن (بر خیز)	bar khāstan (bar khīz)
risk	خطر	khatar
rival	حریف	harīf
river	رود خانه	rūd-khāna
road	راه , جاده	rāh, jādda
roan (horse)	سرخون	surkhūn
roast	کباب	kabāb
robber	راه زن	rāh-zan
rock	سنگ	sang
rocket	موشك	mūshak
roe	شوکا	shūkā
to roll	غلطیدن (غلط)	ghaltīdan (ghalt)
roller (for the roofs)	بام غلطان	būm-ghaltūn
roof	پشت بام	pusht-i būm
»	(vulg)	būm

room	اوطاق	utāq
root	بیخ ریشه	bīkh, rīsha
rope	طناب	tanāb
rosary	تسبیح	tasbīh
to rot	پوسیدن (پوس)	pūsīdan (pūs)
round	گرد	gird
rough	ناهموار	nā-hamvār
row	صف	saff
to row	پارو زدن	pārū zadan
royal	شاهی	shāhī
"	همایون	humāyūn
"	مبارك	mubārak
to rub	مالیدن (مال)	mālīdan (māl)
ruby	یاقوت	yāqūt
rude	بی ادب	bī-adab
ruffian	لوطی	lūtī
— (plur)	الواط	alvāt
ruin	خرابی	kharābī
— (building)	خرابه	kharāba
to ruin	خراب کردن	kharāb kardan
rule	رسم	rasm
to run	دویدن (دو)	davīdan (dou)
rusk (Europ)	نان سخری	nān-i sakharī
— (Persian)	نان خشك	nān-i khushk
rust	زنگ	zang
rusty	زنگ آلوده	zang-ālūda
rye	گندمِ سیاه	gandum-i sīāh

S.

sack	جوال	javāl

sacred	مقدّس	muqaddas
sacrifice	قربان , فدا	qurbān, fadā
sad	دل تنگ	dil tang
saddle	زین	zīn
saddle (lady's)	زینِ زنانه	zīn-i zanāna
— (packsaddle)	پالان	pālān
to saddle	زین کردن	zīn kardan
saddler	سراج	sarrāj
safe	سالم	sālim
safety	سلامت , امنیت	salāmat, amnīat
sail	باد بان	bād-bān
sailor	ملاّح	mallāh
Saint (Persian)	امام زاده	Imām-zāda
salary	مواجب	mavājib
sale	فروش	furūsh
salmon	آزاد ماهی	āzād-māhī
salt	نمک	namak
— (adjective)	شور	shūr
salt-cellar	نمکدان	namak-dān
salt-desert	کویر	kavīr
salute	سلام	salām
salvation	نجات	nijāt
same	همین	hamīn
sample	نمونه	namūna
sand	ریگ	rīg
sapphire	یاقوتِ کبود	yāqūt-i kabūd
sash	شال	shāl
satiated	سیر	sīr

satin	اطلس	atlas
satisfaction	رضامندی	rizāmandī
saturday	شنبه	shamba
saucepan	دیگ	dīg
savage	وحشی	vahshī
to save	رهانیدن (رهان)	rahānīdan (rahān)
saw	اره	arra
to say	گفتن (گو)	guftan (gū)
— (respectfully)	فرمودن (فرما)	farmūdan (farmā)
scales	ترازو	tarāzū
scarcity	قحط	qaht
to scatter	پاچیدن (پاچ)	pāchīdan (pāch)
school	مکتب	maktab
— (high)	مدرسه	madrasa
school-master	آخوند	ākhund
science	علم	ʿilm
scissors	قیچی	qeichī
scorpion	عقرب	ʿaqrab
scout	جاسوس	jāsūs
to scratch	خاریدن (خار)	khārīdan (khār)
to scream	فریاد کردن	faryād kardan
screen	پرده	parda
— (tenting)	تجیر	tajīr
screw	پیچ	pīch
scribe	منشی ,کاتب	munshī, kātib
scull	کلّه	kalla
sea	دریا	daryā
seal	مهر	muhr
sealing-wax	لاک	lāk

seam	درز	darz
season	فصل	fasl
seat	نشیمن	nishīman
to seat	نشاندن (نشان)	nishāndan (nishān)
second	دویم	duyum
— (arabic)	ثانی	sānī
second (sixtieth part of minute)	ثانیه	sānīa
secret	راز	rāz
secretary	منشی	munshī
— (of legation)	نایب سفارت	nāyib-i safārat
sect	فرقه	firqa
secure	محفوظ	mahfūz
sedition	فساد	fisād
seditious	مفسد	mufsid
to see	دیدن (بین)	dīdan (bīn)
seed	تخم	tukhm
to seek	جستن (جو)	justan (jū)
"	پی چیزی گشتن (گرد)	pei-i chīzī gashtan (gard)
to seize	گرفتن (گیر)	giriftan (gīr)
seldom	کم	kam
to select	منتخب کردن	muntakhab kardan
self	خود	khud
to sell	فروختن (فروش)	furūkhtan (furūsh)
to send	فرستادن (فرست)	firistādan (firist)
sense (plur)	حس	hiss
senseless	بی حس	bī-hiss
sentence (gramm.)	جمله	jumla
sentinel	قراول	qarāvul
to separate	جدا کردن	judā kardan

separate	جدا	judā
seraglio	اندرون	andarūn
sergeant	وکیل	vakīl
sermon	وعظ	vaʿz
serpent	مار	mār
servant	نوکر	noukar
to serve	نوکری کردن	noukarī kardan
service	خدمت	khidmat
sesamum	کنجت	kunjit
to sew	دوختن (دوز)	dūkhtan (dūz)
sex	جنس	jins
shadow	سایه	sāya
shagreen	ساغری	sāghirī
to shake	تکاندن (تکان)	takāndan (takān)
shame	شرم, خجالت	sharm, khajālat
shape	صورت	sūrat
sharp	تیز	tīz
to shave	تراشیدن (تراش)	tarāshīdan (tarāsh)
sheathe	غلاف	ghilāf
sheep	گوسفند	gūsfand
sheet (bedding)	ملافه	malāfa
shelter	پناه	panāh
shepherd	چپان	chupān
shield	سپر	sipar
to shine	تابیدن (تاب)	tābīdan (tāb)
ship	کشتی, جهاز	kashtī, jahāz
shoe	کفش, گیوه	kafsh, gīva
— (horse-shoe)	نعل	naʿl
shoemaker	کفش دوز	kafsh-dūz
to shoot	(تیر گلوله) انداختن (انداز)	(tīr or gulūla) andākhtan (andāz)

shop	دکّان	dukkān
— (plur)	دکاکین	dakākīn
shore	کنار	kanār
short	کوتاه	kūtah
small shot	ساچمه	sāchma
shoulder	شانه دوش	shāna, dūsh
to show	نشان دادن	nishān dādan
shrimp	میگو	meigū
shrine	زیارت گاه	zīārat-gāh
shroud	کفن	kafan
shrub	بوته	buta
to shut	بستن (بند)	bastan (band)
sick (I am)	احوالم بهم خورد	ahvāl-am bi ham khurd
side	پهلو	pahlū
siege	محاصره	muhāsira
sieve	غلبیر	ghalbīr
fine sieve	الك	alak
sight	تماشا	tamāshā
signature	امضا	imzā
signet	خاتم	khātim
silence	خاموشی	khāmūshī
silent	خاموش	khāmūsh
silk	ابریشم	abrishum
silver	نقره	nuqra
simple	ساده	sāda
simplicity	سادگی	sādagī
sin	گناه	gunāh
since	از آن که	az ān ki
sincere	صادق	sādiq

sinew	پی	pei
to sing	خواندن (خوان)	khāndan (khān)
"	آوازه خواندن	āvāza khāndan
singer	مطرب	mutrib
single	تك	tak
to sink	غرق شدن	gharq shudan
sinless	بی گناه	bī gunāh
sinner	گناه کار	gunāh-kār
sister	خواهر	khāhar
"	همشیره	hamshīra
to sit	نشستن (نشین)	nishastan (nishīn)
size	اندازه	andāza
skating	یخ بازی	yakh-bāzī
skill	هنر , استادی	hunar, ustādī
skin	پوست	pūst
skirt	دامن	dāman
sky	آسمان	āsmān
slack	سست	sust
slab	تخته	takhta
slate	لوح	louh
slaughterhouse	قصاب خانه	qassāb-khāna
slave	بنده , غلام	banda, ghulām
	زر خرید	zar-kharīd
sledge	کالسکه برفی	kālaska-yi barfī
to sleep	خوابیدن (خواب)	khābīdan (khāb)
sleeve	آستین	āstīn
to slide, to slip	لغزیدن (لغز)	laghzīdan (laghz)
slipper	کفش	kafsh
slippery	لغزنده	laghzanda

slow, slowly	کند ,یاواش	kund, yāvāsh
small	خورد ,کم ,ریزه	khurd, kam, rīza
small-pox	آبله	ābla
smart	زرنك	zarang
to smash	شکستن (شکن)	shikastan (shikan)
smell	بو	bū
smile	تبسّم	tabassum
smith	آهنگر	āhangar
smoke	دود	dūd
to smoke (tobacco)	کشیدن (کش)	kashīdan (kash)
smooth	هموار صاف	hamvār, sāf
to smother	خفه کردن	khafa kardan
smuggler	قاچاقچی	qachaqchī
snake	مار	mār
to sneeze	عطسه کردن	ʿatsa kardan
snipe	نوکدراز	nuk-dirāz
snow	برف	barf
to snow	برف باریدن	barf bārīdan
snuff	نشوق	nushūq
so	چنین	chunīn
soap	صابون	sābūn
sock	جوراب	jūrāb
sopha	نیمتخت ,نیم‌کت	nīm-takht, nīm-kat
soft	نرم	narm
sojourn	اقامت	iqāmat
solar	شمسی	shamsī
soldier	سرباز	sarbāz
some	چند تا ,چندنفر	chand tā, chand nafar

son	پسر	pisar
song	تصنیف	tasnīf
soon	زود	zūd
sorrow	غم	gham
sorrowful	دل تنگ	dil tang
soul	جان	jān
sound	صدا	sadā
soup	اش , سوپ	āsh, sūp
— (broth)	آب گوشت	āb-i gūsht
sour	ترش	tursh
source	اصل	asl
south	جنوب	junūb
souvenir	یادگار	yādgār
to sow	کاشتن (کار)	kāshtan (kār)
spade	بیل	bīl
span	وجب	vajab
spark	اخگر	akhgar
sparrow	گنجشك	gunjishk
to speak	حرف زدن	harf zadan
spear	نیزه	neiza
special	مخصوص	makhsūs
speck	لکّه	lakka
spectacle	تماشا	tamāshā
spectacles	عینك	ʿeinak
speech	نطق	nutq
to spend	خرج کردن	kharj kardan
spice	ادویه	advīya
spider	عنکبوت	ʿankabūt
to spill	ریختن (ریز)	rīkhtan (rīz)
to spin	ریشتن (ریش)	rīshtan (rīsh)

spinach	اسفناج	isfināj
to spit	تف زدن	tuf zadan
splint (of a horse)	قرەقوش	qaraqūsh
to spoil	ضایع کردن	zāyiᶜ kardan
sponge	ابر	abr
spoon	قاشق	qāshuq
spot	لکه	lakka
to spread	پهن کردن	pahn kardan
spring (season)	بهار	bahār
» (spiral)	فانار	fānār
spur	مهمیز	mahmīz
spy	جاسوس	jāsūs
squadron	دسته	dasta
square	مربع	murabbaᶜ
to squeeze	چلاندن (چلان)	chalāndan (chalān)
stable (for horses)	طویله	tavīla
stag	مرال	marāl
stage (on journey)	منزل	manzil
stain	لکه	lakka
staircase	پله	pilla
stale (bread)	بیات	beiāt
stallion	نریان	narīān
to stammer	لکنه کردن	lukna kardan
stamp (postage)	تمبر	tambr (timbre)
to stand	ایستادن (ایست)	īstādan (īst)
standard	علم	ᶜalam
star	ستاره , اختر	sitāra, akhtar
starch	نشسته	nishasta
to start	روانه شدن	ravāna shudan
station	منزل	manzil

statue	مجسّمه	mujassama
to stay	ماندن (مان)	māndan (mān)
to steal	دزدیدن (دزد)	duzdīdan (duzd)
steam	بخار	bukhār
steamer	کشتیِ بخار	kashtī-yi bukhār
steel	فولاد	fulād
steep	سرازیر	sarāzīr
step	قدم	qadam
stick	چوب دست	chūb-dast
to stick	چسپیدن (چسپ)	chaspīdan (chasp)
— (transitive)	چسپاندن (چسپان)	chaspāndan (chaspān)
stiff	خشك	khushk
sill	ساکت	sākit
to stink	گندیدن (گند)	gandīdan (gand)
to stir	هم زدن	ham zadan
stirrup	رکاب	rikāb
stockings	جوراب	jūrāb
stomach	معده	ma'da
stone	سنگ	sang
stony	سنگلاخ	sanglākh
stool	کرسی	kursī
to stop	وا ایستادن (وا ایست)	vā īstādan (vā īst)
store	انبار	ambār
stork	لکلك	laklak
story	حکایت, قصه, نقل	hikāyat, qissa, naql
stout	چاق	chāq
stove	بخاری	bukhārī
straight	راست	rāst
strange	غریب	gharīb

stranger	غریب	gharīb
to strangle	خفه کردن	khafa kardan
strap	قایش ,تسمه	qāīsh, tasma
straw	کاه	kāh
strawberry	توتِ فرنگی	tūt-i farangī
stream	راهِ آب	rāh-i āb
street	کوچه	kūcha
strength	زور	zūr
to strike	زدن (زن)	zadan (zan)
string	نخ	nakh
stripe	خط	khatt
strong	قوی	qavī
stucco	گچ کاری	gaj-kārī
student	طلبه	talaba
study	تحصیل	tahsīl
to stumble	سرِ سم رفتن	sar-i sum raftan
»	ناخن بند کردن	nākhun band kardan
stupid	احمق ,خر	ahmaq, khar
stupidity	خری	kharī
sturgeon	سگ ماهی	sag-mahī
style	عبارت	ʿibārat
subject (of a state)	تبعه ,رعیت	tabaʿa, raʿīat
— (of a book or letter)	مطلب	matlab
sublime	عالی	ʿālī
substantive	اسم	ism
successor	خلف	khalaf
— (plur.)	خلفا	khulafā
such	چنین	chunīn

to suck	مکیدن (مك)	makīdan (mak)
suddenly	ناگاه	nā-gāh
suet	پی	pī
suffering	درد	dard
sufficient	کافی	kāfī
sufficiency	کفایت	kafāyat
sugar (soft s.)	شکر	shakar
— (lump s.)	قند	qand
sugar-cane	نی شکر	nei-shakar
suit of clothes	دسته لباس	dasta-yi libās
to suit	بکار خوردن	bi kār-khurdan
sulphur	گوگرد	gūgird
sum	مبلغ	mablagh
summer	تابستان	tābistān
Summer residence	ییلاق	yeilāq
summit	قله	qulla
to summon	احضار کردن	ihzār kardan
sun	آفتاب, خورشید	āftāb, khurshīd
supper	شام	shām
supplication	استدعا	istidʿā
to suppose	فرض کردن	farz kardan
sure	یقین	yaqīn
surface	رو	rū
surgeon	جراح	jarrāh
surroundings	اطراف	atrāf
suspicion	گمان	gamān
suspicious	بد گمان	bad-gamān
swallow	چلچله	chilchila
to swallow	فرو آوردن	furū āvurdan
swamp	لجن زار	lajan-zār
swan	غو	ghou

to swear	قسم خوردن	qasam khurdan
sweat	عرق	ʿaraq
to sweep	روفتن (روب)	rūftan (rūb)
»	جاروب کردن	jārūb kardan
sweet	شیرین	shīrīn
sweetheart	معشوقه	maʿshūqa
sweets	شیرینی	shīrīnī
to swell	باد کردن	bād kardan
swelling	ورم	varam
swift	تند	tund
to swim	شنو کردن	shanou kardan
to swindle	گول زدن	gūl zadan
swine	خوک ,گراز	khūg, gurāz
to swoon	بی هوش شدن	bī-hūsh shudan
sword	شمشیر	shamshīr
symptom	علامت	ʿalāmat
syntax	نحو	nahv
syringe	آب دزدک	āb-duzdak

T.

table	میز	mīz
table-cloth	سفره	sufra
tail	دم	dum
tailor	خیاط	kheiyāt
to take	گرفتن (گیر)	giriftan (gīr)
tale (see story)		
talent	قابلیت	qābilīat
to talk	حرف زدن	harf zadan
»	گفتگو کردن	guftugū kardan
tall	بلند قد	buland-qadd
tallow	پی	pī

tambourine	دایره	dāira (vulg. dāria)
tank	حوض	houz
tap	شیر	shīr
tape	نواره	navāra
tar	قیر	qīr
tarantula	رتیل	ruteil
taste	مزه	maza
good taste	سلیقه	salīqa
tax	باج ,مالیات	bāj , mālīāt
tea	چای	chāī
to teach	یاد دادن	yād dādan
„	درس دادن	dars dādan
teacher	معلّم	muʿallim
tear (weeping)	اشک	ashk
to tear	دریدن (در)	darīdan (dar)
telegram	تلگراف	talagrāf
telegraph	تلگراف	„
telegraphist	تلگرافچی	talagrāf-chī
telescope	دور بین	dūr-bīn
to tell	گفتن (گو)	guftan (gū)
temper	مزاج	mizāj
temporary	موقت	muvaqqat
tenant	مستأجر	mustaʿjir
tender	نازک	nāzuk
tent	چادر ,خیمه	chādur , kheima
tepid	شیر گرم	shīr-garm
terrace	سکو	sakkū
territory	خاک	khāk
terror	هراس	hirās
testament	وصیت نامه	vasīyat-nāma

testimony	شهادت	shahādat
to thank	تشکر کردن	tashakkur kardan
theft	دزدی	duzdī
thermometer	گرما نما	garmā-namā
thick	کلفت	kuluft
thief	دزد	duzd
thimble	انگشتانه	angushtāna
thin	نازک	nāzuk
thing	چیز	chīz
to think	خیال کردن	kheyāl kardan
thirst	تشنگی	tishnagī
thirsty	تشنه	tishna
thistle (eatable)	کنگر	kangar
thorn	خار	khār
thoroughbred	اصیل, جنس	asīl, jins
thought	خیال	kheyāl
thrashing-floor	خرمن	kharman
thread	ریسمان	rīsmān
to threaten	ترساندن (ترسان)	tarsāndan (tarsān)
threshold	آستانه, درگاه	āstāna, dargāh
throat	گلو	galū
throne	تخت	takht
to throw	انداختن (انداز)	andākhtan (andāz)
thumb	شست	shast
thunder	رعد	ra'd
Thursday	پنج شنبه	panj-shanba
to tidy	جابجا کردن	jā-bi jā kardan
to tie	بستن (بند)	bastan (band)
tiger	ببر	babr
tight	تنگ, سفت	tang, sift

tile	کاشی	kāshī
time	وقت	vakht
— (leisure)	فرصت	fursat
tin	حلبی	halabī
tin-opener	حلبی بُرّ	halabī-burr
tinker	حلبی ساز	halabī-sāz
tipsy	مست	mast
tired	خسته	khasta
title	لقب	laqab
toast	نانِ برشته	nān-i birishta
tobacco for water-pipes	تنباکو	tambākū
— for short pipes or cigarettes	تتن	tutun
to-day	امروز	imrūz
toe	انگشتِ پا	angusht-i pā
together	با هم	bā ham
toll	راه داری	rāh-dārī
tomato	بادنجان فرنگی	bādinjān-i farangī
tomb	قبر	qabr
to-morrow	فردا	fardā
tone	صدا	sadā
tongs	انبر	ambur
tongue	زبان	zabān
tool	آلت	ālat
tooth	دندان	dandān
top	سر	sar
torch	مشعل	mashʿal
tortoise	لاك پشت	lāk-pusht
torture	شکنجه	shikanja
total	جمع	jamʿ

to touch	دست زدن	dast zadan
touchstone	محاك	mihāk
towel	دستمال	dast-māl
tower	برج	burj
town	شهر	shahr
toy	بازیچه	bāzīcha
track	ردّ پا	radd-i pā
trade	تجارت	tijārat
traffic	آمد و شد	āmad u shud
to translate	ترجمه کردن	tarjuma kardan
translation	ترجمه	tarjuma
translator	مترجم	mutarjim
transport	حمل و نقل	haml u naql
trap	تله	tala
trappings	یراق	yarāq
to travel	سفر کردن	safar kardan
traveller	سیاح	seiyāh
tray	سینی	sīnī
treasure	گنج , خزانه	ganj , khazāna
treaty	عهدنامه	ʿahdnāma
tree	درخت	dirakht
to tremble	لرزیدن (لرز)	larzīdan (larz)
tribe	طایفه	tāifa
tribute	باج	bāj
troop	دسته	dasta
to trot	یورتمه رفتن	yurtma raftan
trouble	زحمت	zahmat
troublesome	پر زحمت	pur zahmat
trousers	شلوار	shalvār
trousseau	جهاز	jahāz

trout	قزل آله	qizil-āla
true	صحیح	sahīh
truly	راستی	rāstī
trumpet	شیپور	sheipūr
trunk (of a tree)	ساق	sāq
„ (of an elephant)	خرطوم	khartūm
„ (box)	یخدان	yakhdān
truth	حقیقت	haqīqat
to try	تجربه کردن	tajruba kardan
tube	لوله	lūla
Tuesday	سه شنبه	si-shamba
tulip	لاله	lāla
tumour	دنبل	dumbal
tune	آواز	āvāz
tunic	قبا	qabā
turban	عمامه	ʿamāma
Turk	ترك	Turk
Turkey	خاك روم	khāk-i Rūm
turkey (bird)	بوقلمون	būqalamūn
Turkish	ترکی	turkī
to turn	گردیدن (گرد)	gardīdan (gard)
turner	خراط	kharrāt
turnip	شلغم	shalgham
turquoise	فیروزه	fīrūza
turtle	سنك پشت	sang-pusht
twice	دو دفعه	du dafʿa
twin	توأم, دو غلو	touʿam, du ghulū
tyranny	ظلم	zulm
tyrant	ظالم	zālim

U.

ugly	زشت	zisht

ugly	بد گل	bad-gil
umbrella	چتر	chatr
un-	نه , غير	na-, gheir-
unanimity	اتفاق	ittifāq
unbeliever	كافر	kāfir
uncle (paternal)	عمو	ʿammū
» (maternal)	خال	khāl
unclean	نا پاك , نجس	nā-pāk, najis
under	زير	zīr
undersigned	امضا كننده	imzā-kunanda
to understand	فهميدن (فهم)	fahmīdan (fahm)
»	ملتفت شدن	multafit shudan
undoubtedly	بلا شك	bilā shak
to undress	لباس كندن (كن)	libās kandan (kan)
unfortunate	بد بخت	bad-bakht
unhappy	دلتنگ	dil-tang
uniform (military)	لباسِ نظامى	libās-i nizāmī
— (civilians)	لباس رسمى	libās-i rasmī
uninterrupted	لاينقطع	lā yanqataʿ
university	مدرسه	madrasa
unjust	بى انصاف	bī-insāf
unless	مگر	magar
unofficial	غير رسمى	gheir-rasmī
unpaid	مفت	muft
unripe	خام , نارس	khām, nā-ras
until	تا	tā
unwell	بى دماغ	bī damāgh
unworthy	نالايق	nā-lāyiq
up	بالا	bālā
upon	روى	rū-yi

upside down	وارونه	vārūna
use	فایده	fāida
to use	استعمال کردن	isti'māl kardan
useful	مفید	mufīd
useless	بی فایده	bī-fāida
usual	عادی	'ādī

V.

to vaccinate	آبله کوبیدن	ābla kūbīdan
vain	خود پسند	khud-pasand
valet	پیش خدمت	pīsh-khidmat
valid	بر قرار	bar qarār
valley	دره , جلگه	darra, julga
valuable	قیمتی	qīmatī
value	قیمت	qīmat
to value	قیمت کردن	qīmat kardan
vanity	خود پسندی	khud-pasandī
various	مختلف	mukhtalif
varnish	روغنِ کمان	roughan-i kamān
vault	طاق	tāq
vegetable	سبزی	sabzī
veil	رو بند ,پرده	rū-band, parda
vein	رگ	rag
velvet	مخمل	makhmal
vengeance	انتقام	intiqām
to venture	جسارت کردن	jasārat kardan
Venus	زهره	Zuhra
verandah	ایوان	eivān
verb	فعل	fi'l
verdigris	زنگار	zangār

vermin	جانور	jānvar
— (vulg.)		jūnavar
verse	بیت	beit
very	خیلی , بسیار	kheilī, bisyār
vestige	اثر	asar
veterinary surgeon	بیطار	beitār
to vex	اذیت کردن	azīat kardan
viceroy	فرمان فرما	farmān-farmā
victor	فاتح	fātih
victory	فتح	fath
victuals	آذوقه	āzūqa
view	منظر	manzar
village	ده	dih
villager	دهاتی	dihātī
vine	مو	mou
vinegar	سرکه	sirka
vineyard	انگورستان	angūristān
violence	شدّت	shiddat
violent	شدید	shadīd
violet	بنفشه	binafsha
violin	کمانچه	kamāncha
virgin	باکره	bākira
virtue	هنر	hunar
visible	ظاهر	zāhir
visit	دیدنی	dīdanī
"	دید و بازدید	dīd u bāzdīd
visitor	مهمان	mihmān
visiting card	کارت	gārt
vocabulary	لغت	lughat

voice	آواز	āvāz
volcano	کوهِ آتش فشان	kūh-i ātash fishān
volley	شلیک	shalīk
volume	جلد	jild
to vomit	قی کردن	qei kardan
voyage	سفرِ دریای	safar-i daryāī
vulgar	عام , پست	ʿāmm, past
vulture	لاش خور	lāsh-khur

W.

wages	مواجب	mavājib
waist	کمر	kamar
waistcoat	جلکه	jilaka
to wait	صبر کردن	sabr kardan
to wake	بیدار شدن	bīdār shudan
walk	گردش	gardish
to walk	پیاده رفتن (رو)	piāda raftan (rou)
wall	دیوار	dīvār
wallet	قبل	qubul
walnut	گردو	girdū
want	خواهش	khāhish
war	جنگ	jang
warehouse	مغازه	maghāza
warm	گرم	garm
warmth	گرمی	garmī
warp and woof	تار و پود	tār u pūd
to wash	شستن (شور)	shustan (shūr)
washer	رخت‌شور	rakhtshūr
wasp	زنبور	zambūr
waste	تفریط	tafrīt

watch	ساعت	sāʿat
water	آب	āb
to water	سیراب کردن	sīrāb kardan
wave	موج	mouj
wax	موم	mūm
way	راه	rāh
weak	ضعیف	zaʿīf
wealth	دولت	doulat
weapon	اسلحه	aslaha
weather	هوا	havā
to weave	بافتن (باف)	bāftan (bāf)
wedding	عروسی	ʿarūsī
Wednesday	چهار شنبه	chahār shamba
weight	وزن	vazn
welcome!	خوش آمدید	khush āmadīd
well (for water)	چاه	chāh
well (adverb)	بخوبی	bi khūbī
wellwisher	خیر خواه	kheir-khāh
west	مغرب	maghrib
wet	تر ,خیس	tar, khīs
what	چه	chi
wheat	گندم	gandum
wheel	چرخ	charkh
when?	کی	kei?
where	کجا ,کو	kujā, kū
while	مدت	muddat
whip	شلاغ	shallāgh
whirlpool	گرداب	girdāb
to whistle	سوت زدن	sūt zadan
white	سفید	safīd

who? کہ ki?
whole تمام tamām
wholesome سالم sālim
why چرا chirā
wick فتیلہ fatīla
wicked شریر sharīr
wickedness شرارت sharārat
wide گشاد gushād
widow بیوہ bīva
width پہنائی pahnāī
wife زوجہ ,زن zouja, zan
wild وحشی vahshī
wilderness بیابان bīābān
will مراد murād
willow بید bīd
to win بردن (بر) burdan (bar)
wind باد bād
to wind up کوک کردن kūk kardan
window پنجرہ panjara
wine شراب sharāb
wing بال bāl
winter زمستان zimistān
to wipe پاک کردن pāk kardan
wire مفتول maftūl
wisdom حکمت hikmat
wise دانا dānā
wish خواہش khāhish
to wish خواستن (خواہ) khāstan (khāh)
with با bā
witness شاہد shāhid
witty ظریف zarīf

wolf	گرگ	gurg
woman	زن	zan
wonder	کرامت	karāmat
to wonder	تعجب کردن	taʿajjub kardan
wonderful	عجیب	ʿajīb
wood	چوب	chūb
— (fire-wood)	هیزم	hīzum
woodcock	نوکدرازِ بزرگ	nukdirāz-i buzurg
wool	پشم	pashm
word	کلمه	kalama
work	کار	kār
workman	فعله	faʿala
workshop	کارخانه	kārkhāna
world	دنیا, عالم, جهان	dunyā, ālam, jahān
worm	کرم	kirm
worse	بدتر	badtar
to worship	پرستیدن (پرست)	parastīdan (parast)
to be worth	ارزیدن (ارز)	arzīdan (arz)
worthy	لایق	lāyiq
wound	زخم	zakhm
wounded	زخم دار	zakhm-dār
to wrap	پیچیدن (پیچ)	pīchīdan (pīch)
to wrestle	کشتی گرفتن	kushtī giriftan
to write	نوشتن (نویس)	navishtan (navīs)
writer	نویسنده , کاتب	navīsanda, kātib
writing	خطّ	khatt
wrong	غلط	ghalat

Y.

yard (court)	حیاط	heyāt
— (measure)	ذرع	zarʿ

year	سال ,سن ,سنه	sāl, sinn, sana
yeast	مایه	māya
yellow	زرد	zard
yes	بلی (آری)	baʿlī (vulg. ārei)
yesterday	دیروز	dīrūz
young	جوان ,جاهل	javān, jāhil
youth	جوانی	javānī

Z.

zeal	غیرت	gheirat
zephyr	نسیم	nasīm
zinc	روح	rūh
Zoroaster	زردشت	Zardusht